T0294133

ADVANCE PRAISE

"*Geofusion* is a great and important book. It is a gem and a bridge, connecting the past with the present and future. Readers of all walks of life will be able to understand and connect with the chapters of this book and begin to understand why the future is unlike anything we have imagined thus far. Norbert's thoughts are incredibly powerful, as they illuminate the age of change the world is entering. He masterfully connects each chapter together, painting a picture of tomorrow in a way few authors are able to do. This book is for anyone who has wondered what the future of geopolitics will look like. It is for anyone who has wondered what the future will look like."

Abishur Prakash, geopolitical futurist and
author of *Next Geopolitics: The Future of World Affairs (Technology)*

"The Hitchhiker's Guide to the Future: there is a completely new geography being born. Geography, as the most complex branch of science is revived, is presented by the author to show us the possible outcomes of the changes of the 21st century. How are the mighty wars for power being fought? Why are creativity and innovation gaining revolutionary significance? Unlike the futures depicted by the popular utopist novels, we can learn about a future that presents us models of our ever-changing world, based on the analyses of real data."

Journal of the Hungarian Geography Society

"The winners of the New Geopolitical Age – in one book."

www.novekedes.hu

"The term geopolitics normally evokes a political and military dynamic. It is far more than that as Norbert Csizmadia makes clear in his book *Geofusion*. Aside from addressing the economic sphere, he relates geopolitics to a range of social and technical evolutions. As such, he has made a significant contribution to the study of geopolitics and toward the coherent modelling of the world in its many dimensions."

George Friedman, Founder of Geopolitical Futures (GPF) and
bestselling author of *The Next 100 Years*, *The Next Decade* and *Flashpoints*

Published by
LID Publishing Limited
The Record Hall, Studio 204,
16-16a Baldwins Gardens,
London EC1N 7RJ, UK

524 Broadway, 11th Floor, Suite 08-120,
New York, NY 10012, US

info@lidpublishing.com
www.lidpublishing.com

www.businesspublishersroundtable.com

Translated by: Bence Gáspár and Kata Paulin

Printed in Latvia by Jelgavas Tipogrāfij
ISBN: 978-1-912555-21-5

Cover and page design: Caroline Li

NORBERT CSIZMADIA

THE POWER OF GEOGRAPHY AND THE MAPPING OF THE 21ST CENTURY

LONDON NEW YORK SHANGHAI
MADRID BARCELONA BOGOTA
MEXICO CITY MONTERREY BUENOS AIRES

CONTENTS

INTRODUCTION

THE SPECIAL GEO-MOMENT

The economic and financial crisis that started in 2008 reorganized our world. New values, new meeting points and the unprecedented cooperation of new actors have all emerged, and they have been shaping the world ever since. The models, maps, and recipes that used to work do not function anymore. We need a new approach, and more and more unique solutions are becoming warranted. We live in a special geo-moment: in a century where knowledge and creativity reign supreme, and where new values are developing.

The 21st century breaks with traditional geographical maps, therefore we have to redraw them in these decades of unrivalled opportunities and unprecedented challenges. Almost every day we hear about the results of the accelerating technological progress. In early 2016, the existence of gravitational waves was confirmed for the first time, and a milestone breakthrough was achieved in the development of artificial intelligence when AlphaGo, devised by Google's developers, first defeated man in Go, a game invented in China and considered one of the most complex in the world, containing 10^{170} possible combinations. The results are also encouraging in the field of creating fusion energy, and according to some, technological *singularity* is not far away either. Thanks to the 24/7 global economy of new technologies, talent finds a way of bridging distances. However, the mobility, economic and otherwise, of the individual and of nations, communities, and countries has increased with the advent of the internet, modern public transport, and new industries. Today, just as an economist, a geographer, and an engineer can easily start a business together, countries thousands of kilometres apart can connect on the basis of common interests and economic and political cooperation.

Meanwhile, climate change and our efforts to maintain this under +2°C; environmental degradation threatening humanity's conditions of life; adaptation to the entailing consequences; rising economic and social inequalities; economic crises; international conflicts; migration – the list goes on and on – pose unparalleled challenges to humanity. When examining these phenomena spatially, we can see that economic power is shifting from the former centres to the periphery, therefore the frontiers of the past may become the new centres. Thus, the unipolar world becomes multipolar, while global strategies are replaced by regional cooperation.

We are part of a special 'geo-moment' in both location and time: global space is fragmented, knowledge, creativity, and highly skilled labour are coming to be the greatest value, and former peripheral countries with knowledge-intensive economies may become the new points of reference. In their own field, everyone attempts to determine the winning nations, communities, leaders, and powers of this era. Who will prevail, the large or the small? The strong or the swift? Central or peripheral countries? The task of the explorers and geo-strategists of the 21st century is to provide guidance in this constantly changing period full of tremendous opportunities and global environmental, social, and economic challenges.

This calls for new maps that retain the wisdom and tools of the old and complement them with today's knowledge. This is because the explorers of the 21st century do not need to rely on the North Star for orientation, but rather on innovation clusters, the world's best universities, the latest technological achievements, as well as their spatial connections and networks. And today these maps help us not only in orientation but also in being successful at the personal, national, regional, or even global level. This requires, first and foremost, a new perspective, comprehensive knowledge, unique ideas, and creativity. In order to create new knowledge, we have to familiarize ourselves with the world around us.

Today, we live in an age of fusion and networks. We collaborate with economists, sociologists, geographers, and engineers, since the more varied an approach we take to a challenge, the more easily we will find an answer and a genuine solution.

This book outlines the intersection of the lessons, thoughts, and visions of leading strategic thinkers and their professional studies and memes. It serves as a meeting point for the results of strategic workshops, the guiding ideas of interesting books, and the interpretations of the latest trends. I am convinced that we need geography both as everyday people open to the world, and as professionals engaged in mapping and understanding it. If we would like to define geography in one sentence, we can say that it is a tool for getting to know the world. This is a guidebook in this special geo-moment, for which I seek to provide readers with both a map and a compass.

Let us set sail – *Navigare necesse est!*

Norbert Csizmadia

PART 1

THE GEOGRAPHY OF OUR EARTH: A MAP FOR DISCOVERING THE 21ST CENTURY

CHAPTER 1

WHY IS GEOGRAPHY IMPORTANT IN A GLOBALIZING WORLD?

Globalization is not only a feature of our time, but also a trend that has unfolded over a longer historical horizon. The ancient Roman Empire can be regarded as an undeniably globalized arrangement, unifying a major part of the world as it was known at that time. Major milestones paving the way to globalization have included the great geographic breakthroughs, from the discovery of the Americas to Magellan's first voyage around the world, and, much later, the expeditions to discover the unknown internal territories of various continents up until the 19th century. The unquestionable milestones of globalization were the colonial empires of the 19th century that spanned most of the world, among which the largest, the British Empire, covered 22% of the world's territory and constituted 20% of its population. It was held together in a unified administrative and economic framework when it was at its peak in 1922. Although large empires have disintegrated, with the United States and Russia being the only exceptions, unification has picked up speed and spread at a pace that was previously unfathomable.

Today, human society and the economy along with it have been radically transformed in the wake of globalization. The integration and the rise of networks within the global economy is unfolding at an accelerating pace from one decade to the next. The elimination of the barriers within the economy, the global unification of standards, and the global homogenization of consumption habits have given rise to a global economy that is increasingly becoming a unified whole and behaving like a single unit. This unification is also apparent in the global networks maintained by major financial institutions, spanning global hubs from Hong Kong to New York, and from London to Buenos Aires, allowing capital to flow freely between the different regions of the world. Therefore, it is no surprise that the role of geographic location has also been radically transformed in this new economic and social structure. In fact, the significance of geographic location and physical distance seems to be disappearing completely. In the wake of falling transportation costs and the extended physical reach of technologies, distances are shortening and space is becoming 'denser'.

The end of geography? – O'Brien was wrong

In the early 1990s, British economist Richard O'Brien published his book, *Global Financial Integration*.[1] This provided an analysis of the global financial system, and instantly made O'Brien the central figure in the debate on the role of location within our globalized world. O'Brien argued that even at the time of writing his book, tens of billions of dollars were trading hands on international money markets and, likewise, tens of billions of dollars could be transferred from one point of the world to another in a matter of mere seconds thanks to modern information technology. O'Brien predicted that "a state of economic development where geographical location no longer matters" was not far away.

Today, we can ascertain beyond any doubt that O'Brien (who later became a futurist before trying his hand at a career in music) was wrong. Experience has shown that from 1996-2016 territorial location gained significance within professional, scientific, and economic policy discourse in the midst of global restructuring. Several of the most influential thinkers addressing the world's global socioeconomic questions have dealt with the rising role of spatiality and places, specifically the growing significance of cities. An urban studies theorist, Richard Florida, presented a model where the role of places in general and cities in particular is deemed essential for the rise of the creative class, which is considered the driver of economic prosperity in his book, *The Rise of the Creative Class*. Edward L. Glaeser, professor of economics at Harvard University, wrote about the (economic) triumph of the city in one of his most important books.[2] At the same time, we must also take into account that geopolitical guru Robert D. Kaplan identifies the recognition of the pivotal role of territoriality within global processes as the key tenet of his book, *The Revenge of Geography*, which can be seen as a response to O'Brien.

Today, researching the geography of the world and of its smaller regions is gaining significance in various domains of social sciences. The new economic geography described by Paul Krugman, who was awarded the Nobel Prize for economics in 2008, set up a spatial equilibrium model of growth, and reincorporated geographic thinking into the mainstream of economic discourse.

What is in fact happening within the global economic space?

Globalization has slashed transportation costs, brought distant locations closer to each other, and seen the spatial networks of global production grow into a global web. In the knowledge-based economy, information may appear to disregard physical space and to be capable of being transmitted to any point of the world thanks to the steady rise in digital technologies. It is nevertheless apparent that strong territorial trends of concentration also prevail within the economy: the role of cities has become more important than ever, alongside the so-called 'agglomeration effect'. However, while the majority of product markets have taken on global dimensions, what are known as input markets – primarily labour and technology – remain very much linked to location.

Globalization not only unifies the world, it also divides it. The networks of production span the entire world, while the central zones of the economy are typically engaged in very different types of activities compared with the less-developed peripheries. The key difference lies in the value added that they create. The high wage costs of advanced economies can only be guaranteed by continuous invention and innovation, i.e. the monopoly of new products, while mass production can be relocated to less-developed regions offering lower production and wage costs.

The main consequences of globalization on the spatial aspect of the economy can be summarized as follows: the main globalization processes, i.e. the spread of information and communication technologies and growing deregulation, have created a dual spatial process, the geographic spread of economic activities coupled with stronger local trends. To put it differently, spatial concentration has gained economic significance, while long-term relationships between distant business partners may also be strengthened. The firms of global industries plan their product markets and sales in terms of country groups, and with respect to input markets and production, they think in terms of subnational regions, generally cities and their agglomerations. Globally competing companies have recognized that the sources of their competitive advantages are spatially concentrated, so they must take local action to bolster these advantages.

The competition between new economic geography and regions

According to Nobel laureate Paul Krugman's[3] 'New economic geography' theory, the general equilibrium theory describing new conditions can be expanded in space. Decreasing transportation costs, the growing significance of economies of scale, the role of increasing returns within global industries, spatial monopolistic (and oligopolistic) competition and the externalities of agglomerations describe the new economy operating under these new conditions. According to Krugman's new economic geography, the centripetal force leading to spatial concentration and the centrifugal force of spatial dispersion are the result of these effects, which combine to create spatial equilibrium. Spatial concentration, i.e. the growing significance of large urban economies that function as hubs within the global economy, follows from this theory.

The study of competition between countries and regions has become a major topic of interest of economic and regional studies, sparking much debate. In his earlier well-known argument,[4] Paul Krugman contested the idea that there would be similar competition among countries (and thus regions) as in the corporate sector – for instance, the success of a country would not necessarily come at the detriment of competitor countries. Krugman also considered the early use of the concept of competitiveness to be dangerous, because every country will be a winner in the international distribution of labour based on comparative advantages, with every country seeing an improvement in living standards. Every region's economy will automatically grow if they focus on their specialization based on their relative advantages.

Meanwhile, Michael E. Porter claims that competitive (i.e. absolute) rather than relative (comparative) advantages have become relevant in the competition among regions, similar to the competition between industries. Porter argues that in territorial competition, "competitiveness depends on productivity, i.e. how capital and human and natural resources are utilized locally. Productivity sets the sustainable standard of living."[5] What follows from this is that economic growth is not automatic. Regional competition will have its winners and losers, so programmes based on strategic planning must be incentivized in the context of economic development. Porter claims that cluster-based initiatives will be the ones able to survive in global competition.

Within regional economics and economic geography, it now seems accepted that regions compete, but this competition differs from that between corporations and countries. Roberta Capello writes that "regions compete on absolute rather than comparative advantages".[6] The consequences of regional competition are similar to those of the competition between countries: successfully competing regions see wages rise, the standard of living and employment improve, new investments emerge, and these regions attract talented and creative young people and businesses.

In the wake of this industrial competition, on the one hand the economic role of regions and territorial units is increasing, and there is greater business exploitation of the agglomeration advantages that stem from spatial concentration (essentially external spatial economies of scale). As a result of these processes, several of the initial hypotheses used in economics warrant a reassessment. These include the phenomenon of regional competition and the interpretation of economic growth and development, together with the economic policy and development concepts crafted in response to new challenges.

Where does knowledge grow? Locations within knowledge production

The global economy has entered a new stage of development – innovation, knowledge, and creativity are now the key criteria for successful economic growth.[7] Countries must therefore devise strategies that enable them to move their economies toward a path of knowledge- and innovation-driven development. This is an international competition and those who are unable to make this transition will be left behind and pushed to the periphery of development, synonymous with a permanently low standard of living. The key protagonists of knowledge- and innovation-driven development are the enterprises that are flexible, open, and creative, and are positioned in the forefront of product development. Meaningfully improving the business environment of these enterprises has therefore become a priority for governments.

The level of creativity of communities, regions, and countries is closely correlated with their economic development. The countries that understand the changes unfolding in the environment and view these as opportunities invest in knowledge and innovation. The countries that are unable to generate knowledge will have no other choice but to buy it. And knowledge is becoming an increasingly expensive asset. However, the spread of the knowledge economy has come hand in hand with ambiguity in terms of the role of geography.

In his book, *Triumph of the City*, Edward L. Glaeser emphasizes the importance of personal encounters as opposed to just the rise of the internet and information technology (IT) – the importance of which can be overstated. Glaeser cites numerous studies that confirm the fragility of groups that form and communicate solely electronically and maintains that IT tools should be improving the efficiency of personal meetings rather than being their substitute. Personal relationships are the foundation of deeper trust, greater respect, and more efficient communication and cooperation.

Geographic proximity is also a major factor for patents; it has been demonstrated that the number of patents that refer to each other is twice as high within a metropolitan region. Therefore, geographic proximity has not lost its significance in this age of information technology and information society. The circumstances allowing new ideas and knowledge to be born are still defined by geography (specifically, the geographic configuration of the agents that foster development). Today, geographic proximity continues to have a major impact on innovation and productivity.[8]

Only a portion of our knowledge, referred to as *digitizable knowledge* can flow globally with the help of information technology. However, there is a deeper dimension of knowledge that can only be conveyed – and even created and regenerated – through personal, face-to-face interactions and relationships. This type of knowledge, commonly known as tacit knowledge, a term coined by Michael Polanyi, holds the true secrets of innovation, production through technology and successful economic functioning. In an age where the value of economy is defined by knowledge, knowledge production and innovation arise in metropolises that serve as a backdrop for more concentrated human interactions, and specifically centres that host numerous activities and diversity. This holds true even where urban concentration and agglomeration yields negative impacts such as environmental and social tensions or growth in production and wage costs.

The appreciation in the value of geography is also apparent in the changes in the European Union's cohesion policy. Local developments were prioritized for the 2014–2020 programming period as a result of the Barca Report (published in 2009). In the Treaty of Lisbon – the European Union's unified fundamental document since 2012 – territorial cohesion was identified as a new objective geared toward a deeper understanding and shaping of spatial organization. These policies implement geographically harmonized developments based on territorial strategies tailored to every region. The principle of flexible geography introduced by the new programmes also attests to the rise of a location-based mentality. Space and location have thus become more important in cohesion policy, although they do not necessarily coincide with the territorial units defined by the administrative borders of countries and regions.

Held captive by geography – a changing and unstable world

Globalization has essentially reached everybody. Global correlations directly impact our personal lives in a number of scenarios, such as when our coworkers come from different national backgrounds, when we consume food produced in East Asia, or perhaps when our loan instalments change as a result of the shifting international balance of financial powers. Today, we are living in a changing and unstable world in terms of economy, society, demography, and climate.

The changes are closely correlated with the development of technology and are increasingly taking place on a global scale. This is why the early 21st century is considered to be an exceptionally uncertain period and why geopolitical analyses are becoming more important than ever. British foreign policy journalist Tim Marshall addressed these topics in his book, *The Prisoners of Geography*. Over the course of a career that spans 25 years, Marshall has been present in numerous major geopolitical theatres such as the Balkans, Afghanistan, and Syria. In his book Marshall draws attention to the underlying factors of the events in these theatres, specifically their geographic aspects.

He argues that the decisions of national leaders are shaped by geographic factors to a far greater degree than one would first think. This was true in ancient Athens, Persia, or Babylon, and today geography continues to influence the decisions of every leader.

In today's technological era, when the boundaries of mental and physical space are losing their significance, we are prone to forgetting the importance of geographic factors. Having said this, we are also at a time when we are witnessing quite the opposite in the sense that geographic factors are becoming increasingly decisive in international relations and political debate. And so we are seeing that the geographic laws familiar to Hannibal, Sun Tzu, or Alexander the Great still hold true today. Geopolitical developments impact every nation, during both times of war and times of peace.

The revenge of geography – geopolitics and the new world order

Robert D. Kaplan, former geopolitical analyst at Stratfor (a geopolitical intelligence platform and publisher) and the author of several books including *The Revenge of Geography* (2013), argues that geography holds the key to understanding drivers in the world, and specifically geopolitical and foreign policy conflicts. In his acclaimed book, Kaplan shows why the impact of geographic factors on societies is still active today, and that the Western elite's belief that geography has become obsolete is flawed, and underestimates and fails to take these factors into account when understanding and resolving conflicts. Although we may forget about the power of geographic factors, they do exist, Kaplan argues. Not even technological progress is capable of eliminating them, despite the fact that many believed the contrary. In fact, not only has technological progress failed to result in the 'end of geography', it has given greater significance to certain territorial aspects. The same applies to international relations and foreign policy. While the Western world sees international relations as a mere collection of laws and international treaties, the majority of the world thinks in terms of deserts, mountains, ports, and fresh water. No matter how obsolete this may seem, territory and the associated blood ties play a pivotal role in defining who and what we are.

Many were perplexed when Kaplan presented his theory in the context of our current global political setting, and attempted to outline the expected trends by factoring in geographic aspects in the 20 March 2014 issue of *Time* magazine. The surprise was even greater when Vladimir Putin occupied the Crimean Peninsula in early 2014, driven by exactly the same considerations. Russia took advantage of the fact that Europe had been weakened by the protracted economic recession and internal conflicts when annexing the peninsula in an effort to maintain its influence over Ukraine, playing the 'geographic card' multiple times. It then infiltrated (using indirect tools) the territories of Eastern Ukraine inhabited by a large Russian minority, which happened to constitute a link between Russia and the Crimean Peninsula.

A significant portion of the problems in the Middle East stems from a geographically driven battle between the Shiites of the Iranian

Plateau and the Sunnis of the Arabian Peninsula. The Eastern Saudi and Bahraini political oppression (Western Iraq and Western Syria) is fuelled by the conflict between Saudi Arabia and Iran. When Iran undertook to lay the technological and scientific foundations for building a nuclear bomb, Israel entered into a de facto alliance with Saudi Arabia. Israel in the late 2010s fears the consequences of a zero-sum game in the event of a potential confrontation and, despite its formidable military power, taking unilateral military action against Iran would exceed its capacities.

The most important territory for the United States in the 21st century is Asia, which has become far more unstable compared with the early 21st century. This is partly due to geographic reasons. The countries of East Asia had stabilized by the late 20th century, many of them establishing settled institutional systems and successful and thriving global-standard economies that have allowed and, in many regards, compelled, them to open up toward the rest of the world. Growing military ambitions began as early as in the 1990s. Asia's share of global military imports has risen from 15% to 41% since 1990, and its share of global military spending has swelled from 11% to 20%. Most conflicts have occurred due to the strategically located islands in the East and South China Sea, rich in natural gas and oil.

Although these disputes are often placed in a context of racial and ethnicity-based nationalism, they are not driven by moral or ideological motives, but are quite simply about territory. The tension between China and Japan or the many conflicts between China and Vietnam and the Philippines are so complex that although they could theoretically be resolved through negotiation, they will in fact be held in check by the balance between the Chinese and American navy and air force. The military ships stationed in the Pacific Ocean form a map similar to that of Europe in earlier centuries, enmeshed in a variety of conflicts. Although there is little chance of a war breaking out in the classic sense, East and South-East Asia are shaping up to be an increasingly troubled and complex region characterized by territorial disputes and the fight for controlling natural resources and trade routes.

The huge mountain ranges of the Himalayas have enabled India and China to live close to each other in relative peace. However, shrinking distances since the third quarter of the 20th century have made them strategic competitors in both the Indian Ocean and the South China Sea. In 2001, the election of Hindu nationalist Narendra Modi in India may have marked a more aggressive turn for Indian foreign policy, particularly with regard to Japan and China. China is expected to react with more pronounced and regime-centric nationalism to its economic struggles, disputes regarding maritime territories, and growing internal ethnic conflicts. It remains to be seen how long the Han Chinese, who account for 90% of China's population and inhabit its most prosperous regions, will be able to maintain control over the distant minority-populated peripheries that are now showing economic and social dissatisfaction. The greatest existential challenge facing China will not be controlling its currency, but rather its borders and certain regions, warns Kaplan.

According to Kaplan's vision, if geographic aspects are duly factored in, Western methods – such as the reinforcement of civil society and the rule of law – coupled with decentralization could prove efficient in resolving these conflicts. So, although a thriving civil society may emerge in Ukraine, its geographic position will compel it to maintain a continuously strong and sound relationship with Russia.

The Arab world is also set to stabilize sooner or later, but Western powers will be unable to impose their model on the complex and extremely populous Islamic societies, or only at a great expense. Meanwhile, there is also little likelihood of war breaking out in East Asia, however, ethnic nationalism will have to be addressed within the region.

The good news is that most redrawn boundaries affected by conflict are located within and not among states. For this reason, the cataclysms of the 20th century are not likely to repeat themselves. At the same time, continues Kaplan, civil society can only be reinforced by factoring in geographic attributes, and foreign policy must implement the strategic lessons of the underlying analysis in practice without sacrificing principles, and with a focus on geography.

CHAPTER 2

GEOGRAPHY: A TOOL FOR GETTING TO KNOW THE WORLD

At the beginning, geography referred to the description of the earth. This is reflected in the etymology of the word *geography*, where *-graphy* refers to the descriptive origin of the discipline. In the world's first geography manual, *Geographica*, Strabo, the first geographer and a contemporary of Christ, attempted to describe the known part of the world based on his own travels and the works of other geography writers. Geography later shed this descriptive role, by 'venturing out' into boundaries that integrate a territorial approach and thus created its own subfields.

Geography, the queen of sciences

The flow of knowledge between various disciplines occurs in all directions. The geography of the earth, or more specifically, the spatiality of the earth and its countries and regions, is no longer an area reserved for a small, isolated group of experts, i.e. professionals who deem themselves geographers based on their qualifications. On the contrary, it seems that sciences, particularly a broad range of social sciences, is increasingly turning toward geography, by necessity. As noted earlier, new ideas have been emerging with extraordinary intensity on the boundary between economics and geography.

The reason for this is that as they intrude into mainstream economic mentality, the pivotal role that geographic attributes play in the economic development of countries and the world is becoming ever more apparent. These scientific developments have given rise to new disciplines.

Consider, for example, the transformation of China into a superpower and its economic rise. No matter how we expand the frameworks of economics, it is unable to explain this, let alone forecast it. The same holds true for the other changes that were momentous from the perspective of economics such as the 2008 global economic crisis, the Arab Spring in 2011 and the ensuing migratory pressure, or the rise and fall of various macroregions. The rise of geo-economics at the intersection of geography, geopolitics, and economics is recognition that development on a global scale is often best explained by geographic and historical correlations.[9]

In the wake of these two-directional developments, geography has transformed into a science dealing with all the spatial dimensions, configurations, correlations of and interactions between global social, economic, and environmental processes and phenomena. Peter Haggett's *Geography: A Global Synthesis* is a seminal book for today's geography. The nearly 1,000-page book was first published in 1972, and has been updated and reissued several times to corroborate the synthesizing significance of geography in higher education worldwide.

Haggett offers his own interpretation of geography, grouping his answers into the five topics: location, place, movement, human–environmental interaction, and region. Geography has long shed the closed nature of positivism, and has entered into interactions with the most varied domains.

If mathematics, necessary for scientific knowledge, is the king of sciences, then geography, which attempts to capture the entire world using its spatial concepts and which in its own way has a productive relationship with nearly every other discipline, is unquestionably the most beautiful discipline, that is, the queen of sciences. This mysterious queen is now a discipline, a cultural domain, an academic subject, a mentality, a perspective, and also an increasingly common representation method. And in the approach of this book, geography is the best tool for getting to know the world.

Geographic studies focus on interactions

Geography is the study of interactions in multiple directions. The spatial distribution of various social, economic, and demographic phenomena is shaped by numerous factors, and at first the investigation is aimed at discovering how other elements of geographic space impact the subject of the study. The findings are expressed in the spatial concepts of geography. For example, if the analysis pertains to the spatial distribution of certain communities, then we first assess the location of these communities and their basic data and facts (such as population, the number of births and deaths, the degree of emigration and immigration, the number of commuters etc.).

As a second step, the factors that shaped the specific (territorial) configuration are examined. Therefore, the essence of a geographer's work is to identify correlations and select the most relevant determinants among the essentially infinite number of possibilities. Such an analysis cannot leave out the role of humankind. We should consider humanity's influence while asking ourselves questions such as: why do global metropolises emerge where they do? Because of their coastal location or perhaps because of historical factors, the abundance of resources? In most cases, we can find one or several answers, or a combination thereof, that provide a satisfactory explanation.

The third step of the analysis involves reversing the sequence of questioning: what are the consequences of the described and experienced territorial configuration emerging? If we remain in the realm of cities, we could ask questions such as: how do transportation systems adapt to their configuration? What impact do they exert with respect to political geography? What impact does the presence of a global metropolis have on the natural environment? A thorough analysis can reveal numerous, almost an infinite number of consequences, of which we generally seek the most relevant.

"Geography thus describes where places are and what they are like, answers the questions of why they are located where they are and what has shaped their attributes, and the consequences of their specific location."[10] This is basically the same thing that any other science does, from sociology to chemistry: each of these examines a phenomenon and then attempts to provide an explanation. For geography, we can say that it describes the spatial aspect of phenomena and their system of interaction with space. So, what is the problem with geography? According to some beliefs, geography is not even a science.

Geography does not function according to a pure set of geographic laws, and tends to use laws describing the space-related findings of other scientific disciplines, for instance, physical geography uses facts from geology, geophysics, and meteorology, while social geography mainly uses knowledge from economics and sociology.

The perfect system – the world's physical geography

A key element to examining phenomena from a geographic perspective is understanding and presenting spatial systemicity. The spatial modelling of economic, social, and cultural rules is an important and productive effort of the sciences, one example of which is the almost perfect systemicity of physical geography. This is capable of encompassing the spatial patterns of the climate, geomorphology, the flora, rock structures, soils, and even the resulting economic resources and opportunities. Geographic *zonality* is a good example of this. Within the system of geographic *zonality*, the geographic distance from the equator and the poles (*equatorial zonality*) and the geographic distance from the seas (*maritime zonality*) play a role. These spatial concepts provide an explanation for the global systems of atmospheric circulation and ocean currents, as well as for most environmental features in nature, and the economic attributes built upon these features.

Geographic zonality

How does the geographic explanatory model work in practice? The model can be well illustrated in its use for exploring the background of winemaking and wine consumption, a complex sociocultural and economic institution with a history of more than 6,000 years.

To identify the causes, we must look back very far, as far back as Earth's location in the solar system, and more specifically to the issue of geographic zonality. This emerged because of two fundamental reasons: the Earth's spheroid shape and its axial tilt. Its spheroid shape means that the solar angle of incidence around the equator is nearly 90° (at noon), and nearly 0° in polar regions. As the angle of incidence of the sun's rays is the main factor affecting the rise in soil temperatures, average temperature gradually decreases as we move from the equator toward the poles.

However, due to the Earth's axial tilt, the perpendicular culmination point migrates from one point to another between the tropics, touching each tropic once a year and traversing the area between them twice a year. This creates high temperatures between the two tropics, an area that is therefore called the hot tropics.

The north and south poles are located at the northern and southern extremities of the Earth's axis of rotation and they delineate the areas where the angle of sunlight reaches 0° during certain periods of the year. The thermal effect of the so-called solar zones determined by the angle of sunlight is significantly modified by the geographic distribution of the other elements on the Earth's surface, such as topographic and hydrosphere elements. The interactions between these elements give rise to the climatic zones. Zonality is also characteristic of the ecosystem due to the interactions between specific temperature conditions and air circulation and hydrological cycles, the geological and structural attributes shaping their territorial directions, as well as their soil conditions.

Wine production is dependent on the grape, and only certain geographic regions are able to provide the fertile soil required. The best regions and core winemaking areas are located between the 30th and 50th parallels in the northern hemisphere, which includes the Mediterranean region, and between the 20th and 40th parallels in the southern hemisphere.

Among the geographic conditions forming the foundations of viticulture, the main factors are the climate, the topography, and the soil attributes. In terms of climate, the optimum regions for wine production and viticulture feature average temperatures between 9°C and 21°C throughout the year. Precipitation must reach an annual 500 mm, otherwise irrigation is necessary. However, lower precipitation can be offset using special planting methods. The distribution of annual precipitation is most relevant during the pre-harvesting period; too much rain at this time can significantly damage quality. The optimal amount of sunshine is between 1,800 and 2,500 hours annually, and this figure may even reach 3,000 on the islands of Southern Europe.

However, the explanatory power of geography presumably has its limits. Some 45% of the world's vineyard regions are located in Europe,[11] but traditional European wine-producing countries continue to produce more than 70% over of the world's wine. The discrepancy stems partially from reasons based on natural attributes, farming traditions, and the diverse interactions of the European spirit, taste, and philosophical background. If we dig deeper, it is easy to identify the underlying geographic drivers behind the social and cultural factors, which lead us back to the explanatory model of geography.

Between 2009 and 2014, the European Union produced 167 million litres of wine on average every year, and accounted for 57% of the world's wine consumption and 70% of wine product exports.[12] The top three wine-producing countries are France, Italy, and Spain, and this ranking has remained unchanged for a long time. Other major wine producers in Europe include Germany, Portugal, Hungary, Romania, Bulgaria, and Greece. In recent years, New World wines have been rapidly catching up with traditional wine-producing countries, and the United States (mainly California), Argentina, Chile, the Republic of South Africa, Australia, and New Zealand have become major players in the industry. This trend is also driven by the geographic factors that shape the dynamics of development and change in our societies.

The economic and political impact of El Niño

El Niño, a complex and global weather phenomenon, can be integrated into geographic zonality and used to make forecasts. *El Niño* (which means 'little boy' in reference to the Christ Child, as the phenomenon is most intense around Christmas time along the Peruvian coast) is a large oceanic, atmospheric, and climatic phenomenon in the tropical regions of the Pacific Ocean. Strictly speaking, it is the warm phase of the sea surface between the Peruvian coast and the Indonesian islands, which periodically changes its temperature. It creates storms and flooding in the Pacific coasts of North and South America and the Caribbean region, and droughts in South-East Asia and the western basin of the Pacific Ocean.

El Niño may lead to a rise in inflation, albeit only to the slight degree of 1%, and some countries may even benefit from this. *El Niño* primarily impacts the rate of inflation and the price of consumption items in the short run, but may also shape national politics when coupled with other circumstances. The *El Niño* phenomenon's main feature is an above-average rise in temperatures in the middle portion of the Pacific Ocean.

South America is affected by huge amounts of precipitation. The drought continues in winter and spring in Indonesia, while North America faces higher temperatures and above-average precipitation.

Changes in weather mainly affect mining and agriculture. Drought decreases crop yields, while rainfall hinders the extraction of raw materials, which in turn impacts their price. In South America, ore is affected to the greatest degree, while in South-East Asia, palm oil is the most vulnerable commodity. *El Niño* also affects the price index of other commodities indirectly, causing inflation in the affected countries, albeit of under 1% based on the latest data. According to the International Monetary Fund (IMF), this trend mainly affects Japan, South Korea, Chile, Thailand, India, and Indonesia.

13°C annual average temperature

The example of winemaking has shown how the explanation of economic processes requires the application of geographic aspects. We have just demonstrated the role of complex weather phenomena in the modelling, interpretation, and projection of socioeconomic developments. Recently there has been a growing trend in man-made climate change that can also be captured with geographic concepts. Climate change is something that will have mostly adverse consequences for us, something that both climate sceptics and those fearing climate change–induced catastrophes will agree to. Given this consensus, a paper published in the journal, *Nature* in October 2015[13] caused quite a surprise with its conclusion that climate change may trigger a rise in productivity in developed countries.

The authors of the 2015 paper proposed that an average growth figure should be found with respect to temperature, which would act as a point of reference in identifying unequivocal fluctuations in economic growth.

The authors managed to find this exact value, demonstrating that warmer-than-average years hinder growth in the developed and developing countries where the annual average temperature is 13°C or higher.

According to their analysis, in Brazil, which already has a warmer-than-average climate, a 3°C increase in annual average temperatures would reduce economic output by 3%. Meanwhile, Germany and France, which have average annual temperatures below the optimum cut-off value, perform better during warmer years.

In the United States or Australia, where the annual average temperature is 13°C or slightly higher, warmer years may curb economic growth. In certain regions of the United States, on every warmer day when daily average temperatures exceed 24°C–27°C, average daily revenue per employee decreases by 20%, and this figure rises to 28% on very warm days when the average temperature is above 30°C. The paper by Marshall Burke, Solomon Hsiang and Edward Miguel made great ripples.[14]

According to the World Bank, there are ten countries that have annual average temperatures between 11°C and 15°C. Spain, Afghanistan, and Nepal have annual average temperatures closest to the defined cut-off value. In Europe, Spain and Greece have annual average temperatures that are closest to 13°C. Among global metropolises, Toronto, Boston, Pennsylvania, Seattle, Detroit, Chicago, Porto, Lisbon, Madrid, Marseille, Nice, Milan, Ankara, Tbilisi, Kabul, Beijing, Tokyo, Melbourne, Wellington, and Cape Town have annual average temperatures closest to 13°C. The average temperature for European Union Member States is 9.25°C, and the average temperature in G20 members is 12.64°C.

The *Economist*,[14] citing another paper, also emphasized that in the construction, manufacturing and the transportation industries, temperatures above 29°C exacerbate worker fatigue, meaning they are able to work one hour less on average per day.

In countries with average temperatures of over 13°C, managing warming temperatures and maintaining productivity results in substantially higher costs, because the lower indoor temperatures necessary for effective work must be maintained at an extra expense.

In Singapore for example, energy use by buildings accounts for 40% of the city-state's total energy consumption. Therefore, if we are unable to curb the impact of climate change, then the world's electricity consumption will increase by 83% between 2010 and 2100.

CHAPTER 3

OUR EARTH IN THE 21ST CENTURY

"What place would you advise me to visit now?" he asked.
"The planet Earth," replied the geographer. "It has a good reputation."

Antoine de Saint-Exupéry
The Little Prince translated by Katherine Wood

For the Little Prince, who embarked on a trip on the recommendation of the strange geographer who had no field experience, the Earth hid many more treasures than the other planets he had visited. As we have learned from Saint-Exupéry's novel, the Earth was so huge that a veritable army of lamplighters had to be used to illuminate the six continents. There were a total of about 2 billion grown-ups including 111 kings, 7,000 geographers, 900,000 businessmen, 7.5 million tipplers and 311 million conceited men.

It is clear that these figures were invented off the cuff, in the context of the tale, based on the era when Saint-Exupéry was alive.[15] Profound changes have occurred in the 75 years since its publication, from an increase in the world's population (to 7.4 billion) to our far greater knowledge about the Earth and life on Earth. The Earth that Saint-Exupéry's geographer believed to be permanent and sound seems to be increasingly threatened and threatening in light of our new knowledge and the trends of the 21st century. So what could we say to a Little Prince or a similar stranger falling to Earth in the 21st century?

The Earth is not round after all...

There are many confusing facts regarding our planet. First, the shape of the Earth itself may come as a surprise for many. One of the first milestones for getting to know our planet was defining its shape. The first theories from antiquity represented Earth as a flat disc. Plato and Aristotle, as well as Pythagoras and Eratosthenes, corroborated their theory that the Earth was (more or less) round relatively early. The theory that the Earth was flat then spread again in the Middle Ages, but the great discoveries provided concrete evidence that the ancient thinkers were right; by sailing around the globe, it was proven beyond any doubt that the planet was round, a fact that has since been confirmed from outer space.

However, the Earth is not exactly round: it has a unique spheroid shape, jutting in some places and indented in others. But these are negligible; the Earth would be smoother than a billiard ball if both were the same size.[16] Not even the highest altitudes and greatest depths would influence this to a significant degree.

And yet it moves...

The Earth's surface appears immobile if viewed from above; however, in fact, the entire planet and life on Earth is in constant movement, even in the case of a seemingly stable entity such as the Earth's crust. For instance, the African Plate drifts 2.5 cm toward the north-east every year, while the Pacific Plate drifts 7 cm–11 cm toward the north-west.[17] Movements of tectonic plates (driven by currents in the Earth's mantle) have consequences that are felt on the surface in the form of earthquakes or volcanic activity.

More than 500,000 earthquakes are detected every year, 100,000 of which are within the range that can be felt by humans and 100 of which cause significant damage. Earthquakes and volcano eruptions occur most frequently in geographically clearly definable areas, at the edges of diverging or converging tectonic plates, at transform boundaries or subduction zones.

Japan experiences 1,500 perceptible earthquakes every year. Southern California gets more than 10,000 earthquakes, although most cannot be felt.[18] Destructive volcano eruptions are rarer, with 10–20 volcanoes exhibiting some sort of activity every day. We currently know of 1,500 potentially active volcanoes, of which approximately 500 have erupted at some time during the course of human history.[19] The biggest of these was the eruption of Krakatoa located in Indonesia, with a force four times greater than that of the most powerful explosive device ever created. The eruption claimed 36,000 human casualties, but also had a number of longer-term indirect impacts. The volcanic ash and debris ejected into the atmosphere reduced the earth's average temperature by 1.2°C.[20]

The oil of the future: water

A considerable portion of the Earth's surface is uninhabitable for humans. One third of this area is covered by deserts and two thirds by water, mainly in liquid state, but a smaller area is covered by water in solid state. Water is also present on Earth in the form of vapour, making it the only planet in the solar system where water can be found in all three states.[21] Despite the apparent blue hue of our planet, water only accounts for 0.07% of Earth's mass and only 0.4% of its volume. Merely 3% is fresh water.[22] Ninety per cent of this can be found in solid state in Antarctica, while 20% of the not constantly frozen fresh water is found in Lake Baikal, Russia.[23]

Merely three thousandths of the water found on Earth is suitable for human use.[24] As such, water is a scarce resource but one that we need in every aspect of our lives. It is invisibly incorporated into every product and service that we use, and which we use rather wastefully. Producing 1 kilogram of chocolate requires 24,000 litres of water; producing 1 kilogram of beef requires 15,500 litres of water; a pair of jeans requires 13,000 litres of water; a cup of tea requires 35 litres and one sheet of paper requires 10 litres. All the while, we are so wasteful with water in our day-to-day lives. Flushing a toilet uses 10 litres of water and taking a shower uses approximately 190 litres.[25]

Water shortage is already a pressing issue today, mainly in developing countries. The quantitative and qualitative lack of water and wastewater management causes approximately US$260 million in losses every year.[26] According to the United Nation's (UN) forecast, two thirds of the world's population will be affected by water shortage in 2025. Water consumption per capita is the highest in the United States, followed by Greece, Malaysia, Italy, and Thailand.[27]

The hydrological cycle is a balanced process on a global scale, but it is marked by huge differences on a territorial scale. The Atacama Desert (South America) has not seen rain for as long as humankind can remember,[28] and Antarctica gets 0 mm of annual precipitation as well, while certain parts of the Indian state of Meghalaya get nearly 12,000 mm of precipitation every year. According to the latest research,[29] water can be found not only on the surface of the Earth, but also in its mantle, and the volume of the latter potentially amounts to three times that of surface waters. One should of course not imagine the deep-lying oceans described by Jules Verne, but rather water that is bound chemically to and trapped inside minerals. The inside of our Earth is made up of concentric layers, so-called spherical shells, of varying physical state, composition and size. At its core, Earth is not only almost as hot as the sun and composed of 88% iron, but also has gold content that would be enough to cover the surface of our planet at a thickness of almost half a metre.[30] This gold is of course inaccessible. The same is not true for the minerals and energy sources located in Earth's crust, which are extracted to a growing degree using increasingly creative methods thanks to advancing technologies in order to meet the continuously rising demand.

The fuel for development

Humanity's energy consumption per capita has increased 120-fold since the hunter-gatherer societies.[31] Energy use has not only increased, but has also become more complex because humans initially used energy only for the needs of their own body, and later for keeping animals. Today, Google's energy consumption alone (2.26 million kWh) accounts for 0.013% of the world's energy consumption, which corresponds to the total energy consumption of 200,000 households. A single Google search, of which there are approximately two million every second and more than 100 billion on average per month (2015),[32] uses 0.0003 kWh of energy and leads to the emission of 0.2 g of CO2 into the atmosphere.[33]

Energy use has become extremely diverse; however, the types of available energy sources have remained limited. Early on, only biomass was used, typically in the form of food or wood. Later, renewables (wind and solar energy), fossil fuels, and nuclear energy were added to the energy mix. Over 80% of energy use continues to be fuelled by the limited amount of biomass that has accumulated during earlier historical eras.[34]

This energy mix varies on a wide scale from one country to the next, depending on the available energy sources as determined by geographic or geological attributes, and the prevalence of sustainable energy management considerations. Iceland's geological attributes allow it to obtain 78% of its energy from geothermal energy and the rest from hydropower.[35] Meanwhile, Denmark already used wind power to cover 39.1% of its electricity needs in 2014.[36]

Coal remains the unrivalled leader among the biggest consumers. In the United States, 33% of electricity is generated in coal-fired power plants,[37] and China alone uses half of the world's coal to generate its heat and electricity.[38]

One minute before midnight – the Anthropocene

The Earth's growing population and the increasingly diverse and intense human activity has transformed our planet. To get a notion of the dramatic speed of this process, let us compare the time dimension of humanity's existence with the Earth's age. If we regard the Earth's 4.5 billion-year history as covering a 24-hour time span, then life was created at 4:00:00am and humanity at 11:58:43pm.[39]

The Anthropocene is the term that has been given to the current geological age, defined by the impact of human activity on Earth. Although the distinction of the Anthropocene as a geological period has not yet been officially accepted and there is a lack of consensus regarding its outset, its use is becoming increasingly accepted within geological sciences. Its beginning is marked by the first Industrial

Revolution and the invention of the steam engine, when humanity made a huge leap in progress and the transformation of its environment.

The most conspicuous human-induced phenomenon with perhaps the most severe and complex consequences is the rise in greenhouse gas concentrations, as a result of which the earth's average temperature has increased by 0.8°C since the Industrial Revolution.[40] Many other adverse phenomena have also been triggered, ultimately damaging humanity's standard of living: 13 million hectares of the world's forest are transformed every year into agricultural land, namely in South America, Africa, and East Asia;[41] the world's seas are 30% more acidic today than in the 18th century;[42] 6 billion kilograms of waste, mainly plastic, are dumped into the oceans every year, which may take centuries to decompose, depending on their type;[43] 40% of the world's animal population has become extinct in the 40 years prior to writing, because of the damage caused to natural habitats.[44]

The complex impact on the environment is expressed using the ecological footprint for each individual country. This is the amount of land and water that a human society (or individual) needs to sustain itself and to absorb the waste it produces, in other words, the extent of the impact on the natural environment. The main purpose of this measure is to ingrain resource-conservation and raise awareness in industrialized countries. Measured on an absolute scale, China, the United States, and India have the biggest ecological footprints.[45] At the level of individuals, the United States also tops the ranking. While its population is less than 5% of the global figure, it accounts for 25% of resource consumption and 30% of waste production. If every person on Earth opted for this lifestyle, we would need six planet Earths to survive.[46] The inhabitants of the rest of the developed world, Russia, and the oil-producing countries of the Arabian Peninsula are not far behind the United States in terms of their ecological footprint. Meanwhile, India's and Indonesia's ecological footprint per capita is less than 180 global hectares, and even China's footprint is no more than double this figure.

The growing global population

Although the Earth's population has been continuously growing over time, the greatest increase has occurred over the past century. Since 1950, the world's population has nearly tripled. It stood at more than 7.6 billion on 1 July 2018.[47] According to the UN's average growth scenario, the human population will grow to 11.25 billion by 2100. Lebanon has the highest national population growth rate (9.37%).[48] This demographic trend is driven mainly by the improvements in medical care and the development of infrastructure and public services.

Social, economic and demographic changes have triggered more intense migration processes than ever before. While there were 175 million migrants in 2000, their figure had grown to 252 million by 2013 and the trend is unbroken. Half of the emigrants originate from ten countries, while the five most common destination countries are the United States, Russia, Germany, Saudi Arabia, and the United Arab Emirates.[49]

Facts and data about the global population

- The Earth's population grew from 1 billion to 2 billion over the course of 123 years, hitting the milestone in 1927. The population grew from 6 billion to 7 billion between 1999 and 2012, i.e. over 13 years.
- Twenty-six per cent of the global population is below the age of 15, and by 2015, the number of those aged between 10 and 24 reached 1.8 billion, an unprecedented figure.
- Many European countries are experiencing shrinking or stagnating populations; the 48 least-developed countries account for the bulk of the world's population.
- Asia is of course the continent with the highest population, hosting 60% of humanity, i.e. 4.2 billion people.
- China has the highest population in the world (1.35 billion), followed closely by India (1.25 billion). The two countries together account for 37% of the global population.
- The world's population grew at the slowest pace in 2011, at only 1.1%, while the greatest increase occurred in 1963, at 2.2%.

- Antarctica is the only continent with no permanent human population; its population depends on the research conducted there.
- The ratio of men to women in the world is 1,010:1,000.
- Global life expectancy is 65 years, but there are huge national discrepancies in this regard. Life expectancy in Sierra Leone is only 47 years, while in Switzerland it is 88 years for someone born today.
- If we assume that the average person weighs 70 kilograms, the global population weighs 285 million tonnes.
- Han Chinese is the largest ethnic group in the world, accounting for 19% of the world's population.
- There are nearly 350 cities worldwide with populations exceeding 1 million.

Urban concentration

Over half (54%) of the global population lives in an urban environment, and humanity's largest wave of urbanization will continue in the years to come. Urbanization creates huge changes in lifestyle and shapes landscapes, profoundly increasing work opportunities and access to education and other public services. At the same time, it exacerbates social inequalities, which are expressed in spatial terms with the concentration of the individual social groups in segregated urban zones and informal communities.

Urbanization has also exacerbated social conflicts, therefore policies geared toward managing urbanization processes must incorporate safeguards for guaranteeing human rights for the sake of sustainable development.

In terms of community size, nearly half of the global population lives in communities of under 500,000, and only one person out of eight lives in megalopolises of over 10 million. The ratio of those living in cities of less than 500,000 is highest in Europe (65%), and these smaller cities form a dense urban network across Europe, the Old Continent.

The number of cities with a population of over 10 million, and the population concentrated in them, are both growing. There were only ten cities in this category in 1990, hosting 7% of the global population or 153 million people. This figure had nearly tripled by 2014, reaching 28, which meant that these cities hosted 453 million people or 12% of the global population. According to the UN's forecast, their number is set to reach 41 by the year 2030.[50]

By 2050, Tokyo and Delhi will continue to lead the ranking of the biggest megalopolises, with nearly identical populations. The UN's *World Urbanization Prospects* report published in 2015 predicted that Tokyo's population will shrink from 38 million to 37 million, while Delhi's population will increase from 25 million to 36 million. However, according to the short-term prognosis, Tokyo's population will expand by 5% to 39 billion and Delhi's population by 40% to 33 million, by 2025.

Medium-sized cities of under 1 million inhabitants located in the vicinity of megalopolises in emerging Asian and African countries will grow at the most dynamic rate.

Cities facing diminishing populations are usually situated in high-productivity Asian countries such as Japan and South Korea, or regions in Europe facing diminishing or stagnating populations.

If the world were 100 people...

When the global population reached 7 billion in 2011, *100people.org* repeated pioneering American environmental scientist Donella Meadows' (1941–2001) study conducted in 1990,[51] modelling the characteristics of the world's population on a 100-member group, and presenting the distribution of the world's population by gender, age, and cultural and ethnic attributes.

Business Insider took an interesting approach to the same question: what if the world's population was shrunk to 100 people?

- There would be 50 females and 50 males; 26 would be children, 74 would be adults, only 8 of whom would be 65 and older
- There would be 60 Asians, 15 Africans, 14 people from the Americas, and 11 Europeans
- There would be 33 Christians, 22 Muslims, 14 Hindus, 7 Buddhists, 12 people who practise other religions and 12 people who would not be aligned with a religion

- Out of the 100, 48 would subsist on less than $2 per day, while one in two children would live in poverty
- 77 people would have a home, but 23 would be homeless
- Only 7 people would have a college degree
- 22 would own or share a computer
- 77 would use a mobile telephone
- 30 would be active internet users.

Linguistic diversity in the world

While humanity is quite fragmented in terms of languages, the three great world religions cover more than two thirds of the global population. The above-mentioned *100people.org* study also looked at language distribution in 2011, and found that 12 people of out 100 would speak Chinese, 5 would speak Spanish, 5 would speak English, 3 would speak Arabic, 3 would speak Hindi, 3 would speak Bengali, 3 would speak Portuguese, 2 would speak Russian, 2 would speak Japanese and 62 would speak other languages. Modern linguistic studies have reported diverging figures for the total number of languages spoken worldwide, but estimates put the figure around 6,500–7,000. *Ethnologue*, the encyclopedia of global languages, contains the descriptions of 7,102 languages.

Social progress

The living standards of the global population, including public health, life expectancy, access to education, and income position, have improved considerably in recent times. These conditions, along with other indicators, constitute the basis of the *Human Development Index* (HDI) introduced by the UN.

The UN has been publishing this widely recognized composite indicator for 25 years, during which the HDI has grown by more than 20% in global terms and by 40% for developing countries. This has brought the number of countries with exceptionally high HDI from 12 to 46 between 1990 and 2014, and their population from 0.5 billion to 1.2 billion.

At the level of individual countries, we can find examples of even faster development: Ethiopia, for example, has boosted its HDI by over 50% over the period under review, Rwanda raised it by nearly 50%, while Angola and Zambia increased their HDI by nearly one third between 1990 and 2014. It is not surprising that countries with low HDI in 1990 were able to achieve the greatest improvement, as a lower figure is easier to multiply than a higher one.

It should be stressed that there is no proportional, linear correlation between HDI and income per capita, although greater work opportunities and income per capita (as a sub-index of HDI) played an important role in this.

Social progress actually conceals huge inequalities. Infant mortality in sub-Saharan Africa is still at the level of mid-19th century England. The second cause of death among women in emerging countries is still complications of pregnancy and childbirth. In global terms, nearly 800 women die every day as a result of pregnancy or childbirth, despite the great progress in this area since 1990: by 2015, the proportion of deaths associated with pregnancy had decreased by 45% globally.

CHAPTER 4

THE GLOBAL ECONOMY: THE PRESENT

The United States is the biggest player in the global economy, accounting for 23.3% of it and featuring an economic structure that is dominated by services: 79.7% of its companies in this field, compared with the global average of 63.6%. Meanwhile, agriculture and industry make up smaller-than-average portions of the economy, 1.1% and 19.1%, respectively, compared with global averages of 5.9% and 30.5%. We can also see that in absolute terms, the United States still has the largest industrial sector in the world.

The world's second-largest economy, China (13.9%), is more balanced in terms of its sectoral distribution, although the service sector is currently growing at a rapid pace. The main difference of its economic structure compared with other higher-income countries is its agriculture sector, which is above-average (with a 9.1% contribution), and the fact that its industry and agriculture together contribute more to its economic performance than services. But services will become increasingly predominant in China's growth structure, fostered by the development directions of its 13th Five-Year Plan (2016–2020) announced in late 2015, which introduced a new growth model for the country. This will entail structural transformations in the economy, with the declared objective of increasing the contribution of services and consumption to GDP and reducing excess capacities in industries exhibiting overproduction. This will no doubt result in a decrease of agriculture's share within the economy. The growing contribution of services to GDP is also emerging in India, coupled with an expected decrease in the contribution of agricultural sectors.

The future of the global economy: The economy will quintuple by 2045

According to the analysis of the British Ministry of Defence's economic department,[52] the size of the global economy will expand to several times its 2012 value by the year 2045. This development will predominantly be driven by China, the United States, India, and the European Union. In the European Union, the United Kingdom will expand the most compared with the 2012 figure by 2045, by nearly 86.9%, followed by France by 72.7% and Germany by 46.8%. China will see its economy quadruple, the United States will experience an expansion of 95.5%, India will show a 4.5-fold increase, and the European Union will grow by 75.7% as a whole. Among developed countries, Japan will expand the least, only by 45%, Canada will grow 1.2-fold and Australia 1.5-fold. Russia and Saudi Arabia will see their economies expand at roughly the same rate by 2045, to 1.6-fold and 1.55-fold the 2012 figure, respectively.

According to the estimates, Ethiopia, Nigeria, Egypt, and Kazakhstan have the potential to exhibit the greatest growth rate, while other high-growth countries as compared with the 2012 figure include Indonesia, Turkey, Chile, Algeria, South Africa, and Mexico.

The most robust economies

The world's largest economies (based on nominal gross domestic product (GDP)) in 2015 were the United States, China, Japan, Germany, the United Kingdom, France, India, Italy, Brazil, and Canada. Interestingly, while the United States ranks first based on nominal GDP, it only ranks 11th based on income per capita (average income earned per person). Meanwhile, China continues to exhibit the highest growth rate among the top economies. Although Japan, which ranks third based on nominal GDP, may be seeing a slowdown in its economic expansion, it still ranks high globally in terms of purchasing power, being the fourth economy in this respect. It also ranks fourth based on export output. Germany is the fourth largest economy, ranking fifth in purchasing power, second based on exports and third based on product imports.

The British economy is the second largest in Europe. It is the fifth largest globally, based on nominal GDP, and the eighth largest in terms of purchasing power. France has the sixth highest nominal GDP on a global scale, and the third-highest in Europe. India ranks seventh based on nominal GDP, and, interestingly, ranks third globally for purchasing power. After the economic reforms adopted in 1991, it has become one of the fastest-growing economies in the world. Italy is the 24th most advanced economy globally, but it occupies eighth place among the top economies thanks to its relatively low unemployment and high income per capita. Brazil ranks ninth based on nominal GDP and seventh for purchasing power. Canada comes in 10th based on nominal GDP and 13th for purchasing power.

A web of airways and hubs

The emergence of global economic processes has been largely driven by the establishment of rapid air transport connections, and the spread of information and communication tools and networks enabling diverse data traffic.

The term hub was first coined in transportation geography, and refers to the air-traffic junctures and transit points serving as the biggest assembly and distribution centres. Hubs have gained huge significance in parallel with globalization, and the development potential of certain cities is defined by their capacity to become global hubs. When a city forges cross-continent links, it gains a situational advantage that enables it to better utilize its local attributes. This then creates a direct feedback loop to its role within the global or regional network of communities. This is why the centres that play various territorial roles are referred to as gateways or hub cities, signifying their capacity to 'open the gates' to their region through their large-scale transportation links. Thus a hub plays a significant role in a region's air-traffic network and developments linked to air transport. The patterns of this network also determine the 'winning regions' of the urban competition in the processes of globalization. Based on the miles flown by international air travellers in 2010, the airlines clocking the most traveller miles spent in the air are Dubai's Emirates,

Lufthansa, Delta Air Lines, Air France, British Airways, the Hong Kong-based Cathay Pacific, and Singapore Airlines. The territorial patterns of the air connections operated by these leading airlines also outline the most developed and most significant metropolises within the global economy.

Features of the world's air-traffic network[53]

- Every country, irrespective of its size, can be reached via the aircraft of at least one airline.
- Every airline that has aircraft of adequate size operates flights to New York or London, the latter a consequence of earlier colonial ties. Airlines that serve two United States destinations also operate flights to either Washington, DC or Los Angeles.
- According to traveller traffic data, the Canary Islands are the most popular holiday destination in Europe, followed by Spain and Portugal.
- The leading holiday destinations for air travellers in the United States are Hawaii, Mexico, and the Caribbean.
- Asia's most popular destinations are the Philippines, Okinawa, Thailand, Guam (which is located between Mexico and the Philippines), and Bali.
- The density of flights in Europe far exceeds those in Japan or the United States. Europe boasts more airlines than any other place in the world.
- In terms of flights per capita, Australia comes in first.
- Every Muslim country operates flights to Jeddah located in the Makkah Region on the coast of the Red Sea, often referred to as Saudi Arabia's tourist centre and second most important city, as well as to the capital of Saudi Arabia, Riyadh.
- Eighty per cent of international flights in Central and South America serve United States destinations, with the main urban connection points being Miami, New York, Dallas, Houston, and Los Angeles.
- The African airways are mainly ruled by South African airlines.

- The countries with the weakest ties to the air-traffic network are Iraq, the Republic of the Congo, Zimbabwe, Myanmar, Nepal, and Peru.
- The surprisingly high air traffic of certain regions creates local economic or political issues and conflicts, for instance in Egypt, Ethiopia, Mali, Sri Lanka, Russia, Togo, Ghana, Ecuador, Angola, or Bangladesh.

The new world order according to Kotkin: the 19 new regional tribal alliances of society and culture

The growing significance of global networks does not mean that the world is becoming uniform in every regard. In an article published in *Newsweek* in September 2010, Joel Kotkin describes a new world order that is based not on political borders, but instead on tribal ties, i.e. skin colour, ethnicity, and religious conviction.[54] In this world order, tribal traits, shared history, race, ethnicity, religion, and culture are to replace the borders defined by diplomacy. These ties are as old as history itself, and their impact has been reinforced by globalization. In this world order, borders remain malleable and change over time, and the author has identified 19 groups of countries, economic regions, or cities that are bound not by their geographic proximity, but by their similar attributes.

The 19 regional tribal alliances according to Kotkin

1. **New Hansa**
   Denmark, Finland, Germany, Netherlands, Norway, Sweden
   The descendants of the Hanseatic League of the early Middle Ages share Germanic cultural roots and specialize in the trade of high-value goods. They boast generous welfare systems, high savings rates, as well as impressive levels of employment, education, and technological innovation.

2. **Border Areas**
   Belgium, Czech Republic, Estonia, Hungary, Iceland, Ireland, Latvia, Lithuania, Poland, Romania, Slovakia, United Kingdom
   These countries share the trait of seeking to find their place in the new tribal world. In the past, most of these countries were often under occupation; nowadays, they are fighting for their autonomy against competing zones of influence.

3. **Olive Republics**
   Bulgaria, Croatia, Greece, Italy, Macedonia, Montenegro, Portugal, Spain
   With roots in Greek and Roman antiquity, these lands of olives and wine lag behind their northern counterparts, and almost all have huge government debt compared with the Hansa countries. They also have the lowest birth rates.

4. **City-States**
   London, New York, Paris, Singapore
   These cities are distinct from their environment based on their high degree of development, openness and international nature. They constitute major economic hubs within their respective regions.

5. **North American Alliance**
   Canada, United States
   These two countries are joined at the hip in terms of their economies, demographics, and culture. The region will remain the world's leading economy thanks to its cities, high-tech industry, agricultural output, and freshwater supplies.

6. **Liberalistas**
   Chile, Colombia, Costa Rica, Mexico, Peru
   These countries are the democratic and market-based economies of Latin America, but nevertheless still suffer from low income and high poverty rates. They are trying to join the ranks of the fast-growing economies, but some of them, particularly Mexico, are strongly tied to the United States economy. It is uncertain

whether the weight of the state will increase in these countries, or economies based on the free market will prevail.

7. **Bolivarian Republics**
   Argentina, Bolivia, Cuba, Ecuador, Nicaragua, Venezuela
   These countries are swinging back toward dictatorship and following the pattern of Peronism, with historical antipathy toward the United States and capitalism. They are characterized by high poverty rates. With their anti-American mindset, mineral wealth, and energy reserves, they are tempting targets for rising powers like China and Russia.

8. **Stand-Alones**
   Brazil, France, India, Japan, South Korea, Switzerland
   These countries have diverse and independent characteristics. Brazil has edged away from North America and is seeking to reinforce its relationship with China and Iran. France has uniquely tried to preserve its culture from Anglo-American influence. India's hugely populous economy is growing continuously, albeit at a slower pace than China. Japan continues to remain a leading global economy. South Korea has become a true technological power over the past 40 years, but it must be careful to avoid being sucked into the engines of an expanding China. Switzerland enjoys prosperity thanks to its excellent business climate, ample water supplies, and extensive international relationship network.

9. **Russian Empire**
   Armenia, Belarus, Moldova, Russia, Ukraine
   Russia has enormous natural resources, considerable scientific-technological capacity, and a powerful military. It relies on the strong ties of the Russian Slavic identity when attempting to expand its influence within the region. It is a moderately developed country with an ageing population.

10. The Wild East
Afghanistan, Azerbaijan, Kazakhstan, Kyrgyzstan, Pakistan, Tajikistan
This part of the world remains a centre of contention between competing regions, including China, India, Turkey, Russia, and North America.

11. Iranistan
Bahrain, Iran, Iraq, Lebanon, Syria
Iran could be a rising regional superpower based on its economic potential, but it is hindered by extremist ideology and a poorly managed economy. The region has become a net importer of consumer goods.

12. Greater Arabia
Egypt, Jordan, Kuwait, Saudi Arabia, United Arab Emirates, Yemen
This region's oil resources make it a key economic and financial partner, with great internal differences in development. A powerful bond – religion and race – ties this community together but makes relations with the rest of the world problematic.

13. The New Ottomans
Turkey, Turkmenistan, Uzbekistan
Although European Union integration remains important for Turkey, its focus has shifted toward the Middle East and Central Asia, and trade with both Russia and China is also on the rise.

14. South African Empire
Botswana, Lesotho, Namibia, South Africa, Kingdom of Eswatini (Swaziland), Zimbabwe
South Africa's economy is the largest in Africa. Its good infrastructure, mineral resources, fertile land, strong industrial base, and relative development have propelled it to becoming the region's leading power.

15. Sub-Saharan Africa

Angola, Cameroon, Ethiopia, Ghana, Kenya, Mali, Senegal, Sudan, Tanzania...

These former colonies are divided between Muslim and Christian, French and English speakers, and lack cultural cohesion. A combination of high poverty rates and natural resources will almost certainly turn them into targets for China, India, and North America.

16. Maghrebian Belt

Algeria, Libya, Mauritania, Morocco, Tunisia

This region is characterized by poverty and isolated nodes of development.

17. Middle Kingdom

China, Hong Kong, Taiwan

Han Chinese account for more than 90% of the population in a rapidly developing China marked by a sense of historical pride, and constitute the world's single largest racial-cultural group. This national and cultural cohesion makes the Chinese market hard to penetrate. China's growth coupled with its need for resources makes it an active player in Africa, the Bolivarian Republics, and the Wild East. Its problems, however, are legion: the centralization of power, growing inequality, environmental degradation, and an ageing population.

18. The Rubber Belt

Cambodia, Indonesia, Laos, Malaysia, Philippines, Thailand, Viet Nam

These countries are rich in minerals, fresh water, rubber, and a variety of foodstuffs but suffer varying degrees of political instability. Apart from Malaysia, household incomes remain relatively low, but these countries could emerge as the next high-growth region.

19. Lucky Countries

Australia, New Zealand

Household incomes are similar to those in North America. Immigration and common historical roots tie them culturally to North America and the United Kingdom. But due to their geographic location and production structure, China and India will become their dominant trading partners in the future.

PART 2

GEO-ECONOMICS: GLOBAL TRENDS IN THE 21ST CENTURY

CHAPTER 5

GLOBAL TRENDS IN THE 21ST CENTURY

The name of Andy Weir, the author of the novel *The Martian*, crops up more and more in discussions among various NASA researchers and officials. This is no coincidence. Futurology and trend research are demonstrably among the activities that require the most imagination, and the United States' global predominance in technology is partly due to the fact that it fosters and promotes the emergence and utilization of new visions.

Even among popular trend analysts, Richard Watson stands out: in five of his books, he has attempted to outline and identify the trends that will shape the development of the period ahead. In his book, *Future Files*, Watson presents 50 trends, and points out five of these that will have a radical impact on the coming decades.[55]

Humanity will become stronger and stronger; however, at the same time it will gradually age. Due to technology, more and more diseases will be successfully cured, and more and more money will be spent on healthcare, medicines, and medical tourism. Everyone will be connected more closely. Information and communication technology, cheap travel, and migration will change people's behaviour, work, and mindset. In 50 years, everyone will be accessible to each other worldwide. Meanwhile, localization gains momentum, tribal feelings are developed in the new city-states, local trumps global. We will experience the 'rise' of the machines, and out of the fusion of genetics, robotics, the internet, and nanotechnology, GRIN technology will be born. The shift of power from the West to the East is a huge shaping force:

China and India will be the winners of the coming decades, and Russia, Brazil, and Mexico will increase their clout. Pollution, global warming, and the lack of raw materials and energy sources will cause ever graver problems: countries will become submerged, while the fiercest fights will break out over fresh water.

Who will be the winners of the 21st century?

The unipolar world will once again develop into a multipolar one, and a new world order will arise in the 21st century. This phenomenon can be attributed to several readily observable reasons:

- Ageing and migration have various economic and social implications in both developing and developed countries (the situation of refugees, new consumer groups, pension schemes, diseases, unemployment, poverty, radicals, terrorism).
- The fight for energy and energy independence continues both domestically and abroad, while certain raw materials become ever cheaper. Germany and Italy will become renewable energy superpowers, whereas, for example, in Russia and the Middle East, a diversified economy is considered important.
- Geo-economic interests and economic warfare lie behind the struggle for markets, energy, competitiveness, and knowledge. Both an economic and an ideological (value-based) clash may unfold between the East and the West.
- In the global world based on new technologies, the door is open to everyone. The knowledge flow between developed and rapidly developing economies is a dual process: it forges connections (new alliances, catalysts), and at the same time the employer country increasingly becomes a mere provider of knowledge rather than its producer.
- Global strategies are replaced by regional cooperation. Among the numerous alliances of the multipolar world, smaller countries may often be able to tip the scales.
- Peripheral countries with a flexible and knowledge-intensive economy might act as the new points of reference in the world economy. This assumes that the paramount conditions for successful growth

are a highly skilled labour force, a resilience to crises, and a balance in regional cooperation.

- After the 2008 financial crisis, new value systems will develop, in which maximizing short-term profits will be of secondary importance behind long-term value creation and preservation. In parallel with the transformation of responsibilities, new industries will reshape the markets.

The currencies of the localized but intricately intertwined 21st century are the unique idea, creativity, and knowledge that can easily 'inflate away' if we do not keep up with our competitors.

The countries that fail to create knowledge will have no choice but to buy it, thus getting left behind in international competition and pushed to the periphery of development, which leads to the solidification of their vulnerability. Therefore, every country's long-term strategy should include a vision that puts its own local strengths in the service of sustained economic growth and employment, and improving living standards in the global geopolitical and geo-economic competition.

Key global trends in 2015

At the end of 2014, the World Economic Forum published its *Outlook on the Global Agenda 2015*,[56] containing, among other things, the most important phenomena that would shape our world in the coming 12–18 months.[57] They are dominated by the economic and sociopolitical trends related to environmental challenges, and they mainly highlight problems. Actually, only one topic on the list can be considered neutral.

These eight phenomena were deemed the most prominent in 2015, in order of importance:

1. Deepening income inequality
2. Persistent jobless growth
3. Rising geostrategic competition
4. The weakening of representative democracy
5. Rising pollution in developing countries
6. Increasing occurrence of severe weather events

7. Increasing water stress
8. Growing importance of health in the economy.

The issue of *deepening income inequality*, ranked first in this list, had already appeared on a similar list of the publication in 2014,[58] ranked second. The severity of the problem is illustrated by the fact that nowadays in the United States, for example, those in the top 1% of the income hierarchy own a quarter of the total income. In the past 25 years, the average income of the top 0.1% increased 20 times as fast as the average. The issue of income and wealth inequality was put in the spotlight worldwide in 2014 by Thomas Piketty's bestselling book, *Capital in the Twenty-First Century.*

The unsolved problems related to unemployment were also on the list from 2014 (in third spot); in 2015, they were ranked second in the form of *persistent jobless growth*. Although economies grow all over the world, albeit at varying rates, the number of jobs does not increase in parallel with this.

The top five trends also include security policy issues. Geopolitical and security concerns dominated 2014, from escalating violence in the Gaza Strip through to Russia's intervention in Ukraine and the rise of ISIS. Despite the various efforts to resolve such conflicts, it was highly likely that *rising geostrategic competition* would continue to be a dominant phenomenon in the ensuing 18 months.

The list in the 2015 publication is overwhelmingly dominated by environmental and economic problems, which are inseparable, as the long-term economic outlook depends largely on environmental sustainability. Nowadays, due to short-term economic thinking, we have to face the consequences of the heedless use of resources. Disputes between neighbouring countries about water resources are more and more common, and on account of climate change, certain weather events are increasingly frequent and extreme. The extent of deforestation, the increasing speed of ocean acidification, soil erosion, dwindling agricultural capacities, and the looming risk of a biodiversity crisis are all unprecedented in modern history. Pollution and environmental degradation are global problems, which affect developing countries more acutely. Thus, environmental issues need to play a greater role than ever before in the global dialogue. We are at a crossroads, and the decisions of the period ahead will fundamentally influence the survival and health of our civilization. Fortunately, this manifested itself in the outcome of the Paris Climate Conference in December 2015. The only trend on the list that can be deemed neutral is the *growing importance of health in the economy.*

We take it for granted that if the economic position of a country improves, the quality of healthcare and infrastructure increases. Yet it is less widely known that the reverse holds true as well, i.e. healthcare developments may exert a direct impact on economic growth. In developed countries, this is driven by the ageing population, while in less developed ones, by the spread of infectious diseases.

Intensifying geostrategic competition

After the end of the Cold War and the subsequent democratization processes, it seemed that the rivalry between superpowers was a thing of the past, and that the world had shifted toward a democratic consensus. Due to globalization and interdependence, wars are much less likely to erupt, and international multilateral organizations (e.g. the UN) often manage conflicts successfully. None the less, this does not mean that security policy risks have been completely eliminated. It is important to underline that the current risks are different from those before the 1990s. Since the 1990s we have been concerned about weak states, the dissolution of countries, and the global spread of terrorist organizations without a country, rather than a major confrontation between nations.

However, in the recent period, especially in 2015, in addition to the risks we had known so far, the confrontations between great powers seem to have returned. It is no coincidence that as a result of this, respondents in both Asia and Europe ranked this problem third. A restart of the Cold War is unlikely, but recent developments have opened up rifts in the relationships between countries. Geopolitics and realpolitik[59] are in the spotlight once again, which is expected to have wide-ranging social, economic, and political consequences.

Overall, today's geopolitical situation is characterized by a persistent and multidimensional competition and the parallel weakening of existing relationships. This trend permeates several different sectors and topics, creating an amorphous world order, in which we have to face symmetrical and asymmetrical challenges at the same time. The changes in the balance of power between world powers divert the political energy from the solution of common and important problems (e.g. climate change), and chaos gains ever more ground.

CHAPTER 6

THE AGE OF GEO-ECONOMICS

In the era of wars waged by the use of economic sanctions, competing trade regimes, exchange rates, and the manipulation of the prices of raw materials and currencies, the World Economic Forum (WEF) listed seven challenges that are connected to the appropriate development of geo-economic strategies. Globalization enabled great powers to devise a strategy for the whole world without giving up their regional hegemon status. In recent years, the countries wielding less power have also been concentrating around regional hegemons. However, excessive interdependence may just as easily be the catalyst for war as a force maintaining the fragile security: close relationships, especially when unbalanced, may easily sour.

Geopolitics and globalization

Geopolitical competition transforms the global economy, the global balance of power, and governance. Before the financial-economic crisis, geopolitics mostly played a role at the local level; however, in the 2010s the conflicts between great powers have flared up again. The most important are the tensions between the West and Russia, and China and its neighbours, as well as the increasingly multifaceted crisis in the Middle East.

Although many wars are being waged all over the world from Damascus to Ukraine, the main battleground is the economy. Military action is replaced by economic sanctions, and military alliances are replaced by competing trade frameworks. The likelihood of a currency war is far greater today than that of annexation, and manipulating the prices of certain raw materials (such as oil) is a far more powerful weapon than the conventional arms race. This shows that we are witnessing the rise of geo-economics, a competition in the language of trade but with the logic of war.

Geo-economics is simultaneously the antithesis and the greatest triumph of globalization. The mutual dependency and linkage between countries becomes so strong that exclusion from this system is considered as great a tragedy as war.

The WEF has revealed the geo-economic challenges, and pinpointed the strong trends that will reshape the world and change the conditions of the competition between the countries. These paint a picture of a world where the possession of power will be just as important as chasing profits, and this will be coupled with the increasing economic engagement of the state; economic warfare will undermine economic integration; multilateral systems will regress to the regional level instead of becoming global; oil prices will be low and fickle, therefore countries will compete for markets rather than resources.

The countries and alliances that are able to shape the future to their own liking (China, the United States, and the European Union) are projected to benefit from these developments, while the greatest losers will be the international organizations that can expect neither support from great powers nor the autonomy that enabled them to mediate between these powers. In the absence of global leadership or coordination, global norms and standards are eroding, and new multipolar power dynamics characterized by the dominance of regional powers are forming.

Seven challenges highlighted by WEF

- Economic warfare
- The 'geopoliticization' of trade talks
- State capitalism 2.0
- Competition for closed markets (and not resources)
- The survival of the biggest and the hollowing out of the periphery
- China's infrastructure-driven web of alliances
- Declining oil prices

Economic warfare

Developed countries are ever less willing to pursue their foreign policy objectives through the use of military force, and are using their global economic influence for extending their power to compensate for this. The recent Western sanctions against Russia are the manifestation of the first great-power conflict since the Cold War. Economic sanctions are the main tools of geo-economics, and they may vary widely from stricter health regulations for imports to a full-blown economic blockade. Sanctions are usually double-edged swords, as they also hurt the interests of the country introducing them, and may provoke countermeasures, too.

The ramifications of this trend are not clear yet, but one of its consequences may be the deglobalization of global corporations. This means that multinational enterprises have to return to their national roots and start thinking in an ever-closer relationship with their own country, taking their decisions together in line with the country's foreign policy stance. Another potential consequence may be the transformation of international trade patterns, along the new lines of geopolitics.

However, the outcome of these geo-economic 'offensives' is not a zero-sum game. A stronger economy with a deeper toolkit and more opportunities can wreak much more havoc in the target country than it can expect in return. Nevertheless, sanctions may fail, and often a 'rejoicing third' party will profit from the whole process. Irrespective of whether they are successful or not, sanctions exert a huge economic impact on the given economy in any event: technological progress declines and the population's standard of living diminishes, which ultimately leads to instability and may even topple the established regime.

The other losers of the process may be the Western-based multinational corporations that might lose substantial markets. If they are able to maintain their economic influence, the United States and the European Union will emerge as the relative winners, with China as the 'rejoicing third'. In addition to the sanctioned countries and Western multinationals, international trade organizations are also expected to emerge from the process as losers, since they have little say in the developments, which casts doubt on their credibility.

The 'geopoliticization' of trade talks

New pan-regional, regional, and country-by-country trade talks and agreements emerge all over the world, and they, according to some, may fill the role of earlier World Trade Organization accords, but it is more likely that they will increase the multipolarization and the trade competition between regional blocs. The best example of this is China's and Russia's push to create a new world order through establishing new trade zones and strengthening their influence in neighbouring countries.

China wished to set up a Regional Comprehensive Economic Partnership to counter the now-defunct Trans-Pacific Partnership, while Russia succeeded in creating the Eurasian Union, to counter the European Union. They are willing to provide substantial financial resources for this purpose with the cooperation of the Asian Infrastructure Investment Bank and the Eurasian Development Bank. In the years ahead, reconciling the great-power ambitions of China and Russia with respect to the Eurasian Union and the Silk Road Economic Belt may be interesting, and it is not clear how Central Asian countries will handle this situation.

Certain countries wish to shift the balance of political and economic power in Latin America as well. Four emerging countries, Mexico, Colombia, Chile, and Peru, would like to challenge Brazil's hegemony by creating the Pacific Alliance, which may be a truly powerful opponent if the wealthy Asian countries can be actively involved.

Geopolitics and trade are difficult to separate. If the rivalry in geopolitics will exert any impact on the nature of trade agreements, it will do so by boosting political and economic competition, and the losers from these developments will be global consumers and corporations. The countries on the periphery of regional powers also stand to lose much.

National champions

The revival of state capitalism after the financial crisis of 2008 provided fresh momentum to the fight between countries for power and influence. The fact that countries seek to achieve strategic goals through acquiring ownership in various companies and financial organizations is not a novelty, though they do this with new and more powerful tools than before. One such increasingly common phenomenon is that governments amend laws, policy directions, or standards to support certain key industries or (state-owned) enterprises. These companies become the so-called 'national champions' that may turn into the given country's leading companies with global clout.

Common cross-border or international regulations concerning certain sectors may also play an increasing role in promoting national interests. Setting these norms, for example in the financial sector, or in the field of technology, energy, or trade, has always been a political question rather than a technical one. The leaders in establishing these norms are the countries and alliances whose 'national champions' dominate the given sector (United States, China, European Union). The role of these sectors goes far beyond economic considerations, as it influences the role of countries, companies, and regions with regard to economic independence, political security, and stability. The lines between trade and strategic objectives are increasingly blurred in the case of the sectors such as technology and finance.

The changing role of central banks may especially benefit the United States and other major economic and financial players (e.g. Europe, Japan, and the United Kingdom), as their decisions have implications far beyond their borders. The Chinese central bank may also benefit from this process.

In the era of geo-economics, states will compete for markets rather than resources. This is a highly remarkable transformation. The nature and drivers of strategic competition have changed often over the course of history, and they are also changing now, for two reasons. First, resources are becoming cheaper as technology progresses and new resources are discovered (e.g. shale gas), which decreases dependence on traditional sources. Second, the demographic and economic rise of developing countries is generating significant global demand and relatively cheap qualified labour at the same time. Competition thus has a dual objective. There is competition for outsourcing on the one hand, and for accessing export markets with a large and constantly expanding middle class on the other. The shift in the direction of strategic competition is clearly indicated by the strengthening United States–Indian and United States–Chinese relations as well as China's infrastructural investments all over the world, which are all motivated by the wish to acquire markets.

The winners of the process will be the countries where per-capita income increases, and where the population is large and growing. The countries and companies that are able to acquire market share through controlling social, economic, and communication networks can definitely be considered winners. However, raw material producing countries (e.g. Russia, Saudi Arabia, or Iran) need to prepare for the decline in their power and economic weight. The medium-skilled population of developed countries will also be negatively affected by the process, since they will have to start competing against a much cheaper labour force with similar skills. The countries that are unable to establish political and economic stability for companies and foreign capital will also lose out.

The survival of the biggest and the hollowing out of the periphery

Many believe that the failures linked to global governance and global divisions will lead to a world made up of organized and harmoniously functioning regions rather than a world in a state of chaos. But this is unlikely. It is true that due to the weakening of the global level, several core countries will be bolstered, though they will not use this for creating fair conditions in their environment, but to establish centre–periphery relations in which the centre operates mostly at the expense of the periphery. For now, it is unclear whether these asymmetrical and bilateral relations will bring about the strengthening of regional powers and the hollowing out of the periphery. The three most striking examples of this are the roles of Russia, China, and Germany. These countries are the strongest economies in their broader environment, and they also set the course of foreign policy. In all three cases, the hollowing out of their periphery is under way in terms of both diplomacy and the economy. The greatest fear of peripheral countries is that their opportunity for manoeuvring among great powers and for sovereign action will be lost. Whether this happens or not is influenced by several factors. Among these, geographical position and economic weight may be decisive, just as in the cases of Singapore and Ukraine.

China's infrastructure development projects may be just as important in the 21st century as the protection of maritime routes by the United States in the 20th century. In (mainly) developing countries, funding infrastructure projects have become a foreign policy tool, especially in China, a global leader in this respect surpassing traditional actors (e.g. the World Bank). China's main motivation for this is that it aims to gain access to the markets where raw materials can be found or where it wishes to direct its exports to. This trend manifests itself in China's growing foreign direct investment (FDI) on the one hand, and in the loans extended to the countries where China would like to gain access to raw materials on the other. This can be observed in its neighbouring countries, in the countries of the Indian Ocean, in Africa, and in Latin America. Through these investments, China often acquires ever larger ownership.

Furthermore, China has set up several multilateral organizations aimed at infrastructure development or its financing, and the elimination of the bottlenecks in trade (borders, tariffs), thereby ensuring the flow of the appropriate quantity and quality of raw materials into China as well as the smooth export of Chinese products and services. The winner of this process is clearly China and the exporting countries for which the well-developed infrastructure is useful. At the same time, China may imperil itself by extending its influence too much, as that may spark anti-China sentiment (e.g. in Myanmar and some African countries). Severe indebtedness toward China coupled with low commodity prices may easily trigger political discontent and instability in the given countries, which may lead to terminated contracts or a wave of nationalization.

Declining oil prices

Following three years of unusual stability, oil prices took a nosedive in the second half of 2014. Between June and December 2014, the price of a barrel of oil dropped from US$115 to US$60. This can only be partly attributed to the glut in supply, and it indicates that Saudi Arabia had lost its stabilizing role with respect to oil prices. The process may easily change direction, and increasing demand may push back prices to their earlier level, or even higher. Indeed, by 2018, prices had already recovered about 20% of the loss. Therefore, in the future, the decisive factor may be price fluctuations rather than low oil prices. Until now, the winners of the declining prices were importing countries, and the losers, of course, were the exporters. Russia, Saudi Arabia, but also Mexico and Brazil are also likely to be affected adversely by this situation. The ultimate winners and losers will be determined by the speed and manner of governments' responses to the present situation. For example India has introduced a politically risky but economically long-awaited measure by reducing fuel subsidies after the drop in prices. And Russia has the opportunity to diversify its economy at last. Low prices exert considerable pressure on geopolitically central actors such as Russia and Iran. The vulnerability of the countries is often overestimated, but for them, the geopolitical stakes in this conflict are higher than the economic risks. They definitely have to change tactics, but they will not back down.

Five recommendations for a world ruled by geo-economics

In the absence of efficient global leadership, the erosion of global norms and values, a shift toward a multipolar world can be expected, where great powers will compete and fight using economic means. Regional powers will gain more influence. Great powers will increasingly view every issue through the lens of zero-sum games, and will only cooperate when their interests are aligned.

Geo-economics: Seven challenges to globalization, a publication by the World Economic Forum, lists the following five recommendations:

1. States should develop the rules of economic warfare, similar to the accords and agreements governing the conduct of conventional wars.
2. The state should find a balanced role within the economy.
3. We should be prepared for the strengthening of the biggest and the hollowing out of the periphery. This is especially important for small countries. In order to avoid being sidelined by regional central powers, small countries should unite their forces.

4. For companies, profits on the global market will remain the priority, but they will have to abide by different rules. Fostering globalization is also important, because this may reduce the risks of geo-economic competition, and multinational corporations play a vital role in this. However, they should also have an internal focus, not only an external one, as national roots and their reputation in a given market will become increasingly important for them. The revival of state capitalism may limit the expansion of certain sectors considered strategic, however, new opportunities may arise for others.
5. We should concentrate on regional actors and sub-global politics instead of international institutions. Civil society needs to be more pragmatic about where to look for the solutions to global problems. The forums similar to G7 are obsolete, as they did not prove to be appropriate for taking global action. The collective action that can be used to combat the fragmentation increasingly characterizing our world has to be developed in a different form, using different tools and considering different interests.

The ominous rise of geo-economics

In their article, Nika Prislan and José Ignacio Torreblanca[60] pointed out that the 2008 global economic crisis created a completely new world and launched new processes. In the years after the fall of the Berlin Wall, an unprecedented prosperity and market liberalization began, which created the false impression that we had reached the 'end of history', to employ the words of Francis Fukuyama. All over the world, liberalization and the opening up of the markets led to more advanced and more democratic societies that, for their part, promoted even more open trade and economic conditions. It seemed that nothing would be able to halt this process. The world was not dominated by state actors anymore but the free market and common economic rules.

But all this changed in the 2000s. The first shock to these global processes arrived in 2001 after the 9/11 terrorist attacks, when state actors started 'taking back' control. The final blow to the world order that emerged after 1989 was dealt by the 2008 global financial crisis, and, according to the authors, this was the starting point of the "age of geo-economics". In this age, countries do not wish to promote the free market. On the contrary, they use market tools to increase their own strength, i.e. the economy is an instrument for great-power politics. The logic of globalization has been replaced by neomercantilism. The phenomenon of geo-economics starts to take hold in the politics of more countries, increasingly dominating their foreign policy. In these countries, economic interests take priority over political ones. It is no coincidence that David Cameron's first visit after his 2010 election as prime minister of the United Kingdom was to India, a country with which a deal worth €840 million was in the making. In a similar fashion, Spain has maintained very close relations with China since 2010, which is also no coincidence, as China holds 25% of Spain's government debt.

Geo-economics has a highly negative impact on European solidarity, and one of the main reasons for this is rooted in the 2008 financial crisis. After 2008, Europe experienced adverse effects as the crisis continued to deepen. Since the European Union was unable to offer a pan-European solution to the global crisis, European states turned inward. While searching for the solution, the individual countries relied on the policy of national geo-economics. This means a shift of foreign policy back to the national direction, and as a result, European Union member states have become each other's competitors once again instead of having common goals and interests, as epitomised by Brexit. Over the long term, this process will cause problems for the European Union, because it undermines the opportunities of the common foreign policy. We live in the age of globalization, and in order to continue competing with developing countries efficiently, the European Union countries need to act together.

The lessons from history

'Social and Economic Collapse: Lessons from History and Complexity', an article by Peter Taylor and Noah Raford, was published along with other studies in *Warlords, Inc.* in May 2015. The study of just six pages builds on the axiom that during the course of history, the various societies and economic systems collapsed right at the peak of their development. The reasons behind these collapses varied: they were caused by internal crises, shortages in raw materials, or external attacks.

According to this article, the risk of a swift collapse threatens us in the 21st century as well, especially in the field of energy supply, as the growing world population will consume ever more energy. On the other hand, on account of technological progress (internet, computer viruses), terrorists and criminals find it easier to cause ever greater damage. What is more, according to the axiom, the more integrated a system is, the more prone it is to collapsing, as it has been shown by the economic crisis of 2008. The currently observable unrestrained economic growth and increasing interconnectedness make the system more and more inclined to collapse.

Empires and allies in the new world order

Parag Khanna's first book, *The Second World: Empires and Influence in the New Global Order* published in 2008 argues that today's international system has three empires or centres: the United States, Europe, and China. According to Khanna, these three entities can be referred to as empires, as they fulfil the basic conditions. Nowadays, the prerequisites for an empire include not only military power but also other factors such as population, access to raw materials, national willpower, diplomatic adroitness, and economic influence: technological innovation, productivity, and global market share. However, Khanna claims that today there are fewer empires than before 1945, merely three.

These three empires extend their influence in three different ways: the United States' strategy is based on coalitions, Europe's on consensus, and China's on consultation. In Khanna's view, the hundred countries of the second world comprise those that are not members of the Organisation for Economic Co-operation and Development (OECD), i.e. the first world, but are not part of the category of the so-called 'least developed countries' made up of the 48 countries considered the poorest by the World Bank. In line with these categories, the countries of the second world include Mexico, Brazil, Chile, Egypt, Libya, Iran, Indonesia, Uzbekistan, and the Balkan countries.

According to Khanna's second assertion, the international order is currently malleable and in constant flux, primarily because the United States' influence has considerably decreased in recent years. The author believes that this might be due to Washington's series of flawed foreign policy decisions (e.g. starting with the Iraq War), its domestic polarization, the rising inequality in its society, and the huge number of its incarcerated citizens. Khanna posits that in recent years it has also become clear that the second world can be stable and prosperous despite the fact that the United States' influence has continuously diminished.

Governing the world in the age of the New Renaissance

The West is in decline, the East is rising, and the international order is changing. Khanna's second book, *How to Run the World: Charting a Course to the Next Renaissance*, published in 2011, examines how this new world should be run and governed. According to its central thesis, the currently decentralizing international order will become ungovernable rather than multipolar. In Khanna's view, in this anarchic rivalry between nations, companies, lobby groups, and people, governments, corporations, NGOs, religious and lobby groups, diasporas, and celebrities compete for influence and attention in an increasingly competitive international environment. In this new system, the role of (nation) states is radically diminished, since their power erodes at the expense of subnational, supranational, and private actors. The study predicts that the world is not far from a 'New Middle Ages' in which economic chaos, social tensions, decadence, and religious fanaticism will be the defining trends. Khanna believes that this is not a problem, since a country alone would not be able to provide answers to the challenges of the 21st century, therefore a new system, a 'New Renaissance' has to be born, where these actors form ties on an ad hoc and voluntary basis, finding answers to the aforementioned challenges sooner than in the current cumbersome structure.

According to the author, one of the main developments of recent years has been the 'liberating' break-out from the 'prison' of thinking in national frameworks, and the unstructured nature of the international order is not simply a danger but also an opportunity. The future will be determined by horizontal, interpersonal relationship networks and self-organization rather than vertical, hierarchical systems.

CHAPTER 7

VISIONS FOR THE FUTURE – GEO-VISIONS

Long-term projections and various scenarios have always provided important aspects for understanding the processes of changes in the world's future. That is why the Economist Intelligence Unit (EIU) devised a methodology that attempts to produce a long-term economic forecast for 82 countries,[61] thereby lending insight into the key developments that are expected to influence and determine the functioning of the business world until 2050.

The top ten economies of the world in 2050

China is expected to overtake the United States by 2026, and become the leading major economy by 2050. With an average growth of 5% until 2050, India is projected to rise to third place, while Indonesia and Mexico will join the top ten economies of the world.[62] Western economies are not expected to feature prominently in the top ten. The United States, Germany, the United Kingdom, and France will be ranked lower, and Italy will not be among the world's ten most powerful economies.

The rise of Asian countries

'The rise of Asia', as a phenomenon, is not a novelty, as we have already witnessed the economic ascent of Japan and South Korea in the second half of the 20th century. Between 2000 and 2014 we saw another boom, when the Asian economy increased its share in the world's GDP from 26% to 32%. According to the EIU's report, Asia's growth rate may change but growth will continue, and Asia's final share of the world's GDP is projected to expand to 53%.

The dominance of the world's top three economies

By 2030, the world's top three economies will be the United States, China, and India. By 2050, each of these three countries will be richer than the five countries ranked after them (Indonesia, Germany, Japan, Brazil, and the United Kingdom) combined. Furthermore, due to their economic clout, China and India will play a much greater role in shaping global issues (e.g. climate change, international security, global economic governance). Over the medium term, the dominant global power – or the United States – has to let India and especially China enjoy an ever-larger role and influence in international institutions.

The new era of demographic decline

Based on the average of historical periods, no drastic global demographic decline is expected until 2050; however, we will experience shrinking at all regional levels from 2030. Long-term demographic projections show that the average fall of 1.3% in 1980–2014 will be reduced to 0.5% in 2015–2050. The growth rate of the world's working-age population will decrease from 1.7% in 1980–2014 to 0.3% in 2015–2050.

Population growth will still benefit some countries

Africa and most countries from the Middle East will profit from the expansion of the working-age population. This will be an enormous advantage for them going forward and it will make their growth sustainable. The potential labour force of Nigeria, Angola, and Kenya is expected to almost triple between 2014 and 2050.[63] In Algeria, Egypt, and Iran, a similarly substantial growth is projected until 2050. The countries that utilize the favourable demographic trends and take a growth-friendly course will be successful in providing jobs to the expanding labour force and may achieve long-term growth by doing so. But in the countries, that are unable to employ the growing labour force, the demographic boom may cause political instability.

Population as a source of growth has to be replaced

In most European and East Asian countries, growth will decelerate due to the shrinking labour force. The drop in the working-age population will be the greatest in Japan at more than 25%, i.e. a decline from 66 million to 47 million. In China and South Korea, the labour force is expected to contract by 17%–18%. In Europe, the share of the working-age population is projected to fall by 20% in Greece, Portugal, and Germany.[64] The group of European emerging (developing) countries (including Kazakhstan and Turkey) is also expected to experience decline, ranging between 20% and 30%.

Collective affluence, individual poverty

Growth is forecast to be greater in developing countries than in developed ones, therefore China and India, two countries that will become advanced economies, will surpass the current leaders, i.e. the United States, Japan, and Western Europe. Furthermore, other developing countries such as Indonesia and Mexico will join the leading economies of the world, overtaking countries like Italy and Russia. In contrast, per-capita income, which measures the purchasing power of the individual, will remain the highest in developed countries. In developing countries such as China, India, and Indonesia, per-capita income will increase considerably – in fact, by 2050 China is projected to achieve the level of Japan.

The world in 2030: four trends for the decades ahead

History has not ended, although many have claimed that social and technological progress have achieved everything that they were destined for. In its 2014 study (*Trend Compendium 2030*), the Roland Berger Institute examined what the key trends will be in 2030.

Demographics: increasing urbanization and ageing population

Since 1990, the population of the Earth has expanded from 5.3 billion to 7 billion, and according to estimates, by 2030 nearly 8.3 billion people will live on the planet. However, the growth rate of the population will somewhat decelerate, and the difference between the growth rate of developing and developed countries will increase even more. Developing countries will grow seven times more rapidly than advanced economies; therefore by 2030, 85% of the population will live in developing countries. In parallel with increasing life expectancy, the median age of the world's population will steadily grow. This figure will rise from 29 to 34 by 2030. It is worth noting that in the 20 years between 1990 and 2010, this increase was a mere 4.7 years, i.e. the median is clearly increasing at an accelerating pace. By 2030, the median age of the population of developed countries will be 12 years higher than in developing economies. Due to constantly intensifying urbanization, by 2030, 59% of the population will live in cities, whereas in 1990 this figure was 43%. The overwhelming majority of the increase will happen in developing countries. Cities have to be regarded as large 'trend laboratories' where new solutions are born.

Globalization continues

Globalization continues, and exports and FDI will increase faster than GDP. Economic growth will be the most pronounced in developing countries, and as a result, the share of developed countries in total global production will shrink. By 2030, trade between Europe and the United States will only be ranked sixth at the global level. China's European and Asian trade routes will be the most important. Therefore, Europe has to start watching China instead of the United States. Developed countries can expect economic growth of 1.8%, while developing economies can expect 6.7%, and the share of developing countries in the world's total GDP will decline from 66% to 44%.

Technology and innovation: the age of life sciences and talent

When analysing technological progress and the potential in the various regions, we can draw interesting conclusions from the developments in the number of mobile internet users and their territorial distribution. While in 2010, 1% of the population had access to the internet, by 2030 this figure will rise to 60%, nearly 5 billion people, with the greatest increase in Asia. The basic innovation periods follow each other in Kondratiev waves. The cycle between 1990 and 2010 was the age of the progress of information and communication technology, while the 20 years between 2010 and 2030 will be the era of life sciences. Within life sciences, biotechnology, medicine, and the pharmaceutical industry will show the most dynamic growth. With the ageing of the population, the demand for medicines will steadily grow, as the 65-plus age group consume three time as much medicine as younger age groups. The fact that diseases spread more rapidly is due to intensifying urbanization and global mobility which poses a further challenge.

With regard to healthcare spending, the divide between rich and poor countries will widen. Some 20% of the world's population lives in OECD countries, yet they represent 90% of healthcare spending. Currently OECD countries spend US$3,000 on each person annually, while in the case of African and South-West Asian countries this amount is below US$40. According to the forecast, community healthcare systems will be limited to providing basic services, while other services will be paid for using private funds.

Demand for skilled labour will exceed supply. By 2030, the demand for highly skilled labour will increase, especially in two fields: healthcare and engineering. Even today, 31% of employers complain that they find it difficult to fill a given position with a qualified professional. This problem affects developed and developing countries to the same extent. The countries and regions that are able to offer good conditions to highly skilled workers will be the winners, while others will lose out. According to the WEF, by 2030, Western Europe, the United States, and China will have a shortage in skilled labour of 45 million, 26 million, and 20 million, respectively.

Lack of resources: energy, water, and global warming

In the future, we can expect an increase in energy demand and energy prices. Oil will remain the chief source of energy, but the share of renewables will expand. Based on the International Energy Agency's projection, global energy demand will increase by 26% by 2030; however, its distribution will change. The proportion of liquid fuels will go down from 35% to 31%, coal will be represented with approximately the samc share (26%–27%), just like natural gas (23%). At the same time, the share of renewables will grow from 10% to 13%, and nuclear energy will increase from 5.5% to 6.4%. Developing countries will use 79% more non-renewable energy than developed ones. In OECD countries, the share of non-renewable energy will drop by 8% to 36%.

Assuming that current economic growth continues, global water demand will increase by 53% by 2030, from 4,500 billion m^3 to 6,900 billion m^3, despite the fact that the amount of available water is limited to 4,200 billion m^3 per year (3,500 billion m^3 surface water + 700 billion m^3 groundwater). Therefore, humanity will have to face a water shortfall of 2,700 billion m^3 in the future, which will entail a rise in water's price. Moreover, the water demand in developing countries increases faster than in developed countries by 18% and unfortunately half of the population will live in areas with scarce water by 2030. One of the key goals of research and development investments will be to resolve the difficulty caused by water scarcity, and the most important task for the period ahead will be to foster waste-water management, water purification, and more economical water management. Due to demographic reasons, agricultural water demand is expected to increase by 40%. We need 2,000 litres of water for producing one kilogram of rice, and 14,000 litres of water for one kilogram of grain-fed beef. For drinking water, 2–3 litres are recommended per person per day, and an average household consumes 20–300 litres of water each day. In addition, we can expect increasing demand for food in the future, due to population growth on the one hand, and rising food consumption per capita on the other.

Average temperatures will be higher by 0.5°C–1.5°C by 2030. In the past 20 years they rose by 0.5°C, while earlier they increased by 6°C in total over the course of 18,000 years. We have to prepare for a rise in sea levels of 6-11 centimetres, rising sea temperatures, and the melting of the polar ice caps. Biodiversity has continued to decrease by five points. A 2°C temperature rise threatens 20%–30% of the species. By 2050, natural areas the size of Australia will be lost. They will be replaced by agricultural production or infrastructure investments. The damage to the ecosystem and biodiversity impacts food and water security as well as our health. In order to tackle this harmful impact, humanity spends an amount in the order of magnitude corresponding to the United States' annual GDP. The world's CO2 emissions will increase by 16% by 2030. This rise will be mainly attributable to non-OECD countries, whereas in OECD countries, CO2 emissions will decrease.

CHAPTER 8

NEW HOTSPOTS IN THE WORLD ECONOMY

The BRIC and the NEXT 11 countries will be the new powerhouses

The BRIC countries (Brazil, Russia, India, and China) will be the new powerhouses, as their economies will grow by 7.9%. By 2030, they will account for 36% of global economic output, doubling their current share. The BRIC countries are the future drivers of growth. From the perspective of FDI, India will be the most popular target, followed by the economies of Brazil, Russia, and China. By 2030, the Brazilian economy will overtake Japan.

It is worth noting that as a result of development, the middle class will be substantially strengthened in these countries.[65] By 2025, 75% of the Chinese population will belong to the middle class, in contrast to 40% in the mid-2010s. In India, the share of the middle class will increase from 7% to 57% by 2030, and in Brazil it will grow from 47% to 58%. According to the projections, the share of the Russian middle class will drop from 71% to 41%, but only because many will enter into a higher category.

In addition to the BRIC countries, we should also watch the next 11 promising countries in the world economy[66] and the ASEAN-5, the five leading nations (Indonesia, Malaysia, Philippines, Singapore, and Thailand) in the ASEAN (Association of Southeast Asian Nations). By 2030, the economic clout of the 'NEXT 11 countries' will increase by 5.9%, and the ASEAN-5 countries will also gain in strength.

By 2030, the NEXT 11 countries will represent 11% of the world economy, with the most growth in Mexico, Indonesia, Turkey, and South Korea. With regard to exports, Mexico, Turkey, and South Korea will be in the vanguard. Economic development will also have a social impact: 20% of the world's middle class (760 million people) will live in these countries. In Asia, the largest economies will be Indonesia and Thailand, and the fastest growing economy will be the Philippines.

Asia 2050 – seven countries in Asia

According to a study by the Asian Development Bank,[67] Asia's development will be driven by seven countries: India, Indonesia, Japan, China, South Korea, Malaysia, and Thailand. In 2010, the seven countries combined accounted for 78% of Asia's total population and 87% of its GDP. By 2050, they will only constitute 73% of Asia's total population, but they will generate 90% of its GDP. As a result, by 2050, together they will represent 45% of the total global output, their average GDP per capita will rise to US$45,800, i.e. considerably higher than the world average of US$36,600. Asia's rapid rise has been one of the most successful economic transformations in the recent period. If the continent's development continues as in the past couple of decades, by 2050, Asia may account for half of global GDP, investments and trade, and its per-capita income may increase six-fold, thereby converging toward the current European income level. It may return to the dominant economic position it occupied 250 years ago, and the 21st century would be widely referred to as 'Asia's century'.

PART 3

VISIONS AND SCENARIOS FOR THE FUTURE

CHAPTER 9

THE NEXT DECADE AND THE NEXT HUNDRED YEARS

On the brink of the world's transformation, what does the future hold in store?

It comes as no surprise that the projections about the future are substantially influenced by the person making them and how that person views the world. The next set of examples illustrate this bias in all projections, and the difficulties and the various expectations forecasting experts need to face. In recent years, the futurist studies that garnered the most attention included the American George Friedman's forecast for the next hundred[68] (from 2009) and ten[69] (from 2011) years. As a security policy expert, Friedman views the world from a security policy perspective. His projection focuses on the United States, which, according to the author, only reluctantly assumed the role of an empire after the end of the Cold War, because the foreign policy duties imposed on it by this role conflict with its internal republican structure. The uncertainty of today's American foreign policy is due to this and the domestic economic problems that arose in the United States in the wake of the 2008 financial crisis.

According to Friedman, the role of the state is strengthened everywhere on account of the economic crisis, therefore it becomes even more important for the United States to act as an empire. In this role, the United States' main goal is finding the balance of power.

Friedman's prognosis is primarily centred on Russia, and the Middle East also features prominently. With respect to Russia, Friedman expects the country's economic clout to grow along with its political ambitions. This trend will also be dominant in the situation of Europe as a whole, as Friedman predicts that Germany will focus on its economic interests and attempt to forge ever closer ties with Russia. This will further restrain and hinder European integration and cooperation on the one hand, and it will make Central and Eastern European countries especially important for the United States on the other, particularly Poland and Hungary. Friedman claims that the Middle East will remain a conflict zone in the decade ahead, and that the United States has to concentrate on Cuba and Mexico in the Latin American region. The Western Pacific region will be increasingly significant for the United States' foreign policy. Here the author expects a slump or slowdown in China's dynamic rise, however, due to the ailing Japanese economy, and also due to the country's development, the role of South Korea in the region will be bolstered. In contrast, because of the lack of American interests and the high risks stemming from the poor level of development in the region, the United States should steer clear of Africa.

In his book about the forecast for *The Next 100 Years*, Friedman also constructs his scenario for the future along Cold War-like and actual armed conflicts. He asserts that the 21st century will clearly be the century of the United States, which will itself play a dominant role in its shaping. Friedman claims that the United States' strategy is built on the full American control of the Western Hemisphere and dominance over the world's oceans.

The next decade

Let us take a closer look at George Friedman's forecast for the decade between 2010 and 2020. In the years after the Cold War, the United States involuntarily became a global empire. The chief challenge for the United States in this decade is to learn how to manage its empire without endangering the republic. The tool for managing the empire is thinking in terms of regions and creating and maintaining the balance of power within the regions. In the Eurasian region, the role of Poland will be vital for the United States in preventing a German–Russian rapprochement, and the importance of Hungary, Slovakia, and Romania will also grow. At the western edge of the Middle East, Turkey will become even more important for the United States.

George Friedman seeks to ascertain whether the United States republic will be able to survive the pressure of the empire in the decade under consideration, and whether managing the empire can be reconciled with the republic. Friedman is a staunch supporter of the republic, and believes that the key to its survival is the office of the president. Friedman uses the example of three presidents, Abraham Lincoln, Franklin D. Roosevelt, and Ronald Reagan, to shed some light on this role. In his view, they embodied the Machiavellian presidency, which preferably combines the above-mentioned duality with integrity. Yet Friedman also shows that this combination does not necessarily produce good results, as those also require political greatness.

The author believes that if the United States wishes to preserve its republican character in the next hundred years, it has to understand the nature of power and the art of wielding it. The book sets out to look into the near future in order to help in this.

The next 100 years

In Friedman's vision, the current wars waged by the United States in the Islamic world will end, and they will be replaced by a new cold war against Russia. Domestic social tensions will mount in China and Russia, and social crises will emerge. Mexico will become a new global power, clashing with the United States in the Western hemisphere. By the middle of the century, Japan, Turkey, and Poland will become new superpowers.

Wars in the 21st century will be characterized by the use of advanced technologies, smaller armies, and fewer casualties. The environment and energy will gain importance, and the world's energy supply will be mainly based on energy production systems installed in space. The United States will maintain its advantage – in fact, its advantage will even increase – over the world's seas, as it will control the main maritime transport hubs, which can be closed at any time.

In the Pacific region, the rivalry between China and Japan will become the centre of attention as potentially very dangerous, and the two Koreas and Taiwan will also join in. Russia's efforts will be directed at recreating its sphere of influence. The conflicts and the clashes between the powers will be concentrated around the five global fault lines: the Pacific Ocean, Russian Eurasia (which means two fault lines in the south and the west), the Islamic world, and the border between the United States and Mexico. Europe will not be uniform, so European countries will be divided into the following four groups: Atlantic Europe, Central Europe (German–Italian axis), Eastern Europe, and the Nordic countries. The United States will be interested in dividing Europe to prevent a Russian–German alliance. Space and the Moon will become more important, and the United States will shift its military command centres into space.

Friedman sketches up the following timeline for the main events of the 21st century: by 2020, China's economy will be weakened, and the country will be characterized by crisis, domestic instability, and a conflict with Japan. In 2015, dynamic growth will start in Eastern European countries, supported by the United States. By 2040, Japan, Korea, and Turkey will become major powers, Japan will embark on an aggressive expansion, and Turkey will expand its influence over the Caucasus and the Balkans. In the decades ahead the global economy will start growing substantially, and as a result, the 2060s will be a 'golden decade' for these new powers, and the progress will continue in the 2070s.

Stratfor 2015–2025

The Stratfor forecast for 2015–2025 is the organization's fifth projection, as the think tank has published its global prognoses every five years since 1996.

Stratfor aims to focus on the main trends in its analyses, therefore their forecasts do not cover all regions, as the think tank maintains that they are not clairvoyants, they simply identify certain trends that can lead to various consequences. In the 2015 forecast, for example, Africa and Latin America are not mentioned, and the study focuses on Europe, Russia, Turkey, China, and the United States.

European Union

According to Stratfor, the European Union will be unable to solve its main problem in the decade to 2025, which, according to the researchers, is not the Eurozone (which is currently experiencing a crisis), but the free-trade area. The European Union's economic centre is Germany, which exports more than 50% of its GDP, half of which goes to other European countries. This shows that Germany's productive capability far outstrips its domestic consumption. This means that in Germany, economic growth, full employment, and social stability are all underpinned by exports. According to the analysts, this entails at least two different Europes: an economically less developed Europe including the Mediterranean countries, and a Europe with more advanced industries such as Germany or Austria (it is interesting to note that the analysts are uncertain about categorizing France). These two European regions are vastly different, which makes pursuing a common European policy basically impossible. Measures cannot be equally good for every country: what is a boon to one part of Europe, may be a bane to the other half. This explains the rise of nationalism in Europe. In fact, the authors go even further: Eastern Europe's fear of Russia creates yet another Europe, making four in all, the United Kingdom and Scandinavia, Western Europe, Mediterranean Europe and Eastern Europe.

Stratfor already forecast all this in 2005, just like the rise of Eurosceptic parties, and they believe that these trends will continue. None the less, according to Stratfor, the European Union may survive in some form, but the economic, political, and military relations will be maintained on a bilateral basis, or, if there will be multilateral relations at all, they will be limited. The analysts think that the revival of nation states in Europe will be crucial in the next decade, in fact, their number may even increase.

The analysts also write about Germany's situation. Germany is currently one of the most influential countries in the world, and the fourth strongest economy globally. However, it is extremely vulnerable because it is highly dependent on exports, its customers, and their purchasing power. In this sense, several factors are against Germany. European nationalism will lead to protectionism, i.e. protectionism with respect to capital and the labour markets. Weaker, mostly Southern European countries may set up trade barriers, mainly in agriculture, and, as European producers, are facing constantly increasing international competition anyway. Therefore, according to Stratfor, these processes are expected to lead to Germany's economic downturn sooner or later, which will trigger domestic, social, and political crises, reducing Germany's influence in Europe.

This is when a new regional power, Poland, will emerge. Stratfor predicts that Warsaw will become the driver of economic expansion in Europe over the course of the years ahead, and even now it exhibits highly remarkable growth dynamics. The Polish economy will continue to grow, in parallel with Poland's political influence. Thereby, over time, Poland will become a dominant actor in the Northern European region. The analysts also claim that it will spearhead a coalition against Russia, also including Romania. They predict that in the second half of the decade between 2015 and 2025, this coalition will play a key role in redrawing Russia's borders. As Moscow weakens, this coalition will start dominating not only over Ukraine and Belarus, but also farther to the east.

The Middle East and North Africa

According to the Stratfor forecast for 2015-2025, we will see the fall of the former European colony countries across the whole of North Africa. Power is not held by the governments of the individual countries but by various armed groups. This leads to constant fighting, but there is no solution in sight over the longer term. The various armed groups cannot win these fights, but they cannot be defeated either, which leads to a complete stalemate and constant internal conflicts. Not even the United States can solve this situation, and it will have no intention to intervene in the region's internal issues in any depth, as the developments in Russia will divert its attention from this area.

The resulting situation will present a serious security challenge for the whole region. The United States will not deploy its troops here again, even if the other countries in the region would expect it to do so. Neither Iran nor Saudi Arabia will be in a position militarily or geographically to do so. However, one country has a vested interest in resolving the situation and has the ability to do so: Turkey. Ankara has so far avoided risk, but it will need to change its strategy. It will need support from the United States if it wishes to be successful, and Washington will be willing to help, albeit at a high price. Turkey will have to cooperate and strike a deal with the United States in America's efforts to isolate Russia. Stratfor predicts that Turkey will strike such a deal.

According to Stratfor's ten-year forecast, by 2025 Turkey will become the most important regional power in the area, and it will seek to expand its influence over the northern coasts of the Black Sea as well as the Balkans. Its efforts may prove successful as the position of the European Union wanes.

East Asia

In China, the cycle characterized by high growth and cheap labour will end soon, in the 2010s, and Beijing will enter a new phase. China will continue to be one of the largest global economic powers, but it will not be the driver of global growth as it used to be. It basically treads the same path as Japan, Taiwan, or South Korea did earlier. According to the analysts, China will not display military aggression, but it may shift toward Russia's maritime interests. In this, it will have to compete with Japan. This is because Tokyo will not rest on its laurels either, and it will increase its naval power in the course of the decade. Russia will be unable to protect its maritime interests in East Asia. A three-actor game will emerge: China and Japan will compete, but they will prevent each other from getting the desired territories.

Basically, there is no other country that could take over China's role, but Stratfor believes that a group of 16 smaller countries may match Beijing's strength: these are called the 'post-China manufacturing hubs'. Their combined population is over 1.15 billion. These countries are characterized by poor infrastructure and high-risk factors. They can be found in most parts of South-East Asia, in East Africa, and one part of Latin America. They will gradually take over China's role, and by the end of the decade, they will exhibit remarkable economic growth.

The United States

The United States continues to generate 22% of global economic output, and its expansion has been practically unstoppable since 1880. According to Stratfor in 2015, the United States absolutely dominates the world militarily and politically, and will continue to do so in the decade ahead. Its insularity is America's greatest advantage. Exports contribute merely 9% to its GDP, and 40% of them go to Canada and Mexico. This means that only 5% of its GDP depends on the consumption in other parts of the world. It is less dependent on energy sources than at the time of the 1973 oil crisis, and since then it has become a significant energy producer in its own right. As costs rise in China, industrial production also has increased in the United States.

The United States benefits enormously from global crises (although Stratfor fails to mention that the 2008 global crisis originated from the United States). Therefore, the forecast rests on the basic tenet that the United States remains the heart of the international order. However, it will be much more selective in assuming responsibilities abroad, both politically and militarily. In the second half of the decade, the United States will try to offset these dangers caused by Russia's decline in the same period. Stratfor believes that in general, the United States will not solve Europe's problems: it will not fight against China, and will only make minimal interventions in the Middle East.

CHAPTER 10

STRATEGIC VISIONS

Robert Kagan is less optimistic about the unchallengeable American hegemony. He also focuses on the geopolitical aspects of the world's future, and he does so from a mainly American perspective.[70] According to Kagan, the domestic economic, financial, and social problems may lead – although not necessarily – to America's decline. He believes that the current world order created by the United States and based on democracy and political and economic liberalism is a unique system in humanity's history that is worth preserving. However, this requires continued active leadership from the United States. Either the decline of the United States, or its withdrawal or isolation due to its domestic problems, would lead to a multipolar world revolving around competing superpowers, where autocratic states would be strengthened, and economic cooperation would be replaced by rivalries and increasingly common conflicts.

Yet America's decline and the ensuing negative scenario can still be avoided. According to Kagan, in order to prevent a decline, Americans should not accept it as inevitable, but instead they should find solutions to the country's domestic problems and they should not withdraw from finding solutions to the world's problems.

Brzezinski's strategic vision

Zbigniew Brzezinski, the former national security advisor in the Carter administration, discusses the world's future in a more varied approach than Robert Kagan and from a more realistic perspective than Friedman, but still mainly from the aspect of security policy.[71] His book, *Strategic Vision*, about the geopolitical future of the world attempts to answer the following four questions:

1. What will be the impact of the changing distribution of global power from the West to the East and humanity's political awakening?
2. Why does the appeal of the United States decrease, and what kind of geopolitical reorientation is necessary to revitalize its role in the world?
3. What would be the geopolitical consequences of the United States losing its leading position, who would be the direct geopolitical victims of this, and could China assume the United States' central role by 2025?
4. How should a revived United States determine its long-term geopolitical goals after 2025? How could the United States, together with its traditional European allies, involve Russia and Turkey in creating an even larger and more powerful West? How could the United States strike a balance in the East between the necessity of the close cooperation with China and Asian geopolitics without entanglements?

According to Brzezinski, the world temporarily became unipolar after the end of the Cold War, and today we can observe the distribution of power. While the West loses its global leading role, the East rises. Brzezinski also believes that in the rising but not tension-free East, this realignment may lead to self-destructive conflicts reminiscent of the history of 20th-century Europe, but this is not inevitable. Brzezinski's argument is similar to Kagan's, in that both maintain the West's decline and the East's escalating conflicts can be avoided through the revival of the United States.

However, in the Brzezinski's vision, the process does not end in a uniform world under exclusive American hegemony, but in the peaceful balance and global cooperation between a broader Western alliance and a cooperative East that also achieves its inner harmony due to the stabilizing impact of the West.

In Brzezinski's view, in the world order based on this scenario, the broader West includes Turkey and Russia in addition to the United States and the European Union. The United States remains the leading power in this broader West, in fact, it has to play an active role in its creation. At the same time, it has to support the balance in the East, constructively accepting the strengthening of China's global status. According to the author, the United States has to experience a revival to maintain its leading position, since only a dynamic, strategic-minded United States and a unifying Europe can create a broader, more viable West, which can be the responsible partner to a rising and increasingly self-confident East. Failing this, the divided and self-centred West may experience a decline similar to the 19th-century history of China, while the East will repeat the self-destructive power struggles of 20th-century Europe.

Peace is a key prerequisite for economic development and prosperity, therefore security policy is also an important field. However, the most clear-cut dividing line in every security policy forecast is whether the United States can successfully get through its financial crisis, and the impact this crisis will exert on the other economies of the world.

The endgame of the financial crisis

John Mauldin and Jonathan Tepper, two American economists, analysed the possible scenarios of the endgame of the financial crisis in their book, *Endgame*.[72] According to the authors, the current financial crisis is the end of a debt supercycle characterized by debt mounting for decades, in which the reduction of the current debt levels becomes essential. The general scenario shows that the process is preceded by a multi-year slowdown in the economy coupled with high debt levels, which can only turn into a slow recovery after the substantial reduction of the debt. In the realignment period, the risk of both deflation and high inflation is considerable in the affected countries. Through the drop in demand, the reduction of debt essentially leads to deflation. This is characterized by further diminishing consumption of the savings rate growing due to the significant excess capacities in the economy, high unemployment, and the reduction in the value of accumulated wealth. The destructive impact of deflation can only be prevented by painful government measures, and politicians may find it more appealing to monetize debt by boosting inflation. However, while inflation does not bring about real growth, an increase in investors' yield expectations, or an expected rise in government spending and the deficit, it may entail the risk of hyperinflation, which is the worst-case scenario. Nevertheless, the authors are optimistic for the long term and expect a higher standard of living over a 10–20-year horizon even in the developed world.

By applying the financial projections to security policy and the expected future world order, we can see that a solution to the issues of the global division of power and the new world order is forecast to develop without major shocks, i.e. the future will not be dominated by power struggles and conflicts.

Kurzweil and singularity

The impact of technological change is also interesting for many in connection with the future. Many people are afraid of the expected changes because of the increasing pace of progress, and the fear of the depletion of the Earth's resources and of technology spiralling out of control. In order to address these fears, we should examine an extreme scenario about the expected direction and impact of technological progress described by Ray Kurzweil in connection with the phenomenon he called singularity.[73]

According to Kurzweil, while human thinking describes our environment using linear models, in reality the changes of the world around us are exponential, i.e. constantly accelerating. Singularity is when the pace of the changes ahead reaches a point where we cannot reliably predict their effect beyond a point relatively close in time, i.e. the event horizon. In Kurzweil's scenario, singularity is a future period in which technological change will be so rapid and far-reaching that human life will irreversibly change as a result. Still, we do not have to prepare for a completely new world in every sense, although we should expect fundamental changes in our environment and way of thinking. Singularity ties in with the history of evolution in a broader sense, which, in the author's view, can be divided into six periods.

Kurzweil does not assign concrete dates or horizons to the periods ahead, but argues that they are very close in time on account of the exponential nature of changes. As a result of singularity, human and machine intelligence will merge, machines will become capable of independent development, and in some sense they will be human, with their intelligence becoming similar to that of humans. Nevertheless, our civilization will stay human despite the huge progress in the intelligence of machines and technological devices, because our intelligence is of biological origin.

Is globalization truly unstoppable?

After our foray into global power and technological projections, let us now turn to the prognoses about economic and social changes that are more relevant from the aspect of today's decisions. In connection with these, the most widespread belief is that future economic and social changes will be determined by globalization.

Pankaj Ghemawat, a lecturer at the IESE Business School in Barcelona and a former lecturer at Harvard Business School, calls for caution in connection with this widely held view. According to Ghemawat, this approach based on the advanced state of globalization and its unstoppable, spontaneous further progress is flawed,[74] and it has two detrimental effects. First, due to our flawed hypothesis, we are prone to attributing too many of the negative and positive changes to globalization, and second, we limit our thinking to these two, mutually exclusive options.

While Ghemawat simply wishes to expand our framework of thinking, a book by the American National Intelligence Council on global trends also undertakes to make projections.[75] According to the authors, our future will be shaped by a few important megatrends together with uncertainties – referred to as game-changers – influencing their effectiveness and results. The authors describe four possible visions for the future produced by the interaction of these game-changers.

1. *Individual empowerment*: The reduction of poverty, the expansion of the global middle class, higher qualification levels, the widespread use of communication and production technologies, and advances in healthcare bolster the power of the individual.
2. *Diffusion of power*: There will not be any hegemons, and power will shift to the networks and coalitions of a multipolar world.
3. *Demographic patterns*: The demographic arc of instability, i.e. the territory of politically unstable countries with a substantial young population, will shrink, growth may decelerate in ageing countries, 60% of the global population will live in urbanized areas, and migration will intensify.
4. *Food, water, energy nexus*: Demand for these resources will grow, and managing the problems pertaining to any one of them will be in interaction with the supply and demand of the others.

The impact of megatrends may be influenced by the game-changers. Out of these, the role of the United States and the governance gap require some explanation. The former is connected to the question of whether the United States will be able to appropriately adjust to its changing role, work together with its new partners and overhaul the international system together with them. The second, similar question is whether governments and institutions will be able to adapt fast enough to utilize the changes or if they will be overburdened by the developments.

The authors claim that as a result one of the following four worlds will emerge.

1. *Stalled engines*: In the worst-case scenario, the risk of interstate conflicts rises, the United States turns inwards, and globalization and growth will be stymied.
2. *Fusion*: In the best-case scenario, the United States and China will be able to engage in cooperation in a wide variety of areas, and the two countries will spearhead the broader global cooperation.
3. *Genie-out-of-the-bottle*: As certain countries become winners, inequalities increase dramatically, and inequalities within countries exacerbate social tensions. The United States will not withdraw completely from the world, however, it will not act as the 'global policeman' anymore.

4. *Non-state world*: Utilizing the new technologies, non-state actors will take the lead in managing global challenges.

Our future is shaped by today's trends. However, our current and future decisions impact on them just like the way we adjust to the developments. The phenomena experienced today are actually the result of our earlier decisions and choices. This means that both the direction and the importance of the trends seen today may change the future. This also means that adaptation can be not only passive acceptance, but also a deliberate effort to slow down, halt, reverse, or deflect unfavourable trends.

CHAPTER 11

DON'T WAIT FOR THE NEXT WAR: THE AMERICAN STRATEGY

Wesley K. Clark's book, *Don't Wait for the Next War*, is a comprehensive strategy for fostering long-term American growth and world power status based on the energy industry and without war.

American national strategy has always been a response to a crisis or war (such as World War I or the Great Depression). According to Clark, the biggest question is whether a strategy not based on war can be devised. The first step toward this would be for the United States to tackle its domestic issues rather than the external problems. Clark lists five overlapping challenges faced by the United States: the fight against terrorism; boosting cybersecurity; the regulatory reform of the American economy; rethinking foreign policy toward China; and reviewing the key role of energy in the 21st century.

The United States has to gain strength in all geopolitical areas, it has to hold a 'sharp sword', while still holding a 'protective shield' above those in need. Instead of haphazard measures, the author calls for a modern counterterrorism plan that focuses on long-term objectives. The United States has to be in command of its cybersecurity through greater government involvement but also through boosting cooperation with American companies. Confidence in the government and the American state has to be restored through economic growth, which will also serve as a basis for international confidence. Clark believes that economic growth requires a regulatory reform of the financial system and an energy policy that responds to climate change. He asserts that with an appropriate energy strategy, the United States could achieve a new economic renaissance, create new jobs, maintain its lead in research and development and in innovation, while determining global energy policy that is the basis for its whole foreign policy.

During the Cold War, it became clear that the mere existence of military equipment, a stable locality, and response capacities are more effective weapons than their deployment. Clark argues that the American strategy should be this (military, economic, and energy policy) armament that serves as a deterrent and sets an alluring example at the same time, without concrete and direct interventions, in a strong alliance with Europe. The United States still has the power to implement its domestic reforms and revive its alliances and Clark maintains that the world knows exactly why Americans are fighting – for freedom, acknowledgment and opportunities – and the world expects them to continue on this road and shape the global arena.

America's five challenges in the 21st century

The history of American national strategy goes back as far as that of the United States, which were united in the ideology of democracy and economic freedom. The national strategy initially focused on conquering the continent and competing with the British Empire. Substantial changes were triggered by World War I, the Great Depression, World War II, and the Cold War. Clark concludes that the national strategy of the United States has always been a response to a crisis, in fact, often the greatest disaster provided the country with a goal.

In the 1990s, the United States won the Cold War, and remained the only competitor for world power status. As the crisis and the challenges receded, the national strategy evaporated. There was no clear-cut strategy behind the Gulf War or the Yugoslav Wars: in fact, the retaliatory strikes after the terrorist attack on the World Trade Center in 2001 were ad hoc.

No strategic planning preceded the war in Afghanistan or Iraq either, therefore even if the Americans won, they did not know what to do with the victory. If the United States wishes to keep its world power status, it has to recognize today's challenges, and devise a clear strategy for them that all countries can identify with.

The creation of the national strategy cannot be postponed any further, as the United States has reached an inflection point: government debt is rising, while economic growth is experiencing a slowdown, confidence in the state has been shaken, and the failure of public dialogue has manifested itself in domestic political fights. America's image abroad (and its power) is more stable than its domestic image; however, its foreign influence will soon start to decline.

Terrorism

By military standards, terrorists represent a grave political threat: while close to 60,000 people in the United States die in armed aggression annually, one terrorist attack is enough to engender a backlash from the public.

Therefore, politics treats terrorism as a priority, and a whole industry has emerged for its prevention, analysis, and communication. Clark calls this the 'terrorist-industrial complex', on which billions of dollars are spent by the government and the private sector. Well-paid experts and analysts work under highly centralized control in a Washington-centric system, which is in stark contrast to the decentralized structure of terrorist cells, and both are continuously improving. Terrorist cells are present in close to 70 countries all over the world, recruiting thousands of people every year. Old methods have been retained (e.g. suicide bombers) but they are now complemented with new ones (e.g. ground-to-air missiles). Clark adds that during the regime changes in the Middle East, the 'supported', who later turned into 'radicals', acquired many such missiles. The United States is well ahead of the world in technological competition, but there are more and more terrorists that were born in the United States.

According to Clark, the countermeasures against terrorism have been inadequate, since they were driven by short-term (and often political) goals. Instead, a long-term strategy resembling the one during the Cold War is necessary, that reshapes the Muslim world from the inside. The United States has to fight radical Islamic ideology just as capitalism acted against the ideology of communism. This has to be applied on all fronts, so that Islam undergoes a democratic modernization. Clark believes that, first, order has to be restored in the sending countries of terrorism: preventing the organization and technological development of terrorist cells, showing the irrationality of sects, discrediting the reasons behind terrorism, and bringing sustainable development into the region. The United States has to understand that a major part of the solution has to come from within the Muslim world, from internal reforms, rather than from outside. However, this strategy does not provide an answer to terrorism's technological leap nor to America's domestic security: this leads us to the next challenge, i.e. cyber and internet security.

Cyber and internet security

Since the second half of the 20th century, the global competitive edge of the modern American financial sector has stemmed from communication networks, especially the internet. The internet is open to everyone, without anyone controlling it, and connects everything, which means in the United States alone there are 500,000 potential 'cyber targets'. The lesson from this is clear: the more advanced an economy, the more vulnerable it is. Most exposed are the energy sector and the aviation industry (aeronautics and space technology). And often, indirectly, there are other governments behind the criminals, and among them the Eastern European and Russian hackers deserve special attention. It is ironic that America's offensive force bolsters itself with spy software, while one of the most vulnerable countries is the United States itself.

Transforming the American financial system

One of the most complex financial systems in the world is that of the United States. The operation remains unclear, even to the key figures of the financial sector, yet they continue to pour ever more money through it. Clark believes that one of the greatest challenges faced by the United States is the transformation of its own financial system.

Economic crises are not unique events – they have cropped up periodically during the centuries. However, the real question is why we cannot prevent these crises, and if they do erupt, why we are unable to respond to them effectively.

Clark concentrates on America's economic situation and the 2008 economic crisis because these crises entail national security (and political) risks. At that time, the majority of Americans lost half their savings, and 8.8 million lost their jobs as unemployment surged by 5%. Confidence in the American economy was shattered, the country's international influence declined, while domestic income inequalities rose, which led to heightened internal tensions. Now the shock is over, but the system itself has not changed, and no real reforms have been implemented. Clark proposes stress tests for banks, and 'peacetime engagement' for the whole financial sector, in which he would include the state supervisory authority, the Fed, and the Treasury Department.

While Clark acknowledges that the overregulation of the financial sector may slow down the economy, he notes that ever more economists make the above principle stricter, proposing forms of taxation that would primarily ensure the stability of the financial sector. International organizations (e.g. the International Monetary Fund) play a central role in reforming the economic system, as they can transfer the economic formula of the renewed and strengthened United States to other parts of the world. In this context, the impact of American capital on the economies of developing countries has to be reviewed from a historical perspective.

China

China's astonishing development is unprecedented in terms of its speed and intensity. A similar process could be observed in Japan in the 1980s and Germany's development in the early 20th century. From a territorial perspective, Germany was much smaller than the United States, and it did not have the type of unified political governance that China does today. China is not a 'new Soviet Union' either, as its economy is intricately intertwined with the other parts of the world, especially with the United States. The United States has defeated all these three great powers (by integrating or occupying them or making their economic situation untenable), but China's situation is unparalleled, and neither method would work.

This confusion is indicated by the ambivalent United States foreign policy of 'commitment' and 'distancing' since the late 1990s: one day the United States signed a cooperation agreement with China, then the next day it condemned certain Chinese acts that violated human rights (e.g. Tiananmen Square, Taiwan, industrial espionage). Barack Obama wished to put an end to the uncertainty by making an unequivocal foreign policy commitment, and announcing the policy of the "Pivot to the Pacific".[76] Clark notes that the army (in this case the foreign policy focus) not only pivots *to* somewhere but also pivots *from* somewhere. In the case of the American foreign policy, the pivot to the Pacific reduces America's diplomatic and military clout amassed in the Arab world and the Middle East.

The United States has often found China's way of thinking difficult to fathom, and Clark mentions some examples of this:

- The military term 'pivot' offended China and was perceived as a threat, as, last time, Western societies arrived in the region as armed colonizers.
- China constantly stresses that it does not wish to create colonies or to achieve superpower status through violence, still there are numerous territorial disputes in the area (on account of Taiwan or the islands in the South China Sea).
- China does not understand why America is unwilling to join forces with it in these territorial disputes, as economically China is much more important to the United States than the other parties in the conflicts. In fact, when the United States attempts to manage these situations as a mediator, it irritates China.
- It is interesting that the Chinese decision makers welcome every gesture and advance, but they never initiate anything similar. China steadfastly follows its own long-term strategy.

In contrast to the fight against terrorism and Islamic radicals, Clark underlines that a cold war against China is out of the question. The Chinese are not the Soviets, there is no historical precedent for this situation that could be repeated, and therefore a new strategy is necessary. The United States has to convince China that it is in its best interest to join the world order that has emerged after World War II. E2S, the American energy strategy, may provide an answer to this question. As the world's leading energy exporter with a strong and protected economy, the United States is able to balance Sino–American relations with appropriate global judgment. Together with the European Union, the United States is able to compete with China by exhibiting an attractive international model between interlinked but separate economies. In fact, an even better example has to be set than what China may achieve through a potential Russian (energy) alliance.

If the United States manages to reach a deal with China about a three-way cooperation (United States–European Union–China), that may provide a solution for the Eastern European situation as well (e.g. for the crisis in Ukraine). The United States and Chinese international funds may generate infrastructural developments in Eastern Europe that could considerably reduce Russia's influence.

Clark asserts that the United States has to stand less firmly by its principles pertaining to democracy, and has to provide leeway to countries such as China and its state capitalism, while making it clear that it does not tolerate the violation of human rights. Assertive and patient diplomacy has to be based on a strong and growing economy, a solid system of alliances, and the constant demonstration of power, so that American military capacities are not called into question in the event of a crisis.

This enables the United States to confer the deserved world power status on China, without war, with the United States as an equal party, in the service of the world's prosperity and stability.

Energy needs and climate change

According to oil industry experts, global oil consumption will increase from 90 million barrels to 120 million barrels per day. In a growing and industrializing China, it will be especially important to ensure gas and oil supplies, therefore whichever country leads the global energy industry will be the one to determine Chinese relations. The energy industry and energy industry developments are especially costly, but Clark believes that elected leaders should bear these costs for the long-term benefits, and their decision has to be made clear to the general or even the global public through diplomacy and international cooperation.

Clark clearly advocates mixed energy sources (renewables and fossil fuels), underlining the importance of new, alternative energy sources as the drivers of innovation and research and development. He claims that wind and solar power are able to compete with coal- and gas-fired power plants; however, he sees no chance for new energy sources replacing petroleum products over the medium term.

Under President Carter, the United States dominated the solar power industry, while in the 2010s the centre of the industry is in Europe, led by Germany. China's entry into this market will completely upset the balance of power (which has already started with the takeover of production and manufacturing, and it will continue with the management of planning and innovation). Thus, the United States has to be proactive, and occupy the strategic positions in the energy market. According to Clark, domestic policy, the American economy, foreign policy, and relations with China will all be ultimately determined by the energy policy. Precisely because of this, investments must be made in innovation in the energy industry because these are for the long term and they create jobs and generate easily calculable profits, which may set the pace for the growth of the American economy.

Sustained growth and security in the United States may be guaranteed by energy independence and an economy based on a heterogeneous energy industry investing in new and long-term technologies.

Europe and Russia

President Vladimir Putin designated the energy industry as the basis for Russia's national strategy, which is complemented nicely by energy technology and the export of raw materials and weapons. The next step would be global expansion, which Putin seeks to do by establishing alliances and unions (e.g. supporting the Iranian nuclear programme, the Eurasian Union).

If the United States takes the lead in the global energy market, it will influence European natural gas prices and the global oil market. Thus economic sanctions, although necessary, only make up one (short-term) half of the strategy, while the other half is composed of the (economic) control over the energy market and the economic development of Eastern Europe. The policy of deterrence against Russia has both a military and an economic aspect, therefore the NATO allies need to increase not only their military potential but also their economic 'weaponry'.

This mostly concerns the Balkans and Eastern Europe, but the United States can offer a real alternative to Russia by fostering economic growth and development (e.g. in Slovakia, Romania, or Bulgaria). Propping up the economy are these 'gateways countries' which are of strategic importance, since the less vulnerable their financial systems are, the less they are exposed to Russia's influence. Clark mentions the skilled workforce as an advantage of this region, but the lack of real development plans is considered a disadvantage. The region needs external funds, raw materials and infrastructure.

Would the United States really like to refight the Thirty Years' War?

When asked at his hearing by the Senate how long the war in the Middle East will last, Assistant Secretary of Defence Michael Sheehan answered 'for 10 or 20 years' in addition to the 13 years since the war had started.

In an article titled *The New Thirty Years' War*,[77] Richard N. Haass, president of the Council on Foreign Relations, argues that the current situation resembles the Thirty Years' War in many respects. This is notwithstanding that the Thirty Years' War was a religious clash, while in the present conflict moderate but armed groups face each other, supported by neighbouring powers that wish to protect their sphere of interest and increase their influence in the region. Struggles can emerge not only between but also within countries, especially where governments increasingly lose their leading role and are less able to control the smaller groups and militias.

In the wake of the 2011 Arab Spring, there is a real chance that we are witnessing the early stages of a prolonged, costly, and dangerous conflict, because as things stand, everything can deteriorate. The region is in unrest, most of the public is politically impotent and poor in every respect, and the boundary between the secular and the religious spheres is contested. In addition, national identities often compete due to the differences arising from religion, sects, or tribes. Civil society is weak, education does not teach critical thinking, the presence of oil and other energy sources hinders the efforts aimed at diversifying the economy in this region, and those in power often lack legitimacy.

The new Thirty Years' War

The Thirty Years' War started, in May 1618, with the defenestration of three officials,[78] which was attributed to religious reasons, even though there were substantial economic interests in the background. The war totally devastated Europe, and especially the German principalities. The religion of the people living in an area was determined by the ruler (based on the principle of 'one country, one religion'), and not by the emperor. The conflicts in Iraq and Syria show strong parallels with this: the Sunnis and the Shias live next to each other under the rule of several princes and dictators, while great powers long for their resource-rich territories. There will only be peace when religious tolerance spreads in the region.

In an article published in 2003, Paul Rogers predicted that the oil in the Gulf would be vital for the world in the next three decades. He claimed that should the United States take the region centred on Iraq under Western control, we would face a very long armed conflict. Thirteen years after the conflict, Barack Obama announced a "new" war, or more precisely the continuation of the war against the terrorist organization Islamic State. In a nutshell, Obama's strategy was the following: air strikes against all targets, wherever they are; providing increased support to allied ground forces; counterterrorism measures, with special regard to financing and recruitment; supporting civilians and humanitarian organizations.

Rogers also stressed that the emergence of the conflict was also influenced by Obama's 2008 election and his peace policy, because that was when several soldiers were let go who were able to organize the Islamic States' terrorist organization and who hate America more than anything. Paul Rogers concluded that America had learned nothing from the previous decade.[79, 80]

Why 30 years?

Michael Klare's study, 'Energy: The new thirty years' war' argues that the new Thirty Years' War will be waged for energy.[81] But why 30 years? Klare believes that this is how long it will take for developing the current experimental energy sources and power plants and for them to spread. Why war? The current economic system faces a complete overhaul, and the currently profitable oil companies will have to change sooner or later. Those that are in the right place at the right time will become the next BP or Exxon. The other driver of this process is that energy management is part of national sovereignty, therefore an energy war can easily escalate into a real war. By the 2040s, the great powers may be reconciled, in which the winners will designate the energy boundaries and rules of the new world.

CHAPTER 12

SILK ROAD IN THE 21ST CENTURY

Whose side is China on?

The Americans believe that China is on America's side, but according to Russia, China sides with the Russians. Yet, China chooses a third way: it only relies on itself, and strives to achieve global-power status by peaceful means such as cooperation, transnational developments, infrastructure developments, and investments.

In 2015, it was clear that the priority for Chinese diplomacy was to start implementing its One Belt, One Road (OBOR) economic initiative, i.e. to make the 21st-century Maritime Silk Road and the Silk Road Economic Belt operational. The latter would link China and the other Central and Western Asian countries to Europe, while the former would reach Europe through Southeast Asia and Africa.

The project affects 64 countries – including China – for example Sri Lanka, the Maldives, Greece, Kenya, Indonesia, Afghanistan, Iran, and Italy. The investments are financed by the Silk Road Fund, an international investment fund, established on the initiative of the Chinese government. China has already contributed US$40 billion to the fund.

The Chinese efforts are part of a search for its identity, which arose from the transformation of the economic model in the once-isolated country, and the wish to strengthen regional power status and global power ambitions. China strives for global economic expansion, and at the same time demands a say in the international financial system.

China's grandiose trade and development project is the OBOR connecting Europe and East Asia. The undertaking that affects 64% of the global population and 29% of global GDP is depicted as the flagship of Chinese foreign policy and a part of the great power game in Asia.

Experts try to estimate the changes that China's increasingly dominant presence may bring, for example in the Asian regions where the United States, India, or Russia have traditionally and for a long time had substantial influence. For the time being, it is unclear how the directly or indirectly affected countries will respond to the strategic, political, and security implications of the Chinese initiative.

China aims to accelerate its integration into the world economy, reduce the country's export-oriented stance, boost internal demand, improve employment, and find solutions to the excess capacities in industrial production. At the same time, the strengthening of foreign policy relations with the Asian region and the rest of the world, as well as the opening up to the West, have also gained momentum.

One Belt, One Road: 64 countries

The Chinese government's OBOR initiative is supported by 64 countries, which is a clear political victory for the Chinese leadership. It shows that China's growth and role in the world economy is acknowledged by Western powers as well. However, it is important to make a distinction: this does not mean that Beijing has taken the lead among global powers. In the future, it will be interesting to see how the organization's currency will be determined, as making the yuan an international means of payment is China's declared intention. Beijing has realized that taking the lead in the East Asian region is impossible without making this prospect attractive for neighbouring countries, and acquiring their support. In the past few years, the assertive, or, as many would say, aggressive Chinese attitude with respect to the disputes over the islands in the South China Sea has intensified the already existing fears linked to China's great power ambitions.

Within the framework of the so-called 'rebalancing' policy announced by President Obama and conducted with the leadership of the United States, a defence alliance was set up for China's isolation or at least strategic encirclement. This currently forming alliance includes Japan with its tentative rearmament programme, South Korea, the Philippines and Vietnam, and the latter is hardly considered Washington's traditional partner. Small and medium-sized countries seek to get under America's protective umbrella, and the race for establishing alliances has intensified in the region. On the other hand, nationalism manifesting itself in anti-China sentiment has gained renewed momentum. Chinese President Xi Jinping has recognized the danger these developments entail, and strives to present the Chinese state's security policy manoeuvres in a trade-economic guise.

The two-way trade plan and the corresponding infrastructure development plan, the new Silk Road initiative, became the flagship of this policy. The aim is to create a land route through Central Asia to Europe on the one hand, and to establish a maritime trade route to Europe from the South China Sea through the Indian Ocean, the Arabian Sea, the Red Sea, and the Suez Canal on the other. Due to the previously mentioned economic interdependence, the Central Asian infrastructure developments and investments have a direct impact on the situation of the underdeveloped province. It is also important to halt the spread of Islamic radicalism within the Central Asian countries themselves through fostering economic development.

With the withdrawal of its troops from Afghanistan, the United States has lost its previous weight in the region, and due to the consequences of the Ukrainian conflict, the Russians do not act as real rivals against China. The land-based Silk Road Economic Belt is only realistic in Central Asia, as the route was originally planned to run through Northern Iraq and Syria before reaching Turkey. With the Islamic State terrorist organization fighting in the region, it is difficult to imagine that a major land-based trade route would run here in the near future. The Silk Road has another important side branch, toward Pakistan. China can access the Persian Gulf by bypassing the route running through the Indian Ocean and the Strait of Malacca (Indian Ocean, Arabian Sea), through Pakistan, a traditional ally (and partner in offsetting India's influence). The Gwadar Port (Pakistan's access to the Indian Ocean) built with Chinese funds is suitable for receiving imports from the Arab world. The next step is creating the land-based link to Western China.

What the map shows

If we take a look at the conflicts since 1990, the terrorist attacks, American military interventions and the military, social, and economic conflicts, and superimpose the development areas and route of the Silk Road Economic Belt on this map, the strategic issue becomes evident. Why are American military forces concentrated here, and why is it important for the United States to preserve its global power? The United States rules the seas and the world's oceans. But how does it fare on land? Why is it important for the United States to prevent the establishment of a coherent Eurasian supercontinent with Europe, Russia, and China?

The main point of building the 21st-Century Maritime Silk Road is to strengthen the Chinese presence in the waters to the west of the Strait of Malacca, primarily against Indian positions, which is key in preventing the United States-led isolation already mentioned. This maritime trade route is also about strengthening the ties between Africa and China. For Hungary, this maritime route may be important because Chinese exports and imports arriving to the Mediterranean would partly run through the Balkans toward Western Europe. It is no coincidence that China is interested in developing the railway network in the Balkans, and that it supports the building of a high-speed rail connection between Belgrade and Budapest. The OBOR project is to be supported by the China Development Bank to the tune of US$890 billion, and this is not an isolated initiative. The Asian Infrastructure Investment Bank, the New Development Bank, and the Contingent Reserve Arrangement monetary fund are all parts of a Chinese great power policy that uses foreign trade tools for its expansion.

According to some analysts, the OBOR initiative may be China's 'Marshall Plan', which may facilitate the region's economic integration and create new business opportunities for Chinese companies. In connection with the investments already under way, it can be clearly seen that China is not preparing for providing aid to its partner countries as an act of philanthropy, but plans to finance market-based investments that promise guaranteed returns. Nevertheless, just as the historical Silk Road enabled more than the transport of goods for almost 2,000 years, the OBOR will play a crucial role in making trade ties stronger, but also in cementing the cultural and technological link between continents.

China has made it clear from the outset that the Central and Eastern European countries will play a major role in its strategic success.

In order to maintain the competitiveness of Chinese exports on European markets despite the growing costs of production, the primary concern is reducing transport times. Owing to earlier investments, Chinese products do not need to be transported to large cities in northern Europe anymore, since the ships can directly reach the partly Chinese-owned Port of Piraeus. This reduces the average transport time between China and Europe from 30 to 20 days. Thanks to the development of the railway lines running through the Balkans, the transport time can be decreased further, which ultimately bolsters the competitiveness of Chinese products.

What is more, the infrastructure developments along the OBOR such as the strategically important Gwadar Port established at the strategically important end of the China–Pakistan Economic Corridor (CPEC) and the road and railway developments linked to that may provide answers to several challenges that Chinese companies have faced in the recent period.

China's opening up to the West: the impact of the Silk Road

China's declared intention is to conclude 'win-win' deals with the countries in the region. The main point of the OBOR strategy is to create land-based and maritime trade routes similar to the historical Silk Road that help China in maintaining its ties to European, Asian, and Middle Eastern countries. The effects of the OBOR project on the countries concerned are the following:

1. *Market stimulation effect*: The OBOR connects the regions within China not only with each other but also with the areas outside China, therefore it stimulates production and trade, creating a market worth over US$4 billion.
2. *Knowledge stimulation effect*: The OBOR places special emphasis on next-generation information technologies, making the information flow between the different regions even smoother.

3. *Efficiency increasing effect*: The flow and optimized distribution of labour, capital, and technologies between the areas is considered a priority in the OBOR project, which considerably increases efficiency.
4. *Cooperation boosting effect*: In a comprehensive view of the issues pertaining to the development of the individual regions, cooperation between the countries and regions is vital for implementing the OBOR project.

Asian Infrastructure Investment Bank

In April 2015, a new development arose in the strategic struggle between the United States and China. Until now, no outright winner could be declared in the dispute, but as the deadline expired for the application for the permanent members of the Asian Infrastructure Investment Bank (AIIB), for the first time, China chalked up the first clear-cut win over its rival. Among the founding members, there are 44 countries from the region (Asian or Pacific) and 24 countries from outside the region. These countries include key United States allies such as the United Kingdom, France, Germany, and Italy, but in the end Australia, Thailand, and South Korea also joined.[82] Only the United States and Japan stayed clearly outside the AIIB (the membership application of North Korea was rejected on grounds of transparency issues with respect to finances and general government).

PART 4

THE AGE OF FUSION

CHAPTER 13

WE LIVE IN THE AGE OF FUSION AND NETWORKS

New stars are born: the energy of fusion

Fusion energy is in fact the inverse of the energy created during nuclear fission. Both are nuclear reactions that produce energy with different applications. In nuclear fission the nucleus of an atom is split into smaller parts resulting in the release of energy. Nuclear fusion is the process where two light nuclei combine together creating two to three times more energy than nuclear fission. We witness the process of nuclear fusion day in, day out since, this is how the sun generates its energy. Fuel from nuclear fusion is not toxic, fossil, or particularly rare, as fusion develops using hydrogen atoms, the most common element in the universe. If any problem arises, the fusion simply stops. It produces no or minimal radioactive waste and its by-product is helium, which can also be utilized.

Unfortunately, research into fusion is slow, overly cautious, and yields few results from a lot of effort. Stepping up research into the options for implementing fusion energy in practice would be welcome, as our world direly needs clean energy.

Humanity needs vast amounts of energy, which entails an equally vast environmental impact and consequences. We need an energy source that is cheaper than fossil fuels, one that does not result in carbon dioxide emissions, and is at least as reliable as the current system. In other words, we essentially need an energy miracle. Viable commercial fusion energy is now just a matter of time, as the opportunity uncontestably exists. The creation of fusion energy will be a human feat comparable to flying or man's expedition to the Moon – seemingly impossible until accomplished.

From the peripheries to hubs

The study of geology and palaeontology shows that change always occurs at the periphery of water and land, which gives rise to new phases and new eras. Just think of the emergence of amphibians and reptiles during the Devonian and Permian geologic periods, followed by the spiralling progress of evolution, shaped by environmental impacts and the conditions of adaptation.

Peripheries also have the most active tectonic movements, the most active volcanoes and earthquakes, just like the peripheries of science provide the soil for the most interesting technological innovations, companies, and regions. In the realm of science, new scientific domains, new subject areas, new discoveries, and new technological achievements, start-up technologies, and the best new universities emerge at the such meeting points.

The *Map of Sciences* created by researcher Johan Bollen, shows how various subject areas relate to each other and how they create fusional meeting points and hubs.

In the 21st century, new life sciences are becoming particularly important, combining medicine, engineering, natural sciences and economic sciences. The internet is another area of similar complexity.

We live in the age of networks

In this modern age, networks are ubiquitous. Anyone who works on a computer essentially relies on a workplace connection to perform any type of task. When we turn on our computers, we log on to the network of networks: the internet. We use a network, often the very same information and communication network, to make telephone calls. The energy needed to power these devices comes from yet another network, the electrical grid. Our drinking water and the gas used to heat our homes also come from networks. We use networks of roads and railways to visit friends and family. Modern life could not exist without networks, so the concept of network is often instinctively associated with modernity, while in fact networks have always been present throughout humanity. Water pipeline networks already existed more than 4,000 years ago in Mohenjo-Daro, and roads, or at least networks of paths and routes, are also as old as humanity itself. Ubiquitous networks have therefore always been important. But they have become far more important nowadays as increasingly sophisticated networks have emerged and spread in the realm of technology. While networks found in nature developed organically and function almost imperceptibly by themselves, man-made networks must be designed and rendered functional by us. This requires understanding how networks function, as the better we understand them, the better we are able to create effective structures that support our objectives.

The growing significance of networks

The network-like interconnectedness, linkage, and functioning of things has thus become increasingly apparent with the emergence and spread of man-made technical networks. While our nervous system works even if we are unfamiliar with its architecture or functioning, or if we do not even think of it as a network, the same does not hold true for a computer network, which people must build and render operational.

Networks multiply our power and our opportunities. Just like a group of people of a certain size can achieve more as a cooperative community compared with a set of individuals thinking and working in an isolated manner, the capabilities and opportunities of our technical equipment are also multiplied when they are configured into networks. In other cases, the network itself is what gives rise to a function. Just think of the electronics that control cars. The sensors and controllers located in various points of a vehicle are unable to execute the same functions independently as tied together into a network. In a situation like this, information from various points of the network must be collected and processed to give the right control response.

Once technical designers started thinking in terms of and dealing with networks, an increasing body of network-related knowledge and experience was amassed. With the emergence and spread of technical networks and the rise of network-based thinking, we started noticing networks in other places as well. In order to design and build technical networks, network models had to be developed, in other words, a descriptive language and mental framework had to be created for correctly modelling networks. With the spread of networks and by leveraging this new knowledge, networks or network-like functioning has been discovered in other areas, as a result of which network models have become decoupled from specific, concrete technology and become more abstract and generally applicable, and a new science of networks has been born and continues to evolve. This step has allowed us to investigate the logic, features, and functioning of networks in an abstract manner, independent from the associated technology or other media such as the nervous system. This has allowed us to distinguish the features of a network architecture from the features inherent to the physical embodiment of the network in the study of network functioning.

Abstraction enables the computerized modelling of networks and the computerized simulation of their functioning, and further improves our capacity to understand networks, deepening our knowledge of them. This greater understanding in turn creates a positive feedback that makes the learning process self-reinforcing. We are building better and better networks and are gaining a deeper understanding of phenomena (including natural phenomena) with network-like functioning, for instance in the realm of biology and even human relationships.

This process is far from complete. Networks are popping up in more and more places around us, but there still remain untapped areas. The technology for using networks is often already available, for example in living areas or on clothing, but their use has not yet truly taken off. After the age of the steam engine, the internal combustion engine, electronics, and the computer, we now live in the age of networks.

Networks everywhere

What makes a network a network? How can we recognize networks? A network is defined by its unique structure, which is fundamentally very simple. Networks consist of a set of nodes that connect to each other in some way. These nodes and the links between them are diverse and thus so are the networks themselves.

In terms of the diversity of communication and computer networks, they can take on many different forms and be interpreted in many different ways. For instance, the open systems interconnection (OSI) model is used to describe seven different layers of computer networks. The same physical network is examined from a different perspective at every level of the model, each perspective yielding a different logical network. The essence is that anything that is logically a network or exhibits network-like behaviour, anything that can be described with network-like features can take on many different physical forms, in other words the nodes and their links are not necessarily tangible or visible. Why is this relevant? Because this shows that networks are far more ubiquitous than we think. Even human relationships can be described as networks and analysed and broken down into different layers, just like computer networks. The lower layer could be the people we could theoretically reach because we have their telephone number in our address book. The next layer could be the people we know personally. Higher layers could represent the level or type of acquaintance, or the contents of interpersonal relationships. The economy can also be seen as a network, with economic agents constituting its nodes linked via various connections. For instance, if we try to represent a macroeconomic model graphically, to explain the relationship between a model's elements using a figure, we obtain a figure very similar to electrical circuit models not only because macroeconomic models were in fact inspired by technical models, but also because both follow the same network logic.

The fundamental features of networks

Functioning and apparent systems like networks have features that stem specifically from their network-like nature and are thus universal to all types of networks. Identifying, exploring, and understanding these characteristics not only enriches our abstract knowledge of networks, but also helps us understand and design network-like systems or grasp the interactions between connected systems.

Albert-László Barabási, a Hungarian physicist, is a renowned researcher of network sciences. In his book,[83] Barabási presents the mathematical and graph theory fundamentals of network research alongside the general structure of networks and some of their key attributes.

In connection with networks, we gain insight into the self-organizing mechanisms that are responsible for many of the characteristics of the world surrounding us. Barabási sheds light on the central points located within networks and their connections, as well as the significance of the connections that transform smaller networks into more extensive ones. The book reveals that one of the most interesting and important traits of networks is that every network has prominent central points that have many connections, while the majority of these central points are only directly linked to a few other central points. Many other features of networks and their functioning, from their robustness and capacity for regeneration to their vulnerability, stem from this one important attribute. In addition to presenting the different structural types of networks – random or scale independent, centralized, decentralized, or distributed networks – Barabási explains what leads to the emergence of specific types of networks and what characteristics stem from different structural types. Based on these attributes, we can understand why a specific network structure is the most advantageous or most viable given the circumstances and can thus gain a better understanding of how things work and the sometimes-surprising background of events and phenomena.

The fundamental significance of our growing knowledge about networks stems not from the opportunities for concrete application, but much rather from the fact that our knowledge and science are developing just like a network consisting of nodes and new links between them.

By better understanding networks, we can thus find and identify more effective and better ways to expand humanity's knowledge.

The complexity behind fusions and networks

Cesar Hidalgo (MIT) and Ricardo Hausmann (Harvard University) laid new foundations for interpreting economic development, basing this on the average complexity of the goods manufactured by a country. According to the theoretical foundations, complex economies are characterized, besides their stability, by the availability of more diverse and types of knowledge (acquired based on an implicit, explicit, or objective basis) for producing various goods that are able to interact with each other and thus fuse within an individual or an organization.

The basis for researching this economic model was first published in the journal *Science* in 2007, in a paper written with the collaboration of Albert-László Barabási and Bailey Klinger. *The Atlas of Economic Complexity* was published in 2014[84] as an extension of this paper, incorporating the economic complexity index created by Hidalgo and Hausmann at the national level, alongside a country-by-country analysis. This metric of economic development measuring complexity is used, among other things, to study the number and diversity of the goods produced and exported by a country. The analysis is based on the foreign trade statistics of 123 countries stretching back to 1965. The index value also factors in how widespread and how unique the goods are, based on the number of countries that manufacture a specific good. The indicator is also used to forecast economic growth.

In this regard, prosperity stems from the quantity, quality, diversity, and unique nature of the skills and knowledge accumulated by a country's labour force. Accordingly, economic development is the learning process that allows a country to produce increasingly complex and complicated goods. At an individual level, this hinges upon workers having the skills and knowledge to produce the most complex and highest value added possible. At a corporate level, higher prosperity depends on the knowledge, work experience, and know-how of workers. These factors enable economic entities to react quickly to processes unfolding in the economy, to adapt and continuously renew their products or services (innovation capacity) and to continuously improve their productivity.

More complex products and services can emerge in a legal and institutional framework that fosters a higher level of cooperation skills, promotes the diversification of attributes, and stimulates the forging of connections. This is conditional on a higher level of trust, the capacity to cooperate, and a certain culture of abiding by the rules within society, coupled with the creation of an economic framework capable of developing an authentic ecosystem from players operating in different forms of economic cooperation through a higher degree of network formation.

The increasing role of locations in the age of fusion

The value added by human resources and knowledge is the driver of economic growth; economic development and capacity to prosper stem increasingly from the growing complexity of products and services. Accordingly, the economic systems and communities where the harmony of the conditions in the social, economic, and physical environment enables the continuous and rapid flow of learning and new information and knowledge transfer, and which foster personal interaction among individuals are those able to develop continuously. Harmonizing these conditions for connection in space and time is a decisive factor in creating a robust development path for a community. Due to the nature of human sensation, our environment has a major impact on our decisions and thinking, including the physical expression of our environment in the built environment and the totality of impulses coming from the people surrounding us. For this reason, geographical space remains an essential element within knowledge-intensive and innovation-based activities and its significance has barely declined in the wake of technological innovation.

Furthermore, economic processes are changing because our day-to-day lives are growing increasingly complex and this complexity permeates more and more levels. Creating integration calls for establishing shared interfaces that enable rapid connection and smooth flows.

Higher density urban spaces and the virtual spaces of cloud-based solutions provide solid foundations for network-building operations and integration among social relationships and various economic activities. The conscious building of these contributes to greater relationship density. While the digital economy and online spaces are spreading within the economy, the offline interfaces and physical spaces that foster personal meetings remain the most effective environment for cultivating human relationships and knowledge transfer.

The emergence of new ideas and knowledge remains geographically defined

In the age of globalization and information technology (IT) devices, it is becoming an accepted fact that besides the infrastructural and institutional framework, social, community, and economic connections, the density of these networks and the quality of interactions are decisive factors in the development of a region. Shaping relationships between individuals, changes at a social level, and launching changes in corporate cultures and the resulting creation of new social capacities are among the greatest challenges facing the developed world.

However due to human nature, connecting in cyberspace will never replace the experience of personal interaction because humans learn most effectively by experiencing through all senses (such as seeing, hearing, or smelling). This is because personal relationships are the foundation of deeper trust, greater respect, and more efficient cooperation. So, although communicating through IT supplements and makes personal meetings more efficient it will not replace them.

The territorial pattern of the spread of patents sheds light on the role of geographical space in corporate and institutional innovation processes. The number of patents that cite and quote each other within a metropolitan region is twice as frequent as in other areas. In this age of information technology and information society, contrary to earlier predictions, geographic space has not lost its significance and the circumstances allowing the birth of new ideas and knowledge are still defined by geography (specifically, the geographic configuration of the agents of development) and geographic space still has a major impact on innovation and productivity. The territorially defined factors that foster innovation processes are:

- economic life, the scientific world, and the territorial configuration and concentration of the geographic location of the institutional players involved in knowledge transfer; and
- the recognition and exploitation of the local and positional features of regions (including their natural and climatic attributes alongside the shaping of the physical environment).

Another essential point for the qualitative improvement of social capacities and relationships is supporting grassroots initiatives and defining development strategies based on the identification of the common interests of local players, the implementation of which builds on the internal motivation of the players shaping the region's development.

In a nutshell, economic development driven by knowledge and technological innovation offers an advantage to the regions (and cities) that have excellent higher education and knowledge transfer institutions and also the right climatic conditions. Changes in economic structure, the shift toward higher value-added activities, and simultaneously accelerating urbanization affect the lives and living space of millions.

Location as a basic platform

Jan Gehl, Copenhagen's former chief architect and the founder of people-centred urban design introduced the premise that the shaping of the built urban environment impacts the behaviour and conduct of its inhabitants. Gehl's work emphasizes the living areas between buildings instead of the buildings themselves, the quality and form of public spaces, and, through them, the improvement of urban living standards, which help to identify the tools of the built environment that contribute to liveable cities. Gehl interprets the transformation of urban spaces through the competition of functions, where the first step involves the gradual reshaping of transportation methods and networks, with particular emphasis on pedestrian and cyclist interconnections. A key condition for reinforcing local communities is the creation of comfortable community spaces with high usage value that provide a platform for hosting programmes geared toward community activity. Rapid pedestrian and cyclist access to these public spaces is paramount. In terms of location, the focus should be on creating suitable spaces where people spend time. Architectural design fundamentally determines the reinforcement of community functions: high-quality public area furniture and seating, and their adequate positioning, are key factors influencing how leisure time is spent in community areas. The frequent connections between high-activity public spaces and people, and the fine-tuning and development of pedways between buildings create a more inspiring environment.

Broadly speaking, cities characterized by peaceful social cohabitation share the following features:

1. *Full of life*: Providing inspiration for using ground-level public areas and personal meetings by establishing primarily pedestrian and cyclist connections.
2. *Safe*: Safety can best be improved by changing the lifestyle of the city's users and by creating pedestrian connections increasing the usage of spaces.
3. *Sustainable*: With the changing mobility habits and forms of transport, the city's structure promotes the covering of shorter distances, which in turn results in a healthier environment with lower carbon dioxide emissions thanks to pedestrian and bicycle transport.
4. *Healthy*: A key component of urban health policy is promoting daily exercise as an integral part of people's lives with the right environmental conditions.

The guiding principle of an urban policy aimed at achieving these attributes is prioritizing the continuous improvement of people's quality of life, health, and the overall situation and integration of urban society. The transformation of cities along these guidelines results in a physical environment that fosters personal meetings, more and better-quality relationships, while establishing environmentally and economically sustainable living standards and living conditions.

The phenomenon of disruptive innovation

The most characteristic phenomenon of the corporate world's transformation is that valuable companies today operate with relatively few employees. In the mid-2010s, Apple, the world's most valuable company, was worth US$772 billion but only employed 110,000 people worldwide.

Disruptive innovation occurs when markets accustomed to innovation in small increments are shaken up by radically new ideas that satisfy consumer needs to a far greater degree. In the majority of cases, more established companies come to terms with such radical ideas when it is already too late for them to adapt, and they are often crowded out of the market. The products of disruptive innovation share two typical features: they carry some type of new value, often following a novel business model, and are sometimes accompanied by new, smaller scale technological modifications.

With the increasingly deeper social and economic integration of technological changes, entire professions may disappear. Drones used by Amazon to ship books, or to deliver pizzas in Italy, are examples attesting to the impact of these developments on employment. Bank of America's innovation of replacing investment advisors with algorithm-based robots is another example of using technological solutions to replace live labour. Furthermore, the use of robots and the replacement of live labour may spread in the domain of healthcare.

The fourth Industrial Revolution

While professions were relatively stable in the labour market of the past, they have undergone deep structural changes in parallel with the shifting economic processes. British sociologists Alexander Carr-Saunders and Paul Wilson wrote a book during the recession in 1933 entitled *The Professions*. They hailed the emergence of specialist domains and professions as being vital for preserving the achievements of society and the long-term guarantees for passing on traditions, although these professional structures are undergoing a restructuring stemming from the fact that efficient business processes require an increasingly complex knowledge background from workers.

The Future of the Professions, a book written by Oxford researchers Richard Susskind and Daniel Susskind published in 2015 was the latest to shed light on this restructuring. The book blames the spread of information technology for this growing instability. These technologies have disrupted the slow, self-paced development of professions.

The 'mechanization' and the automation of IT to a certain extent contribute to the spread of knowledge content, the continuous expansion of the boundaries of human knowledge and the integration and high-level utilization and application of this knowledge. Machines and other devices have taken over certain tasks from nurses and doctors in much of the healthcare sector, particularly diagnostics. Online consulting has become ubiquitous in this sector; the patient–doctor relationship can be made far more direct and intense using smartphone applications. Electronic rulings and decisions are also spreading among lawyers and judges. For instance, eBay already uses such an application to pass decisions in large volumes, in roughly 60 million consumer complaint cases every year.

According to the Oxford duo, the spread of these processes will result in the total disappearance of certain traditional professions. Technology makes the knowledge of more complicated domains accessible to and understandable by the general public. However, the arguments made in the book sparked much criticism. Some of it pertains to the handling of complexity. According to the counterarguments, it is not true that machines handle complex issues more efficiently, furthermore uniform administrative systems situated in the above professions are the best solution in certain areas, such as taxation, in line with current practice. Moreover, the authors fail to take it into consideration that certain jobs cannot be replaced with machine-like mechanisms for emotional and empathetic reasons; for instance, personal interaction lends far more sensitivity to the communication of bad news. Many hold that the Susskinds ventured too far in their book and failed to take it into account that as they become richer, people tend to prefer more intense human contact.

The authors' assertion, corroborated by many others, is that the structure of professions will change more over the upcoming 25 years than in the three previous centuries. Along these trends, subdomains such as knowledge engineering will emerge within sciences, which can be used to build scientific thinking, scientific findings, and philosophical thoughts around integrated automatisms, shaping them into software. The status of an expert standing above professions is also a new area of activity, aimed at identifying the diverse application opportunities for sciences. In terms of the impact of the process, it is important to emphasize that the restructuring of professions affects the wealthiest groups of society. For example, the top three social strata accounted for 57% of the students enrolled in healthcare higher education institutions in Great Britain in 2011. The most important question is how the restructuring of these viable and stable social groups will impact continuous and peaceful social progress.

Creative capitalism

In an article entitled 'Creative Capitalism',[85] *The Economist* looked at the link between Hollywood's movie industry and the economy, as many are prone to taking Hollywood and the movie industry less seriously compared with other economic sectors. These organizations are exemplary in terms of not only product development and their marketing methods, but also in the management of creative labour.

The basis of the similarity among industries is mainly in product development methodology. The production of food and other consumption goods is only just now adopting an approach that movie studios have long used: focusing on a narrower range of blockbusters and allocating more time to the promotion and management of these movies and products.

In many industries, from electronics to the automotive industry, the pace for rolling out new products and brands is accelerating, so the Hollywood method of building huge hype around certain movies is a valuable lesson. Movie production is a bona fide American success story, and the United States maintains its leading global role within the industry – which is almost unparalleled – generating US$16 billion in export value annually.

Cooperation is paramount for product development.

Every firm that employs creative labour must tackle the challenge of harnessing their creativity for commercial gain without stifling their free-spiritedness, and this is something that Hollywood has a century's experience in.

For every production, movie studios recruit a fresh team of creative people and allow them to work together intensively. The studios only intervene when something is clearly going wrong. The possibility of intervention from a higher level and untethered community-based work generates both a feeling of control and commitment to the project in team members.

Mark Young, faculty member of the USC Marshall School of Business, argues that people work hard and collaborate well in the movie business as freelancers because they have little job stability, work on a project-by-project basis, and must prove themselves continuously to secure future work, and also because they firmly believe in what they do.

The products and movie productions created develop organically, with the input of many people and shaped by internal and external feedback. But this process often results in an outcome that differs from the objectives defined at the outset of the project. For this reason, Ed Catmull, the founder of Pixar, says that every film starts out as an "ugly baby", growing through countless changes into an adult.

Mobile telephone app companies and Silicon Valley technology firms use similar methods in product development. A fresh product is introduced to the market quickly and then fine-tuned continuously based on intensive consumer feedback and testing, undergoing additional developments before being released in a more sophisticated version.

For the sake of better profitability, film studios focus on increasingly fewer projects, typically action-packed 'franchise' films featuring comic-book characters, which sell well abroad and lend themselves to sequels. Similar to Silicon Valley, Hollywood relies heavily on outside financing, sharing the profits from hits but also the risks, reducing investor losses per unit of cost when a film flops. Hollywood's product development model has a proven track record of success. The industry has managed to maintain its leading position on a global scale in the long run.

CHAPTER 14

DATA WILL BECOME THE NEW RAW MATERIAL FOR THE ECONOMY

'Big Data' refers to the large quantity of information accumulating in various information systems, and the classification and structuring of this data. Big Data fundamentally emerged simultaneously with the automation of information processing: although companies had already made strategic decisions based on accounting data, analytics, and surveys in the past, there is far more information available today than merely statistics and projections. Companies can rely on up-to-date structured and unstructured data packages broken down to every individual. The great challenge and opportunity of our age is how we will use these data.

The Gutenberg revolution of our age

The question of how a society treats its accumulated information has emerged again and again throughout history (from cave paintings through cuneiform script to book printing). The codification of laws (Hammurabi) and automated book printing (the Gutenberg phenomenon) were considered as a form of Big Data structuring in their own time. These revolutionary innovations created new industries and catalysed existing ones, including education, sciences, the economy, and politics. However, the scale, quality, and utilization opportunities multiplied by the 21st century, and the scientific community is expecting an even greater catalysing effect from Big Data. Nevertheless, Big Data does not promise an immediate and unconditional breakthrough;

the data must be acquired, stored, and processed, which calls for technology and experts. Big Data systems are only as good as their creators, so an increasingly saturated market of experts and software is emerging, marked by sharp competition.

Managing the unmanageable

There are four major challenges posed by data, referred to as '4V':

- *Volume*, i.e. the quantity of data: 40 zettabytes (43 quintillion gigabytes) of data will be generated by 2020, which is 300 times the quantity existing in 2005.
- *Variety*, i.e. the variety and diversity of data: the quantity of data generated by healthcare reached 150 exabytes in 2011, the quantity of data shared on Facebook reached 30 billion pieces of content, and more than 30 billion hours of video are uploaded to YouTube every month.
- *Velocity*, i.e. the speed of data flow: the New York Stock Exchange uses 1 terabyte of data during each transaction, and a modern car has close to 100 sensors to monitor all items such as oil level and tyre pressure.
- *Veracity*, i.e. the credibility of data: one out of three businesspeople does not trust the information they use to make decisions. According to a survey, 27% of respondents were unable to say what percentage of the data they use is not fully credible or reliable. Low data reliability costs US$3.1 billion for the United States annually.

How big is Big Data?

When the Sloan Digital Sky Survey was launched in 2000, it collected as much information during the first weeks as astronomy had during its entire previous existence, and accumulated 140 terabytes of data over a decade and a half. The Synoptic Survey telescope installed in 2016 collects the same amount of data every five days. United States retail chain Walmart[86] executes more than one million customer transactions every hour, generating an incredible volume of over 2.5 petabytes of information, which is 167 times of the amount all of the books within the American Library of Congress. Mapping the human body's entire genome took ten years in the past, but just one week in 2003. These examples all show that the unmeasurably vast amount of information obtained from the world in the digital environment is increasingly easily managed. This allows us to do many things that were previously unimaginable: we are able to prevent diseases or crime, and identify business trends. If data is managed correctly, we can discover new sources of economic value and achieve scientific breakthroughs.

Never enough data?

Adam Farquhar, of the British Library, warned in *The Economist* that "if we're not careful, we will know more about the beginning of the 20th century than the beginning of the 21st century". Despite rapid technological progress, the volume of collected data already exceeds the available storage capacity. A similar problem is that "many of the digital objects we create can only be rendered by the software that created them", said internet pioneer and Google staff member Vint Cerf. In other words, not just raw information, but the software needed to processes the information must also be archived. Besides technical issues, even more serious legal restrictions prevent the collection of data. Laws require licences for libraries to store certain content, and there is simply no capacity to obtain these licences. On the other hand, users are very quick to waive the protection of their personal data in exchange for a single service, putting legislators between a rock and a hard place.

The future of Big Data

Joe Hellerstein, professor of computer science at the University of California in Berkeley, argues that we are experiencing "the Industrial Revolution of Data". This impact can be felt everywhere, from the business world to scientific life, from state governance to the arts.

Scientists and information technology engineers came up with the term Big Data for this phenomenon. In recent years, Oracle, IBM, Microsoft, and SAP have spent a total of more than US$15 billion to acquire software companies specializing in data management and data analysis. Estimates predict that 4.4 million IT experts will be needed worldwide by 2025 just to deal with data management, and that 1.9 million of these IT jobs will be located in the United States. The industry is estimated to be worth more than US$100 billion and is growing at an annual rate of 10%, roughly twice as fast as the entire software sector.

Data will become the new raw material for the economy, representing a new input that may be equal in value to capital and labour. "The data-centred economy is just nascent," admits Craig Mundie. "You can see the outlines of it, but the technical, infrastructural, and even business-model implications are not well understood right now."

The new industrial revolution of data

The essence of economic progress is finding increasingly better solutions for satisfying people's needs and necessities. On the one hand, this means that today's products are able to better fulfil a greater number of functions and are better adapted to user needs than earlier products. On the other hand, producing them requires increasingly less material but increasingly more intellectual resources, the latter in two different senses. For one, designing and manufacturing a technically more complex and sophisticated product is a more complex process. Consumers and users also have to learn more in order to use a device or product, but this investment is recovered in the course of its subsequent use.

As a result of all of this, information is becoming more significant within the economy, while raw materials are losing significance. Technologies, production processes, technical solution descriptions and documentation, and their data content, are increasingly growing to embody value for companies as opposed to raw materials, machines, and equipment.

The economic role of data and information is also enhanced by the increasing amount of free time we have on our hands thanks to development, even if it sometimes does not feel that way. One of the reasons for this is that it is now much easier to spend our leisure time meaningfully in an entertaining manner, thanks in part to data itself. Movies, TV series, and YouTube channels are essentially made up of data, their true content. Content is what entertains us, not the device used to channel this content. This also holds true for live performances, concerts, theatre, and even sporting events. The content transmitted at these events is essentially information, because what truly matters is not physical contact with the actors, but the enjoyment of the content conveyed. This becomes even clearer if we consider that live performances are seen by more people through electronic channels than those present on location, which also requires the transmission of data. Data is therefore becoming an important input for goods and services, whether it be media content, manufacturing know-how or information on consumer preferences geared toward better meeting consumer needs.

The most spectacular progress has been made in the area of electronics, not only because we have witnessed truly great changes in this domain, but also because the change has unfolded literally before our eyes.

One of the star products of the 1980s, essentially yesterday on the scale of economic history, was the Commodore 64 computer. It was one of the first computers for home use, featuring 64,000 bytes of memory with no internal storage, yet relatively few people owned such a device at that time. Data could be saved on magnetic tape and later to floppy disks the size of two palms, in relatively small quantities. The cathode ray tube monitor was able to display 160 × 200 pixels (in 16 colours) and 320 × 200 monochromatic pixels.

By contrast, smartphones that are capable of displaying 16 million colours at a resolution of 1920 × 1080 or more, with memories that are 15,000 times greater than the Commodore's capacity and with internal storage chips of up to 100 billion bytes that are the size of a fingertip are ubiquitous today, on a scale so small that they fit in our pockets. These devices are far more sophisticated, use far less raw materials and hold information content that is greater by orders of magnitude. They can run multiple software, rendering them multifunctional, and mobile internet that can be accessed anywhere allows data to be exchanged between any two points in the world.

Some services, such as the internet, telecommunication, and media content services are directly linked to data. Data are also present in the personalization of services and industrial products, as consumer needs must be known at an individual level, handled and processed for orders, in a suitable manner for the industry. Such data has become indispensable input for inventory management, manufacturing, and production planning. Finally, data is also becoming more important in agriculture, in the more advanced production technologies, in maintaining and operating the European Union's subsidy system and monitoring farmers and farms, for example for processing data obtained from remote sensing via satellite or for the trading of and market planning of produce.

The World Economic Forum's annual *Global Competitiveness Report* groups economies into three stages of development. As one stage develops into the next, the role of data also becomes more important in terms of competitiveness. The levels can be described as:

- The factor-driven level: growth at this level relies on the growth of production, with growth materializing through brute force.
- The efficiency-driven level: organization and the use of technological solutions become more valuable together with the role of the required data.
- The innovation-driven level: here the focus shifts from increasing the quantity of factors of production to improving quality, and from adopting technical solutions to creating new ones.

The latter in particular is fundamentally based on data in the sense that innovation is what represents value.

All of this goes to show that the rising value of data within the economy is inherent to and a consequence of development. The growing value of data and innovation goes hand in hand with the growing value of humans within the economy, both as resources and consumers. Development means both goods and services are more closely tailored to individuals as consumers, as well as procedures and technologies that are less of a burden on humans. 'Public good' is serving the welfare and prosperity of individuals organized into communities. So, if one considers humans and human communities as the most important value within a continuously developing and modernizing economy, one must work on fostering natural economic development and breaking down any barriers to this development, as this process is specifically centred around humans, their prosperity, and the thriving of human communities.

The rising value of data and information is synonymous with the rising value of people within the economy. As Julian Lincoln Simon wrote in his book *The Ultimate Resource*, the most important, fundamental and ultimate resource of the economy is not some physical resource, but the innovation and adaptation capacity of people.

CHAPTER 15

PERSONAL EXPERIENCE: THE NEW SERVICE OF THE 21ST CENTURY

The 21st century has launched a new and exciting era of technological progress. It is evident that the communication revolution achieved through technological innovation has abolished geographical distances today. But it is important to note that it is precisely the abolition of geographical distances that has increased the worth of the unique (social, environmental, economic, and cultural) values of places and spaces in the globalizing world.

The Earth, turning into an open economic and social space, has created challenges (such as competitiveness) for economies and societies that were not a major issue for nations in the past. In the course of history, there have more or less been deterrents (such as natural borders, or political or war-related events) that provided a certain degree of artificial protection for countries and nations. Another important process was the shift of the world's operating mechanisms in the geographic and spatial sense from the level of nations to the level of cities, in other words the role and constraints of the macrolevel have gradually decreased relative to the microlevel.

The most important of the changes unfolding within society has been the increasing role of individuals. Technological progress has made a major impact on the generation born and growing up in the past decade,[87] where the role of the individual, self-fulfilment (self-realization, self-expression) and freedom as a general idea and principle (access to information, mobility, etc.) is more pronounced and reflected in society than ever before.

Geographic and social changes, where the microlevel and individuals have taken priority, are making an impact in the closely related economic mechanisms. What matters today is reacting to individual needs instead of mass needs, emphasizing quality (unique, handmade products or products made in limited quantities) over quantity (mass production) transforming the economic and production mentality and mechanisms of the past, which were centred on the price of goods, the size of markets, and costs. Instead, the focus today is on attracting the consumer as a target group, gaining the loyalty of and retaining consumers, who must be incorporated into processes in order to be reached, providing a special experience when using a product or service. Experience can be directly tied to individual happiness, which might be one of the most important goals of today's generation.

This mentality has increasingly filtered through to the economy in a broader sense, the world of design, services, education, and business, resulting in a radically new perspective and attitude which ultimately introduces experience as the new service of the 21st century.

'Experience' at the service of the economy

How has *experience* managed to become decisive? The answer must be sought in the relationship between human psychology and the digital revolution. The quantity of visual and audio stimuli affecting people has multiplied and external influences (sophisticated business and marketing communication, thorough familiarity with, and utilization, of human psychology and behaviour etc.) has increasingly exposed consumers to influence and control. So, bringing the concept of *experience* to life has become a reality, and this could of course be used as a competitive advantage (both in an economic and business sense). *Experience* became an increasingly integrated and decisive factor in personal decision making, thinking, and everyday life for us. Richard Florida's assertion that the quality of people's lives is measured and defined not based on material assets, but on the experiences consumed, confirms this.

Alvin Toffler had forecast the growing economic and social role of experience, and predicted the importance of experience and the rise of the experience industry in his 1970 book *Future Shock*.

Two decades later, in 1992, Gerhard Schulze published a similar book, *Die Erlebnisgesellschaft – Kultursoziologie der Gegenwart*, on the impact of experience on society and the emergence of 'experience society', which became a fundamental work on the topic.[88] Progress in the economics-focused interpretation of *experience* has also been made, alongside the social perspective. In this regard, *The Experience Economy* written by B. Joseph Pine and James Gilmore, sparked much debate and was a major breakthrough by introducing the concept of the *experience economy* to a broader public. The definition of an experience economy is essentially linked to the currently unfolding economic structural change, which, according to Pine and Gilmore, means that the service economy will be superseded by the age of the experience economy.[89] This tendency can be observed mainly in countries where society has reached a certain level of social welfare. In essence, this means that society has a need not only for satisfying goods and services, but also for gaining experiences,[90] where a business activity or service is provided in a 'theatrical' setting that draws the buyer into the activity and provides a bespoke and memorable experience in which the buyer plays the leading role. We can achieve an economic advantage by emphasizing people,[91] which ultimately creates a certain additional value for companies.

It is also important to note that the last step of economic supply is not the experience economy, but the *transformation* economy that implements the principle of *customization*. Achieving this requires an economy and economic environment that is prepared to adapt experience-basedness, without which it is impossible to stay competitive.

Other examples of 'experience-basedness'

The role of experience has become important not only in the economy, but in many other domains, including education. The objective of the learning process, that is, of acquiring and internalizing information, is to make students active participants in the process (as opposed to just passive subjects) lends an experience-like aspect to the learning process. This is why the new form of learning, as opposed to classic forms, has been dubbed *experience-based learning* and is gaining ground in educational systems.

The concept of *gamification*, which has been spreading in the business world, is also based on the logic of experience-basedness and consists of drawing consumers (buyers), participants, employees – that is – people, into corporate and/or business processes and decisions. Playful methods and tools are used in an attempt to achieve this objective, which allows participants to think of the cooperation process as an experience (entertainment) rather than an obligation.

Experience has popped up in such fundamental places and levels as website design or what is referred to as the *customer experience*, the latter guarantees that the product or service is designed in a way that strongly incorporates customer experiences and feedback.

Of course, this also includes classic economic sectors such as tourism where the experiences are far more tangible and more easily put into practice. In this case, the true challenge is how the different types of tourism (rural tourism, conference tourism, medical tourism etc.) will be able to incorporate the 'experience' into their own strategy. It is therefore apparent that in terms of future trends, finding the experience will be an increasingly integral part of our everyday lives, and the capacity of sectors and segments to adapt this requirement to create and bolster a competitive advantage in a relentlessly competitive market environment will be a pivotal question for the economy.

CHAPTER 16

THE CENTURY OF KNOWLEDGE AND CREATIVITY

In the wake of the change in economic structure, industrialization and the subsequent rise in services and the emerging information revolution, the value added by human resources and by knowledge is increasingly becoming the driver of economic growth. However, numerous researchers, including Richard Florida, who studied urban regions, and Mihály Csíkszentmihályi, creator of the *flow* theory, demonstrated that besides knowledge and information, creativity is the factor that is best able to boost the utility and value of knowledge.

Knowledge, innovation capacity, willingness, and creativity, which represent the new economic forces, are demonstrable determinants of growth both on a global and national scale, and within country groups representing various alliances of interest in the developed world. These simultaneously result in occupational restructuring, an increasingly large proportion and level of society's participation in education, rising research and development spending, a greater number of registered patents and the spread of intellectual property rights, and, broadly speaking, the increasing contribution of cultural and creative industries to GDP.

With this shift toward creative activities, culture becomes an integral part of the economy. The transformation of culture in the form of a creative cultural service industry has created a new dynamically developing leading economic sector that builds on cultural heritage, the intellectual capital and creative talent accumulated by human resources.

In the early 2000s numerous models and approaches were applied to give a more accurate description of the creative economy, which defined creative industries based on specific predominant features.

Culture, the creative economy, and competitiveness

The culture economy and the development of the creative cultural service industry have a positive impact on both national culture and economic growth. The utilization of cultural heritage and the spread of the associated industries are thus not only the result of sociocultural movements, but also an economic strategy that boosts European competitiveness. The utilization of cultural and intellectual heritage through creative industries also creates value from an economic perspective. In recent years (despite the economic recession) cultural and creative industries have become the most dynamic sectors in Europe, so their stimulating impact on economic growth materializes directly in many cases.

The cultural industry not only contributes to local job creation and generates value added within the national economy, but also reinforces the labour retention capacity of communities. Communities that have a developed cultural industry offer higher quality of life and have greater labour retention capacity, especially with respect to highly qualified and younger generations. From a labour market perspective, culture possesses powerful tools to foster non-formal and informal learning and talent management, which greatly contribute to developing the skills and capabilities of human resources, especially at a young age, which lay the foundations for long-term sustainable economic development. Social experiences and connectedness to networks may represent new economic factors of competition in the long run.

The role of the creative cultural industry as a driver of innovation prevails in education, telecommunications, information technology, and the development of innovative products and services.

According to the data included in the *Creative Economy Report* regularly published by the United Nations Conference on Trade and Development (UNCTAD), creative and cultural activities have become drivers of the economy in many countries worldwide on account of their high value added. The report published in May 2013 claimed that the world's creative products and services amounted to a record export value of US$624 billion in 2011, roughly doubling from 2002.[92]

According to UNCTAD's *Creative Economy Report*, creative economic sectors enjoyed growth averaging 8.8% annually between 2002 and 2011, growing at an even higher rate of 12.1% annually in emerging countries. In terms of creative product exports, handmade goods, designer products, and new media (software development, video games, digitalized creative content development) exhibited the greatest growth between 2002 and 2011.

The World Intellectual Property Organization (WIPO) survey of 45 countries that includes both developed and developing nations assesses the national economic weight of industries that are strongly dependent on intellectual property rights and copyrights.

The WIPO Guide published in 2013 compiled the best practices in intellectual property rights management from 40 countries, and emphasized that in most countries, the significance and national economic weight of creative industries is greater than suggested by earlier assessments and statistical data. Another major finding of the WIPO Guide is that sectors relying heavily on intellectual property rights make quite a significant contribution to economic performance (GDP).

Among the core sectors, publishing and literary activities contribute the most to GDP (38.6%), followed by database and software development sectors (22.42%) and television and radio services (14.75%). Having discovered this growth potential, developing and supporting creative and knowledge-intensive industries has become a cornerstone of growth strategies in many countries. This is not only motivated by economic considerations; increasing investment into creative and cultural sectors contributes greatly to social progress, community welfare, individual quality of life, and life satisfaction.[93] But this also highlights the fact that the positive impact of rising creative and knowledge-intensive sectors can only be partially described with statistical metrics.

Creative industries have a demonstrable economic power in the global economy, contributing to growth, employment, and income creation. The features of cultural and creative industries differ substantially from the work culture and activity frameworks customary in earlier times. The main characteristics of creative and cultural sectors are the following:[94]

- they are based on forms of self-employment and micro-enterprises;
- they have a high uncertainty factor stemming from the sector's nature; and
- they can only thrive in a social environment where communities have a high level of competencies and acceptance from a cultural perspective.

An accepting environment in a knowledge-based society that fosters continuous learning and development also means, beyond the tolerance of cultural differences and opinions, a social environment that tolerates failure and trial and error, where people can learn from each other.

Flow and discovery

Mihály Csíkszentmihályi defines creativity as the process that changes a symbolic area within a given culture. Individual capacity, luck (the presence of a relationship network), and an inspiring and supportive environment all play an important role in it. Before changing a chosen segment of the world, creative individuals must master the knowledge accumulated within that domain in order to apply the best and most suitable methods in the course of their own creative activity. In addition, they must also have a certain degree of self-criticism, humility, passion, and curiosity in order to separate the good from the bad, the ideas to be followed from those to be rejected.

Csíkszentmihályi showcases exceptional individuals through interviews and 30 years of work experience in the field of psychology, presenting artists, scientists, and Nobel laureates who have successfully impacted on their environment and how we view the world. The essence of the creative process is the concentration of attention in the interest of both success and individual satisfaction.

Csíkszentmihályi distinguishes three elements of the creative process:

- a culture that incorporates symbolic rules;
- the individual who injects novelty into a specific area; and
- experts (of the same area) who recognize and acknowledge the individual's innovation.

The creative process consists of the following phases: first, one has to become immersed in a problem that sparks interest and curiosity. This requires earlier experience and acute interest, without which significant novelty cannot be created. Nobody can be creative without becoming disillusioned with the knowledge experienced and acquired in their specific area (of speciality), spurring them on to continue seeking. This is followed by an 'incubation' period when problems churn around below the threshold of consciousness – during this phase, it becomes apparent that those who occupy themselves day and night are mostly not creative, because the problems do not have sufficient time to mature. The idea connections created in the subconscious merge into a complex entity that provides insight into the problem at hand. This is followed by assessing whether further analysis is worth the energy investment. Then comes the performance of the task itself, the immersion in it. This requires the satisfaction of four conditions:

- individuals engaged in a task must remain open and flexible to new discoveries and the way of looking at the problem;
- they must keep an eye on the objective and listen to their intuition for the process to blossom;
- they must remain connected to the knowledge accumulated within the domain in order to use the best methods available; and
- they must listen to their peers, who will check and evaluate the workflow and the outcomes achieved.

In addition, financial welfare and a stable relationship background are also conducive to creativity. These alleviate the individuals engaged in the task from the burden of getting by day to day, and giving them the opportunity to channel their attention into the task at hand, in a motivating and not overly burdensome environment while leaving another portion of their attention free to allow the subconscious to churn thoughts and knit the necessary connections between them. The best environment for this is found in cities or places where cultures meet and people are exposed to numerous impulses and ideas. Csíkszentmihályi also emphasizes that although individuals are the makers of their own destiny, everybody needs a supportive society that fosters and values creativity in order to be truly successful.

The experience of *flow* is related to creativity and it refers to an activity being carried out for its own sake, with enjoyment and full involvement, almost automatically, and fuelled by curiosity and concentrated attention, similar to creativity. Happiness can be achieved when the action guided by *flow* leads to complex new challenges or contributes to the enrichment of the individual and the broader culture.

What is a creative personality like?

Creative scientists share certain clearly identifiable character traits like confidence, openness, dominance, independence, and a capacity for introversion, as well as a streak of arrogance and hostility. Experience suggests that creative individuals are generally outsiders – socially deviant, diverging from the mainstream and the average. According to the standpoint theory, people develop their perspectives based on their situation and social experiences, which may have a significant impact on their opinion, decisions, and opportunities. Authority stems from knowledge, so if someone's perspective is considered 'better' it gives them greater power to shape the world from their own vantage point. Being an outsider is a key element of perspective. Because people with an outsider perspective have different experiences and expertise from the majority of society, they can turn their attention toward new directions.

The leading character traits of the visionary

Mihály Csíkszentmihályi has researched the life and work of some of the world's most creative people, including the writer Madeleine L'Engle and the scientist Jonas Salk, as well as biologists, physicists, politicians, business leaders, poets, and artists. He has also leveraged his work experience of 30 years, using the flow theory to attempt to dissect the process of creativity. His interviewees mostly exhibit dialectic character traits, among which the creative individual must find the right balance, for instance between intelligence and the curiosity of naïveté, extraversion, and introversion. In addition, these people were not necessarily successful or popular in their youth, as popularity necessarily makes one a conformist. They were also not necessarily more brilliant than their peers. But what made them special was the concentrated attention that persisted throughout the rest of their career, narrowing and sharpening further over time.

Flow refers to a state when a person is fully immersed in a creative value-generating activity, not in the hope of an external reward, but for the sake of the activity itself. This also requires the right leadership skills according to Csíkszentmihályi: what counts is not the task of the individuals or how a leader exerts control, but what the leader must become to manage people adequately.

The traits of a creative leader are optimism, a strong belief in the importance of integration, ambition to rise to challenges, curiosity (interest in and willingness to learn), empathy, and the expression of respect toward others.

The new explorers and compasses of the 21st century

In our changing world, it is no longer enough for leaders to create and govern; they need new and credible attitudes and beliefs that reflect that they have a different view about leadership values, mentalities, problem-solving, communication, and communities.

In his 2009 book *7 Lessons for Leading in Crisis*, Bill George[95] has already argued that the 2008 financial crisis resulted and escalated in large part due to the flawed approach of the decision makers of the time. Leaders were only motivated by short-term interests, they tried to resolve tasks and problems in secret and by themselves, failed to assume any personal responsibility, did not place sufficient emphasis on truly resolving problems, and they were ill-prepared and only sought survival, ignoring diverse (consumer, employee) or other interests.

The 2008 global financial crisis created a new dimension for the role of leaders in crisis management. The global shockwaves led to the broad recognition of the need for new leadership in the 21st century. Unfortunately, this realization came at a high price for society.

George outlines the characteristics of this new class of leaders and claims that credible leaders ('the new explorers') will be the cornerstones of the 21st-century society of leaders. These leaders are not only interested in success and profit, but also in building lasting organizations, factoring in all stakeholders in their decisions and not only recognizing, but also acknowledging the importance of serving society and the community. The most important trait of credible leaders is their assumption of responsibility and their most important function is to guide people and/or organizations with a trusted team and their own internal compass.

Maria Giudice and Christopher Ireland identify a similar leadership mentality in their 2013 book *Rise of the DEO: Leadership by Design*. The authors write that leaders of the 21st century are the drivers of change, think in terms of systems, dare to undertake risk, are socially sensitive, intuitive, and not afraid of work, and take part in the work themselves rather than just giving orders.

The age of task-oriented leaders (CEO, chief executive officer) will be superseded by the age of solution-oriented ones (DEO, design executive officer). DEOs typically think in terms of systems, they are experienced and capable of improvising and adapting, they learn from their own mistakes, and they are open to new experiences and solutions. The new leadership class defined by Lawrence Susskind and referred to as 'facilitative leaders' shows great similarity with DEO leaders.[96] These leaders place leadership principles and objectives on new foundations that contrast with the traditional tactic of the 'strong hand'. The fundamental principle of facilitative leadership is to help the work of teams (organizations) and to forge connections (networks) between employees, to resolve problems creatively and to face unexpected challenges and dangers together with the entire organization.

Design thinking

New leaders will also exhibit new approaches and methods alongside a new mentality. Complex problems exist in every area of life for which 'turnkey' solutions are no longer suitable. Instead of turnkey solutions, we must adapt and improvise, build from the bottom up and move in baby steps.[97] The implementation of the solutions and the new DEO leadership mentality calls for a new approach that is referred to as design thinking. This emphasizes creative and cooperative problem-solving, but as a process; it does not insist on strictly following specific steps, but is far more flexible and can therefore be adapted to numerous environments. In terms of the new approach, far more efficient tools[98] are used that offer a more effective solution for addressing organizational problems as they are based on the core principle of cooperation.[99]

The process of joint value creation is becoming increasingly characteristic of new leaders, which is also reflected in cooperation negotiations. This calls for a revision of the win-win negotiation tactic, and an entirely different approach to the needs and objectives required by the negotiation tactic: joint value creation, taking into account personal or corporate needs and interests, and forging long-term relationships.

Finally, the greatest advantage and also the greatest virtue of the leaders of this new age is that they know themselves[100] and are aware of where they are headed, i.e. they listen to their own internal compass. If we confidently follow our own path, we will have the courage to make the necessary decisions and will exude an aura of self-confidence and total harmony.[101] Think of Steve Jobs, who had been the embodiment of the leader of this new age of the 21st century both as a private individual and a corporate leader.

New values in the 21st century: the Athena Doctrine

American CEO and author John Gerzema examines how leadership ethics and corporate culture impact consumer behaviour and financial performance through the lens of social studies. He has extensively addressed the role of women in leadership and the defining character traits of modern leaders. Gerzema is a writer, strategist, speaker, and advisor, and several of his books have been featured on the bestseller lists of *The New York Times*, *The Wall Street Journal*, *USA Today*, *Fast Company*, *The Washington Post*, *Bloomberg Business Week*, *The WEEK Magazine*, and other publications.

Based on the available data, Gerzema defines in a pioneering manner the idiosyncrasies of social changes, upcoming or already under way, and regularly acts as advisor to various companies on how to best adapt to these changes. There is a tangible disappointment with earlier leadership strategies and character traits. There is increasing aversion to aggression, selfishness, and the lust for power, generally associated with reckless risk-taking, warmongering, and repeated political and public scandals. These traits are generally considered masculine. By contrast, new traits such as wisdom, courage, humanity, and collaboration are increasingly gaining significance, which Gerzema associates with the Greek goddess Athena. These are traits that we are increasingly expecting from good leaders.

Gerzema and D'Antonio conducted a study of 64,000 people spanning 13 countries to investigate these changed expectations. They identified a trend whereby currently traditionally feminine leadership and values are far more popular as opposed to aggression, the lust for power, black-and-white thinking, and risk taking. These have been replaced by empathy, collaboration, and kindness. The research found that two thirds of respondents thought "the world would be a better place if men thought more like women. This includes 79% of Japanese men, 76% of people in France and Brazil, and 70% of people in Germany". The study also revealed the expectations about modern leaders: being expressive, open and honest, approaching problems with patience and rational arguments, and seeing victories not in an egocentric manner, but as a means of bolstering collaboration, shared with the entire group. Besides having pride, new leaders are also loyal, i.e. more committed to the matter at hand than to themselves. There is also a need for intuition from leaders, which allows them to walk a mile in the average person's shoes.

Besides emphasizing the importance of feminine traits in leadership, Gerzema also stresses that this is not synonymous with men's downfall. It is merely that a successful leader must have the right balance of masculine and feminine characteristics. This not only results in greater employee satisfaction, but there is also a clear correlation between a state's economic development (countries where feminine thinking prevails in leadership exhibit higher GDP per capita).

Searching for the values of Athena

Intelligence, agility, qualification, fairness, with the capacity to lend civility to situations and strategically resolve conflicts are the traits of the Greek goddess Athena, who Gerzema and D'Antonio regard as the embodiment of the new social and corporate leadership ideal in the post-crisis era. Based on their earlier work *Spend Shift*, which achieved great success, the authors investigated the changes not only in consumer conduct in the wake of the financial crisis, but also the reactions and behavioural changes stemming from the crisis and the shift in values. Gerzema and D'Antonio found that honesty, empathy, communication, and collaboration, seen mostly as feminine traits, are paramount.

They found that explicitly masculine values (defiance, strength, aggression, dominance, bravery, and arrogance) are not found in any of the four categories. But those such as decisiveness and confidence, are 'less masculine' and fit the neutral category. The authors also found that empathy and attentiveness often found in women is a huge advantage in times of crisis, especially because women, and men who think like them, handle risks with far greater wisdom and prudence, which inspires trust in people. Needless to say, this requires the right balance of feminine and masculine traits.

Although women remain relatively underrepresented on the boards of major corporations, the values associated with women are clearly gaining prominence not only in the professional and corporate leadership world, but in society as a whole.

- According to 81% of respondents, the challenges of our time require both a masculine and feminine approach.
- The most important values are attention, collaboration, and innovation.
- 58% of respondents said that greater economic growth could be achieved with female leaders.
- 79% said that a successful career requires collaboration and knowledge sharing.
- 60% believe that female leaders would create a fairer society.
- 85% feel that local communities are more effective than the state.

Masculine and feminine traits outline different but identifiable values, and the authors show why femininity will be the determinant of 21st-century recovery. Building on feminine values (collaboration, attentiveness, sharing, caring), we can find new solutions to the most pressing issues in business, education, and public governance.

PART 5

GEOTECHNOLOGY

CHAPTER 17

THE NEW CAMBRIAN MOMENT

About 540 million years ago (in the Cambrian period), life conditions on Earth were radically transformed,[102] and life forms, living organisms, started differentiating. The period is sometimes referred to as the Cambrian explosion, due to the rapid evolution of the biosphere. In an article published *The Economist* in 2014, Ludwig Siegele compares the rapid spread of companies in the digital sector (start-ups) to this Cambrian explosion. This is because these companies are able to transform whole industries with their novel services and products. Today this 'digital frenzy' has become global.

According to Josh Lerner (Harvard Business School), the basic elements of digital services and products (internet, web language, the opportunity to share various content and services online in real time) are so advanced, cheap, and ubiquitous that they can now be combined and constantly recombined. Google's chief economist calls this the "combinatorial innovation", which start-ups use to apply already existing technologies to find solutions to new problems.

Technology also contributed to the entrepreneurial explosion in other ways. The internet has made the information necessary for setting up and developing a business more accessible and uniform. Global standards and norms and the uniform language and programming tools that have evolved in the world of businesses enable entrepreneurs and developers to think global. In several metropolises (e.g. Berlin, London, Amman, Singapore), there is a vast start-up community (start-up ecosystem), hosting hundreds of start-up schools (accelerators),[103] co-working offices and work spaces. These start-up ecosystems are all highly interconnected. Today anyone who is able to use and code online content can join in and become an entrepreneur in this sector.

Economic and social changes in the drawn-out regeneration after the 2008 financial crisis made the labour market seem hopeless for fresh graduates born in the 1980s and 1990s, as many of them have been unable to find work as employees. Therefore, they are forced to strike out on their own, and they either start a business or join a start-up. The change in cultural attitude of the generation (dubbed the 'millennials') is also pointed out by a new survey in which two thirds of the interviewees were between the ages of 18 and 30 and claimed that they see becoming an entrepreneur as an opportunity.

Start-ups are also substantial drivers behind the new migration to cities. The diverse city centres provide a place and space for these up-and-coming businesses. Another difference compared with earlier times is that while enterprises used to be based on a product idea, today most of the businesses arise out of a team where members often know each other well and their skills complement each other.

However, the author Siegele notes that not all new businesses are start-ups. Steve Blank, a renowned expert in the topic, argues that start-ups are companies that grow swiftly and profitably. They strive to operate as 'micro-multinationals', i.e. on a global scale, but without becoming large. Most of them are small businesses using digital technologies, but the number of social enterprises is increasing steadily. With the help of ubiquitous IT services and software (cloud-based IT), a prototype can now be prepared in days, which also explains the resounding success of the so-called start-up weekends ('hackathons').

The first hackathon was organized by a volunteer team in 2007, and since then they have arranged more than 1,000 weekends with over 100,000 participants in 500 cities, including remote places such as Ulaanbaatar in Mongolia and Perm in Russia. The development of start-ups is supported by targeted supplementary services, one of the most important being testing (e.g. consumer testing, which gives the most effective control over the further development).

Business communities, entrepreneurial ecosystems

In Singapore, the seven-storey building previously in industrial use that became known as 'Block 71' was planned to be demolished a long time ago. That it still stands, is due to the fact that at least 100 start-ups operate in the building officially, and perhaps even more unofficially. After the dot-com bubble, many investors were wary of investing in an internet-based business, and only a fraction of such enterprises based on Singaporean venture capital survived the bursting of this bubble. In the city, the surviving start-ups and those that were founded later cluster in Block 71. Therefore, the government added another building to Block 71, thereby expanding start-ups' office space. With respect to businesses, Singapore is the most densely populated territory in the world, and has one of the best start-up ecosystems globally. Citing Bowei Gai (co-author of the *World Startup Report*), Siegele claims that young Singaporeans are almost forced by the government's policies to become entrepreneurs.

The chief element of the entrepreneurial ecosystem is that it is systemic, and its system consists of market, policy (state), and cultural elements. Some people complement these with talent, funding, and infrastructure, too. Silicon Valley was the first most advanced start-up ecosystem, but since then similar or comparable systems have emerged in several parts of the world. Such cities include Berlin, Boulder, London, and Amman – the latter being one of the most surprising 'hotspots', yet the capital of Jordan hosts several start-ups despite the Syrian conflicts and turbulences. It is interesting that the number of start-ups per capita is leading in tiny Israel.

The state (governance) as a platform

Governments need to adapt as well. Competition and market authorities need to pay attention to the large (market) platforms, since these function as quasi-monopolies, controlling huge amounts of data and information (such platforms include Amazon, Facebook, and Google). The state, too, has to find its role in this new system.

Today, state services are considerably limited; they can mostly be compared to a vending machine. States could adapt to the situation if they became a sort of platform and offered government services as basic components that could be widespread. In other words, the state should provide fewer services, but it should improve its standards. In the future, large enterprises and governments – as the controllers of huge platforms and the supervisors of the ecosystem – will play very similar roles.

All in all, platformization will have an immense impact. Those who interpret the current developments as merely another dot-com bubble may have to think again, because today's digital primordial soup contains all the ingredients that can be used to create the economy of the future or even the future model of governance.

Balance in innovation

Based on his research at Harvard Business School, Ryan Raffaelli argues that technological revival is best exemplified by Swiss mechanical watches, which were almost wiped out by the dumping of cheaper digital watches in the 1970s. Still, the industry currently enjoys unprecedented success, constituting the third largest source of exports in Switzerland after mechanical and pharmaceutical articles. Other examples of emerging technologies include the revival of fountain pens, which began to disappear after the spread of ballpoint pens in the 1950s, as well as the renewal of track-based transport concepts, which has become reality in 30 American cities and is being established in several other communities. Vinyl production in the United States also exhibits a similar trend. Output skyrocketed between 1993 and 2013 from almost nothing to 6 million discs. The increase in the number of independent bookstores also bears testimony to this phenomenon. It is also interesting that the output of Scottish Harris Tweed established in the early 1900s more than doubled between 2009 and 2012. The company produces clothing from 100% tweed, and it is also peculiar as it is the only brand protected by an Act of Parliament.

In the context of innovation processes, the business rationale behind reviving these old technologies is to redefine the value and significance of these products. Swiss watches are status symbols, i.e. their main function is not to show the time. Independent bookstores define their identity as new meeting points for booklovers and new places for networking.

Business activities and brands are being redefined with a delicate balance between tradition and changes. A crucial feature of revived business activities is that such firms have strong ties to both their manufacturers and their clients.

In addition to preserving traditions and maintaining a close relationship with manufacturers and buyers, change is also necessary. In the case of the Swiss watches, this meant redefining mechanical watches as fashionable accessories and luxury items. And in addition to having a café and a stage, the Politics and Prose bookstore in Washington installed a printing machine for its customers to print their e-books on demand. Of course, changes also demand sacrifices, for instance relinquishing a certain market share to new entrants or consumers. Turning toward emerging markets is also a novelty, and the Chinese are demonstrably enthusiastic buyers of Western heritage.

At the same time, reviving technologies also show that 'disruptive innovation' can emerge in various forms: some traditional products such as sailing boats and physical books are present in a constant form, the case of Swiss watches illustrates that there are products whose value needs to be redefined, and there are other products that are continuously present but are perpetually revived and made more efficient by technology. Furthermore, it is being widely acknowledged that people do not buy a certain product because it provides the most efficient solution to a given problem, but because it is aesthetic and invokes pleasant feelings. This leads to a paradoxical situation, since the more widespread efficiency-enhancing economic solutions driven by the internet become, the more the demand for traditional, durable, and quality products produced in small quantities will increase.

Redrawing our maps

How much do digital mapping technologies influence our everyday lives (e.g. GPS, Google Maps)? Just like the first map and atlas, today's mapping technologies reshape the geopolitical balance of power in a novel way.

Nowadays, with the help of Google Maps and other tools, people have unparalleled opportunities for taking part in creating maps. The latest online platforms (e.g. Ushahidi) enable the mapping of humanitarian crises and natural disasters in real time, providing vital information to humanitarian organizations for managing the crises (as exemplified by the events after the 2010 Haiti earthquake). The community projects similar to OpenStreetMap let users create maps covering the whole globe in a cooperation that was not possible before the advent of digital technologies. Tiny communities draw the map of their own district or living environment, which they can use to discover new services or safe routes, and they can literally put themselves on the map. They only need a laptop or a smartphone for this.

However, the impact of digital mapping goes beyond making our lives easier. As maps have become more widespread and are used for more purposes, governments are losing their control over mapping. The power of mapping has always lain in the capacity to create, organize, and disseminate knowledge. This power was redistributed in a revolutionary way by users taking part in community mapping and the internet companies with ever greater influence (such as Google). It is currently unpredictable what kind of effect this radical expansion will have on our future. On the one hand, we are much less likely to lose our way in the world around us with the digital maps, but on the other hand, our uncertainty may be justified with regard to the way new technological tools reshape developments in the international economic sphere.

The hummingbird effect or how Galileo invented timekeeping

Although today we take the technological achievements of the modern age and the comfort provided by them for granted – such as artificial lighting or clean tap water – *How We Got to Now* by Steven Johnson[104] perfectly illustrates the creative trail behind the discoveries and achievements that make modern day-to-day life easier. According to Johnson, the most fantastic thing about innovations is that they accelerate the unforeseeable changes, that may arise much later than they are realized, going beyond the original domain, problem, or the epicentre of innovation.

Johnson coined the term 'hummingbird effect', as an extension of the well-known butterfly effect, to describe these complex chains of influence. The essence of the butterfly effect is that a change, be it initially ever so imperceptible and undetectable as the flap of a butterfly's wing, later may exert as huge an impact as a hurricane. Further to this, the hummingbird effect can be explained like a rifle shot: when it is fired, the bullet (i.e. the innovation) breaks through different places or spheres, while the original effects and intentions often fade into oblivion. If we examine these starting points when immersing ourselves in a subject, we can better understand the process, as the often-unintended consequence and the subsequent change triggered by innovation.

Johnson proves this with a simple story. Legend has it that in 1583 a 19-year-old university student sitting in the Pisa Cathedral suddenly realized that the chandelier was swinging rhythmically back and forth. He also saw that the chandelier covered the same distance over a given time. Lacking any instrument for timekeeping, he used his pulse to measure the swing of the chandelier and prove his observation with numbers. The student was Galileo, who later created the first pendulum clock. This shows what processes can be launched by often seemingly useless or insignificant information or observations.

Almost a century after Galileo, Europe's life changed as the timepiece was created, although the hummingbird's wings continued to flap with almost incredible speed, as time was still impossible to measure accurately to the minute. Time intervened in everyday life, accelerating economic life. The Industrial Revolution ran on working hours, with public clocks being built to help workers get to the factories on time. The introduction of rail travel necessitated the end of local time and standardisation on clock time, to permit the existence of train timetables. People found their lives adhering to the clock as never before.

According to Johnson, the next perceptible flap of the hummingbird's wings was the invention of the first quartz watch in 1928, which facilitated much more accurate timekeeping, and which contributed significantly to the subsequent emergence of the information society. Whenever you look at your smartphone to check the time, the phone uses wonderful technology to receive signals from satellites, and it determines its position and shows the time with the help of GPS.

This is what makes the hummingbird effect so brilliantly powerful, and this power is summarized by Johnson as follows: just think how much background information is necessary for telling the time, from the operation of atomic clocks through the microwaves emitted by the satellites to the mysteries of IT, and all these are required for the information to reach the device you hold in your hand. Of course, we do not have to know all this to tell the time by looking at our phone, but the process of development is like this: the wider the range of scientific and technical discoveries we create, the greater the effect of synergy among the new results. The best part is that often we do not even know where the process started – in our case, with Galileo who initiated idea of timekeeping in people's heads with the swing of the Pisa Cathedral's chandelier.

The discovery of gravitational waves

On 11 February 2016 in Washington State, the researchers at LIGO (Laser Interferometer Gravitational-Wave Observatory) announced that they had managed to detect gravitational waves. The discovery was preceded by the almost 100-year-old theory of relativity, decades of instrument development, and investments of over US$1 billion. A basic result facilitating the better understanding of the universe has been achieved in science, which demonstrates the remarkable success of basic research.

Gravitational waves are ripples in space-time, the existence of which was deduced by Einstein as part of the general theory of relativity. According to the theory, moving masses generate gravitational waves, which detach from their source and spread at the speed of light, changing the 'curvature' of space-time in their path, i.e. the distance between the points in space. The most important antecedent to the discovery is considered to be Einstein's general theory of relativity described a hundred years ago. The existence of gravitational waves was indirectly confirmed in the 1970s. In 1974, Joseph Taylor and Russell Hulse found a pulsar and a neutron star orbiting each other, forming exactly the type of system that produces such waves. As the generation of gravitational waves requires energy, the neutron star has to lose some of its mass. This happened exactly as the theory of relativity forecast. This indirect but convincing proof earned the pair the Nobel Prize for Physics in 1993.

The discovery

As we have seen, the existence of gravitational waves had already been proven indirectly; however, we had been unable to observe them until much more recently. This changed on 14 September, 2015 at 9:51am UTC, when at LIGO both detectors, whose sensitivity was considerably improved in 2015, picked up the same signal at the same time. The gravitational waves detected by the LIGO's detectors originated from the collision and merging of two black holes in a galaxy situated 1.2 billion light years away from the Earth. Actually, any mass can generate gravitational waves, but they are only perceptible when very large masses move at very high speed in a very small space. This was the largest energy event observed in the history of astronomy. The incident has violently 'shaken' space-time, and the tremendous amount of energy was transmitted by gravitational waves. The characteristics of the observed waves also show that the merging of the two black holes was a dramatically rapid process. After orbiting each other for millions of years, the last eight orbits took merely 0.2 seconds, with the last one lasting only 1/150th of a second. At the moment before merging, the two objects were 210 kilometres apart when their event horizons met.

The significance of the discovery is compared by many to getting a new sense for the observation of the universe. Until now, we could only observe it through our eyes, i.e. the various manifestations of electromagnetic interaction such as light, radio waves, or X-rays. However, now we can also hear it, as we will detect events that could not be observed on an electromagnetic basis, for example the merging of black holes.

What can we expect next?

The Advanced LIGO with increased sensitivity has been collecting data since September 2015. The first data collection period ended in January 2016. In the more distant future, the sensitivity of the detectors will be enhanced and interfering noises will be reduced, and events ever further away will be attempted to be observed. In addition to qualitative developments, quantitative improvements can also be expected: in 2018, a third gravitational-wave detector, Virgo, went live in Italy, and two more detectors are projected by the end of the 2020s (the Japanese KAGRA (Kamioka Gravitational Wave Detector) and the Indian INDIGO (Indian Initiative in Gravitational-Wave Observations)). The next steps in the more distant future are to install gravitational-wave detectors in space, where they will be able to detect completely different wavelengths. NASA and ESA researchers are also working on LISA (Laser Interferometer Space Antenna).[105]

Hybrid future: the balance of innovation

In their book published in 2012, *Hybrid Reality*, Ayesha Khanna and Parag Khanna concluded from their research that innovation has a more profound impact on the future of a nation than its military power or the size of GDP. This is because technology has become a major part of people's physical and social life, therefore disregarding it as a driver in the policy planning for education, healthcare, and security is almost impossible. The book claims that grassroots initiatives exert the most marked effect on the markets and the economy. A wide range of opportunities await the greatest thinkers and companies all over Asia, Africa, Eastern Europe, and Latin America for expanding creativity and accessing innovation. In this context, if individuals realize what personal responsibility and opportunity they have for bringing about change and achieving their goals, and they institutionalize it in some form, this process will lead to the downfall of autocratic, oppressive regimes. According to the Khannas, China and America will no longer be superpowers in this system, as they will be replaced by Technology, where the capital 'T' also stands for transparency (technology's role will increase in the realignment of power). Parag and Ayesha Khanna believe that in education, hybrid solutions will gain prominence, combining traditional education and home-schooling, and utilizing both online and offline sources. The key is using technology in a way that helps children understand the world and acquire new knowledge. The Khannas hope that future generations will be able to respect technology, use it responsibly, and at the same time realize and take advantage of its inherent possibilities.

CHAPTER 18

THE FUTURE OF EDUCATION, THE EDUCATION OF THE FUTURE

The Quacquarelli Symonds (QS) World University Ranking of universities is usually considered definitive and QS examines more than 2,000 institutions and ranks more than 800 of them, taking into account and weighting numerous factors while compiling the list.

The academic factor measuring the publication activity of teachers and the international response is worth 40%. The other important factor, the opinion of employers, represents 10%. For example, if someone graduates as a French major, the satisfaction of employers employing French majors is measured. In the case of modern languages, this is decisive. Material conditions, the teacher–student ratio, the share of foreign students, the research potential, scientific citations, and the institution's scientific domain also count. In the fields of medicine and natural sciences, other factors are taken into consideration as well.

When compiling the 2015 ranking, 46,000 teachers and students were surveyed online about the 30 universities in the given scientific domain they considered the best. This outlined professionals' opinion about the most prestigious institutions. In the 2015 ranking,[106] similar to the 2014 list, the Massachusetts Institute of Technology (MIT) is the leading university in the world followed by Harvard, with Cambridge University in third place. Fourth is the University College London (UCL), while Imperial College London comes fifth. The sixth best is also British: Oxford University. Similar to earlier rankings, the vanguard is dominated by American institutions: Stanford is seventh, Yale is eight, and the University of Chicago is ninth, while the California Institute of Technology (Caltech) and Princeton share the tenth spot.

'The top five trends' in international higher education

In the first half of the 2010s, we could observe five trends that triggered the greatest change in the world's higher education institutions after the crisis.

1. The number of foreign students has continuously risen. In 2011, 4.3 million students studied outside their home country, and most of them were from Asia, especially India, China, and South Korea.
2. Universities focusing on science and technology stand out. The most obvious change was exhibited by MIT, which jumped from ninth place in the 2008 QS World University Ranking to first in 2011.
3. Changing educational hierarchy in Asia. The first half of the 2010s brought crucial changes in the Asian educational system. Some countries work hard and consider development and internationalization in this field important. However, most Asian universities have slid down in the rankings.
4. The superficial stability of European universities. The institutions here fare worse and worse compared with the universities in the United Kingdom, despite the fact that the countries on the continent have strong educational systems and a massive cultural and scientific heritage.
5. The 'visibility' of universities. Bigger countries strive to improve their visibility and to get their universities on the QS World University Ranking list.

Ten universities will remain in the whole world?

The most important educational experiment in recent decades has been the spread of massive open online courses (MOOCs). Even the most conservative opinions claim that these courses are democratizing the world of universities. Others deem it possible that as a result, in 50 years only ten universities will remain in the whole world. The MOOC phenomenon was launched by Stanford professor Sebastian Thrun, who advertised his course on artificial intelligence online, letting anyone join over the internet. In the United States this was no novelty, as universities focusing on online lectures started to rise in 2010, led by the University of Phoenix with 250,000 students.

In early 2012, Sebastian Thrun founded Udacity, a website specializing in online courses. Other providers joined in and this was followed by Coursera, edX, Lynda, Udemy and Apple's iTunes U. The initiative that shows famous professors lecturing over the internet for free has become a huge success in American higher education, as millions started registering for the MOOC courses. In Europe, FutureLean is the dominant MOOC provider, with more than 7 million registrations by 2017. Worldwide, there were 23 million MOOC registrations in 2017, bringing the total number of students since the Stanford courses took off in 2011 to 81 million. However, for the first time, registrations have slacked off.[107] But how do students take tests? What certificate do they get at the end? How is the system controlled? What is the value of a MOOC certificate? How do universities profit if knowledge is provided free of charge, when otherwise hefty fees are demanded from their students?

The open and free lectures draw masses, but since students do not pay for the courses, only 10% finish them. Exams and tests are conducted online, and it is almost impossible to check how much knowledge students have acquired, therefore in itself a MOOC certificate is of no particular value. According to MIT professor Walter Lewin, many courses cannot be completed online from home, since students need to use and apply the quite expensive equipment in MIT's laboratories during the courses. Although a MOOC certificate does not replace a Harvard or MIT degree, it clearly indicates that those who complete such a course wish to update their skills. In the United States, workers that keep pace with the world are highly valued. MOOCs may also play a central role in company training, and are important elements of universities' long-term strategy.

The world's best universities are not threatened by the free, open online courses, since the videos and tests that can be accessed over the internet are not enough for the professions that require complex theoretical and practical knowledge and experience such as medicine.

CHAPTER 19

ALL THE WORLD IS SILICON VALLEY

The monopoly of Silicon Valley has been challenged by new innovation centres all over the world since the early 21st century. These technology start-ups operate increasingly easily, which is due to the new financing solutions as well as the economic crisis, which prompted a 'mass migration' of labour from traditional industries to creative ones. And this mass is principally concentrated in the world's metropolises.

In the last decades of the 20th century, Silicon Valley was the unparalleled centre of high-tech innovation. Other regions attempted to imitate it, but none of them managed to produce similar results. For example Sophia Antipolis, near Cannes, founded on the initiative of the French government, has never moved away from its role as an average technology park, despite its mystical-sounding name, its climate being very similar to that in California, and the unrivalled gastronomic culture in the region.

However, in the 21st century, Silicon Valley faced several challengers that all added 'Silicon' to their name: e.g. Silicon Alley in New York, Silicon Wadi in Tel Aviv, or Silicon Sentier in Paris.

The events follow a similar pattern all over the world. In Berlin, new start-ups are said to emerge every 20 minutes on average. Paris is currently developing Europe's largest incubator centre, and in Tel Aviv the 'start-up generation' has become economic reality from a political slogan.

Global Challenges in Innovation

- Nowadays, close to 80% of the value of all products is intellectual capital. The value of raw materials is less than 20%. (The reverse was true 100 years ago. The true value of a product was determined by the raw materials, and the share of the intellectual capital invested was infinitesimal.)
- Science has been developing exponentially since the second half of the 20th century, and societies in various countries find it difficult or impossible to keep pace. From this perspective, the situation of less developed regions or those with an ageing population is especially difficult, because as they drop out of the global innovation chains and processes, the gap between them and developed regions or those with younger populations widens.
- Science had already become globalized in the 20th century (e.g. the use of a common language).
- Innovation time (from the discovery and laboratory work to the product) has shortened considerably (to between five and seven years on average).
- The impact of the real economy on scientific research grows.
- The share of interdisciplinary projects expands.
- The significance of broadband networks continues to increase. The demand rises for collaboration between research groups working far removed from each other in space as well as for all the technical and IT-related conditions for this.
- Among the companies in the innovation sector, small and medium-sized enterprises have gained priority over large enterprises because the former can be established and expanded rapidly and they can respond to market developments in a short time.

In the United States, the so-called unicorns (start-ups valued at over US$1 billion) are not considered rarities anymore, even though this seemed unthinkable well into the 2010s. Young people are ready to realize their novel ideas in several parts of the world, and venture capital firms in the United States have a penchant for buying stakes in companies across the Atlantic. This can be attributed to several reasons. In the increasingly globalized world, venture capital flows have intensified, and innovators can find not only traditional forms of investment but also other sources of finance, for example with the help of the ever more popular crowdfunding websites. Ideas spread more and more rapidly, and the internet offers huge potential in this respect.

The methods for physically realizing ideas expand at a similar pace, since global supply chains and new technologies (such as 3-D printers) simplify these processes substantially. At the same time, the 2008 financial crisis exerted a devastating impact on many traditional industries, providing an opportunity for the emergence and liberation of excess creativity. As the highly mobile and skilled workforce willing to take risks is concentrated in urban hubs, the diversity of urban life, the availability of creative work spaces, and the supporting mechanisms all helped maintain this situation in innovation.

The lively living space of metropolises is extremely attractive. This was one of the factors that Michael Bloomberg, the former mayor of New York, based his strategy on when during his time in office he supported the creation of Silicon Alley in New York with substantial funds. In its latest report, the World Economic Forum underlines that metropolises are not only the drivers of innovation, but also the research grounds for new technologies. According to the report, the 'proliferation of innovation' is probably only the beginning. As the internet permeates more and more walks of life, it is slowly becoming ubiquitous, and in the end the digital world will be indistinguishable from the physical world. Whether the era of 'Silicon Everywhere' dawns is only up to us, and it is starting to take shape in the world's metropolises.

The state's role in innovation

Opinions about the state's role in innovation policy differ in the international discourse. Several recent research articles have emphasized the importance of the countries where research and development and innovation spending by the private sector exceeded that of the state. However, it is increasingly argued that state engagement is vital for the successful economic growth of a country, especially in the areas of basic research, but also in other fields, e.g. the protection of intellectual property rights, economic regulation, and regional and urban development policy.

Mariana Mazzucato, a professor of economics at the University of Sussex, advocates active state engagement. Mazzucato argues that innovation does not work as a system based on symbiosis (win-win relationships) but rather like a parasitic system: high-risk basic research is carried out with the help of state engagement, then knowledge is provided to private companies cheaply, since these activities improve productivity and expand human capital overall. Mazzucato uses American and British examples to prove the significance of state engagement: in both countries, three quarters of the new active substances developed in the pharmaceutical industry between 1993 and 2004 were produced by state-financed research institutes. For instance, in the United States, a quarter of R&D spending and 60% of basic research is sponsored by the state. The author explains this phenomenon with the fact that private companies are not willing to face the risks and uncertainty surrounding scientific innovations or the corresponding costs and long production times.

The success of the strategy of substantial R&D spending at the national level is shown by the examples of Germany and China. After the 2008 financial crisis, Germany increased state R&D spending by 10%, and China has planned to invest US£1.5 billion in seven key industries (including green and IT technologies) during its 13th Five-Year Plan (2016–2020). Despite the crisis, these funds guaranteed the market-leading position for both countries in the machine tool industry and the IT sector.

A good example of the role the state can play in the growth of pivotal companies with respect to innovation is Nokia, the growth of which was supported directly by the Finnish government through an investment agency. However, this form of targeted support has become outdated. As a result of trend changes, the life cycle of the companies in innovative sectors has become increasingly unpredictable, for example due to rapid market developments. The emphasis on increasing the value added in activities has shifted toward complexity, thus successful state assistance aims to support common initiatives and institutionalized cooperation instead of providing subsidies favouring a single actor operating in isolation

The state's regional and community development policy plays a vital role in fostering the institutionalized interconnection between the actors in the development on a territorial basis, as well as in enhancing the collective learning process and the culture of innovation. The state can contribute to the goals in several ways including by:

- financing science and technology parks,
- pursuing a policy of decentralization,
- encouraging large enterprises and those engaged in R&D to move to science parks,
- ordering projects,
- monitoring the long process of the science park's development, which can take decades, and
- providing continuous assistance where necessary (that is why only a few science/technology parks can exist in small, moderately developed countries).

Mazzucato also proposes that state R&D funds be provided to programmes, capital funds, and schemes from which the state can recover a larger proportion of its investment, even if only over the long term. Capital can be returned to the government sector as follows: through targeted state funds and programmes; by establishing a royalty system; by extending more income-based loans; and by increasing the transparency of such public investments and measures. Mazzucato recommends the following strategic measures aimed at increasing the state sector's role in innovation:

- *Growth and innovation*: the government has to focus on economic activities that would not be realized without it.
- *Market creation*: the state should be the catalyst of the knowledge-based economy, i.e. the leading investor in the economy (moving away from its function of fixing market failures, its almost exclusive role until now).
- *Revisiting performance indicators*: the indicators used to measure economic performance and rewarding the most innovative companies need to be redefined.

- *Animal spirits in investment decisions*: the government has to employ tools and measures that bolster investors' willingness to invest from the perspective of emotion-based decisions ('animal spirits') (for example cutting state spending on education, culture, and healthcare indirectly, but substantially, diminishes investments through the heightening social tensions).
- Priority: citing the Chinese and German examples, the researcher underscores the importance of increasing R&D investments as soon as possible, which would not only serve new developments but would also strengthen the position of the countries in the global competition.

Science and technology parks

The expression 'science and technology park' is used to denote areas based on the tripartite cooperation between companies interested in technology, research and development institutions, and universities. In its physical form, a science and technology park is mostly concentrated in an isolated or enclosed space in a fancy environment. Nowadays, 'science park' is the most common term, which can also be used as an umbrella term for science and technology parks, innovation centres, research parks, and even technopolises.

According to Georges Benko,[108] a technology park is a centre of technical and industrial activities, a cluster of innovative and dynamic companies that are the engines of the economy. Pierre Laffitte, the founder of Sophia Antipolis in southern France, believes that a technology park is the cooperation of the most advanced technology, research, companies, universities, and financial organizations in the same place. As their emergence is influenced by the social and economic conditions of the given country, science/technology parks differ from each other considerably in terms of their size, the type of companies in the parks, their ownership, and geographical distribution.

The first science park, Stanford Research Park, was established in the United States in 1951, and it became the starting point for the industrial agglomeration in Silicon Valley. The subsequent wave of science park building worldwide mainly utilized the lessons from the American example. An important territorial difference is that while in the United States, France, China, Japan, and South Korea science parks sprawl over large areas, in Europe there are more parks but they are smaller in size. Around 35,000 companies have moved into the world's science parks, attracting mostly French firms (40% of all the firms in the parks are from France).

As the international examples clearly show, the establishment of science parks not only boosts economic development but also aims to contribute to regional and community development as the parks are often placed in sparsely populated, rural regions, or in debilitated neighbourhoods to revitalize them with the help of the multiplier effect.

Overall, the economic performance and competitiveness of regions and science parks depend on whether collective learning and the culture of innovation emerge in the area. This process needs to unfold to enable the actors in the region to respond rapidly and flexibly to the new technological challenges. This collective learning process in the industrial/science/technology parks can be initiated and expedited artificially, by involving external resources, therefore these parks are important building blocks of an innovative environment. The parks stand for modernity.

Very often the success of industrial and science parks is only measured by the growth of the park (the number of employees) and the modern sectoral structure of the companies and institutions that have moved in. This means that even a successful industrial and science park can function insularly, without any roots in the region, and it can easily suffer a crisis or cease operating as large or successful enterprises with mainly external ties move away. Science parks can only be consistently successful if they not only function profitably as establishments, but also foster the emergence and development of the preconditions for the collective, community learning process in the region, and if they also take part in the process.

Technology, innovation, and research parks in the world

Boston Innovation District (Massachusetts, United States)

The idea of the innovation district was conceived by Mayor Thomas M. Menino. He aimed to transform a 1,000-hectare, run-down, unutilized waterside area in South Boston into a liveable and inspiring urban environment that fosters innovation, cooperation, and companies. The district is a meeting point for technologies, a space for co-working and an ideal environment for start-ups at the same time. Furthermore, it also offers tremendous opportunities in culture, gastronomy, architecture, and transport, thereby encouraging educated workers and entrepreneurs to move there. In the first five years after its establishment in 2010, the district developed rapidly, as attested by the following figures:

- 5,000 new jobs were created at 200 new companies,
- technological companies, the creative industry, and the green technologies and life sciences represent a share of new jobs of 30%, 21%, and 16%, respectively,
- 11% of the new firms are in the educational and the non-profit sectors,
- 40% of the new firms operate in incubator houses and work spaces suitable for co-working, and
- 25% of the firms are small enterprises with less than ten employees.

Silicon Valley (California, United States)

Silicon Valley is a region in the San Francisco Bay Area that concentrates the dominant technology companies from not only the United States but the whole world, whether multinationals or innovative start-ups. It is the world's leading technology centre. One third of the American venture capital investments are concentrated here. In contrast to the world's technology parks or districts, it did not emerge on the government's initiative but as a result of a bottom-up, organic development. Its foundations were laid by Stanford University, its graduates, and the companies founded by them (e.g. Hewlett-Packard). The region's long history of naval and military research also proved to be fruitful in the process.

Kansai Science City (Japan)

The central government decided to establish Kansai Science City (also known as Keihanna) in 1978. Construction works started in 1987 on a 15,000-hectare area covering three prefectures (Osaka, Kyoto, Nara) and eight cities and towns (Kyotanabe, Seika, Kizugawa, Hirakata, Shijonawate, Katano, Nara, and Ikoma). The creation of the city was underpinned by three principles:

1. the establishment of an environment conducive to scientific and cultural developments and research;
2. forging connections with cultural, scientific, and research development all over the world and channelling them in to foster economic development;
3. the creation of a creative and intellectual city serving as a gateway to the future.

The city can basically be divided into two zones, a scientific core and the surrounding periphery. The scientific zone includes public buildings and those with scientific research roles. The 3,600-hectare zone is further divided into 12 districts, each with its own function. The surrounding areas are made up of support services and the green belt. The various areas in the city are connected by a well-designed transport network to form an organic whole.

Daedeok Innopolis (South Korea)

The South Korean government established the Daedeok Science Town in 1974, then a flagship of Korean research and development activities. Several state research institutes, higher education institutions, and private companies have moved in since, and their common operation has shaped the technology centre to create the 'Innopolis' it has become. It stands out with respect to world-class research results and registered patents (30,000). Around 232 research and educational institution can be found here, including 18 state research institutes. Approximately 18,000 researchers work in the centre, 5,000 of whom have a PhD. This is 11% of the country's population with a PhD and that 15% of the country's R&D spending is concentrated in the city.

The city hosts the KAIST (Korea Advanced Institute of Science and Technology), ICU (Information and Communications University), and Chungnam National University, which provides a steady supply of highly skilled workers. In 2011, two further cities, Gwangju and Daegu, also joined, and an Innopolis network emerged, in which the activities of the three cities complement each other and strengthen each other's effects. The two integrated cities have formed the centre of the South Korean manufacturing industry since the 1960s, and now they are repositioned to establish the industries of the future that generate huge value added.

Sophia Antipolis (France)

The technology park between Nice and Antibes was created between 1970 and 1984. It is Europe's leading technology park, hosting the most innovative sectors generating the most value-added technologies for IT electronics, pharmaceutical industry, and biotechnology.

There are also many higher education institutions and support services, and the park has the following features: it stretches over 5,750 hectares, which is a quarter of Paris's territory; 1,452 companies operate here; 31,000 jobs can be found here, 53% of which require highly skilled labour; 4,500 researchers work in the park; there are 170 foreign-owned enterprises; 40% of the companies are also engaged in research and development, and more than 5,000 students study at the higher education institutions in the area.

National Technology Park (Limerick, Ireland)

The park, created in 1984, is Ireland's first technology park. Today it hosts over 80 high-tech knowledge-based companies employing more than 3,000 highly skilled people. The composition of the firms in the park is balanced. There are multinational and Irish companies, as well as R&D institutions and support services. The park places special emphasis on strengthening the ties between the firms operating the park and the local higher education institutions (University of Limerick and the Limerick Institute of Technology) and on encouraging cooperation. The sectoral profile of the park is dominated by information and communication technologies, the healthcare industry, and e-learning. The 650-hectare park is managed by the National Technological Park Plassey Ltd owned by Shannon Development. This is a digitally connected incubation centre, providing an integrated environment for knowledge-based firms with high growth potential.

Matam Park (Haifa, Israel)

Matam Park was founded by Haifa Economic Corporation in 1970, and it has been developing steadily ever since. One of the first companies to move in was Intel, which established its R&D centre in 1974. This still functions and now employs 2,000 people. Matam Park has become internationally recognized as a significant technology centre, hosting the research and development activities of the world's top technology firms (Intel, IBM, Microsoft, Yahoo!, Philips, Google, Qualcomm, Zoran Corporation, NDS Group, Elbit Systems, Aladdin Knowledge Systems, NetManage, Neustar, and NetApp) and employing 9,000 people. Some 51% of it is owned by the Gav-Yam Bayside Land Corporation, and 49% is controlled by the Haifa Economic Corporation.

CHAPTER 20

THE NEW ENTREPRENEURIAL REVOLUTION: THE START-UP GENERATION

Reaching out to new companies and the so-called bridge generation, and the development of the start-up culture, all contribute to economic growth and social progress. Start-ups have introduced a completely new corporate culture, and they want to have as many communities without corruption and based on knowledge and performance as possible. This generation builds bridges between the overseas and the domestic business culture, and start-ups may be the links connecting young entrepreneurs or fresh graduates with the world built on creativity and innovation. The spread of start-ups will gain momentum in the years ahead, which can be attributed to the following factors: the start-up generation of 20-somethings differs from that of their parents with respect to how they make money as well as their global world view, linguistic skills, and character traits. Due to their constant demand for learning, this is a highly skilled social class, whose enthusiasm and eagerness to act can be utilized well in the start-ups. Their stimulus threshold is high, they crave innovative things, and they are influencers and trendsetters rather than followers. They are ready to take part in project work and participate in professional competitions. In the start-up world, successful people are flexible and their thinking is complex, parallel. Spontaneous problem-solvers achieve their goals and succeed more easily in the start-up world. The small-team characteristic of start-ups (initially) fulfils this generation's strong desire for feedback and acknowledgment and provides an opportunity for development.

Why is now the best time to start a business?

Entrepreneurship reshapes the economy and inspires people. It has become the key to the recovery from the global financial crisis, the employment of young people without a job, and, in developing countries, to rising out of poverty, which is also promoted by state policies. In connection with this, Veronika Pistyur, the head of Bridge Budapest, argues[109] that experiences can be more easily shared like this, reaching many people and providing them with inspiration to take a leap, leave their comfort zone, and dare to realize something they crave. The process of establishing and developing businesses has become widely known. The internet has contributed immensely to radically simplifying the creation of start-ups, which changed the nature of these companies. What used to depend on great business plans and their implementation is now the result of a series of several smaller experiments. In the form of a social enterprise, one can manage several social problems (e.g. gender equality, poverty): this is because the culture of donations is changing, in fact, 'donor fatigue' is often mentioned in connection with this. The World Entrepreneurship Forum claims that instead of individual donations, teaching those in need is more important, in line with the 'don't give them a fish, teach them how to fish' principle. This can be profitable even from a business perspective.

Bridging the gap: female entrepreneurs in the world

The Global Entrepreneurship Monitor's 2012 Women's Report points out the following developments with respect to the Middle East and the whole MENASA region (Middle East, North Africa, South Asia):

- in the United Kingdom, 44% of female entrepreneurs consider themselves social entrepreneurs;
- 30% of business ventures in the United States are majority female-owned;
- in developed countries, 32% of female entrepreneurs are innovators, producing products and services that did not exist before;

in the Middle East, 23% of female entrepreneurs create innovative products, while in the case of males, this share is 18%;
- in the MENASA region, 43% of female entrepreneurs were originally motivated by necessity;
- in Abu Dhabi, 92% of female enterprises are managed from home, and in Sub-Saharan Africa, 52% of women plan to start a business in three years.

Haifa Al Kaylani, the Chair of Arab International Women's Forum[110], a London-based foundation aimed at helping Arab women advance, offers a good example of careers popularized by the foundation. The organization seeks to create as many cooperations as possible, building a cultural bridge between the female entrepreneurs of the Arab and the Western world. By 2015, the initiative included 45 countries. The goal is to ease the male dominance of business communities, and create more equality for women. In order to achieve this, the number of female decision-makers has to be boosted centrally; regulation supporting women has to be developed, for example by increasing the allowances and benefits after childbirth; flexible working hours and remote work need to be facilitated for women to help them find the right balance between work and private life. A good example of helping women catch up with respect to technological knowledge is Reshma Saujani's 'Girls who code' initiative, within the framework of which women are trained to code computer programs and encouraged to forge relationships with other successful entrepreneurs, spurring them on the obtain a greater share in one of the most unequal sectors from the perspective of genders, i.e. the IT world.

The traits of successful entrepreneurs[111]

Joe Robinson identified seven traits, writing on the *Entrepreneur* website:[112]

The University of Maryland's Dingman Center for Entrepreneurship examined the traits dominating entrepreneurship and the entrepreneurial spirit in an analysis of 23 research studies. It was shown that in contrast to general opinion, the workaholic, perfectly organized so-called 'straight-A' type of personalities prone to overachievement were not necessarily suited to establish a successful business venture. According to Elana Fine, past managing director of the University of Maryland's Dingman Center for Entrepreneurship, Type A's often do not take the necessary risks to become entrepreneurs, and often the Type C's, i.e. less good students, tend to become better entrepreneurs. The series of studies demonstrates that successful entrepreneurs have all the necessary traits (ability to tolerate risks, openness to new things, innovation capacities, curiosity, conscientiousness, motivation, self-discipline, and stress tolerance) for what it takes to become one. The research, in contrast to earlier studies, focused on practical and cognitive characteristics (the capacity for acquiring new knowledge) that help entrepreneurs in risk taking and risk management, not the traditional characteristics such as risk appetite, performance-oriented nature, and other, often innate traits. The research mainly aimed to identify the traits that are necessary for managing constantly and radically uncertain situations, limited resources, and rapid changes, and that contribute to transforming ideas and ambition into a genuine business.

Tenacity
Businesses need to face a multitude of uncertainties and hurdles over the years, and they have to get over their inevitable mistakes, starting anew after every failure.

Flexibility
Swift adaptation to market conditions is vital for the survival of businesses. In addition, entrepreneurs need to realize and honestly admit if something does not work, and then they need to change it.

Passion
It is commonly assumed that entrepreneurs are materialistic, yet most of them are passionate about their product or service and solving the arising problems, i.e. to make life easier, better or cheaper. Studies have shown that enthusiasm and faith help businesses even during hard times.

Tolerance
This classic trait determines the capacity for risk taking and rising above fears and uncertainties. According to Michael Sherrod,

a staff member at the School of Business at Texas Christian University, it all comes down to managing the sense of fear.

Vision

One of the crucial factors of entrepreneurship is the ability to recognize good opportunities and having visions that others do not. Curiosity puts entrepreneurs in the forefront of innovation, since their vision projects a different world, which they describe effectively to investors, their customers, and employees. On account of their often peculiar ideas about the future, they may encounter many detractors who do not believe in the success of their innovation.

Self-confidence

Self-confidence and entrepreneurs' faith in themselves, their products, and services are crucial traits. Proving that the world needs their products and services is essential to convince detractors. Researchers call this essential factor 'task-specific confidence', which helps in risk management by assisting the entrepreneur in making others believe that enough prior research, resources, and expertise are available to get the job done.

Rule-breaking

A study by Ross Levine (University of California, Berkeley) and Yona Rubinstein (London School of Economics) conducted among incorporated entrepreneurs identified a mixture of smart, aggressive, illicit, and risk-taking activities and traits. Doing something that the majority does not do is in the nature of entrepreneurship.

Start-ups and the national strategy

The significance and value of businesses and the business climate and entrepreneurial spirit characteristic of a given economy are often highlighted during times of crisis. Not only because in most modern economies the majority of jobs are created by entrepreneurs, especially small businesses, but also because the entrepreneurial spirit, a good business climate and efficient businesses provide the stamina and the vitality to viable economies recovering from the crisis.

From the perspective of recovery and the capacity to adapt, one of the chief factors is the willingness and capacity to start new businesses, and from the perspective of economic policy, the establishment and maintenance of a conducive environment. One of the instruments for this is fostering the establishment of new businesses – in addition to bolstering those that already exist – which is not only important because it directly creates jobs but also because it helps restore faith in the future, which stimulates innovation and investments. Therefore, we will now examine two successful promising strategies and programmes for fostering the establishment of businesses.

Israel, the start-up nation

Israel has always been in the vanguard of technological innovation, but only recently has it become one of the most dynamic cradles for new businesses. It is called a start-up nation for two reasons. One of them is the book by Dan Senor and Saul Singer published in 2009,[112] and the other is the economic policy that turned Israel from a country distrustful of capitalism and leaning toward socialism into a paradise for new business.[113] Senor and Singer seek to establish how Israel, a country of merely 8.5 million founded 70 years ago, surrounded by enemies and constantly forced to wage wars, and lacking natural resources, was able to become home to more new businesses than such large, peaceful, and stable countries as Japan, China, India, South Korea, Canada, or the United Kingdom.

The authors use the examples of the country's leading inventors and investors to demonstrate how Israel's adversity-driven culture fosters the emergence of the unrivalled combination of innovation and entrepreneurial intensity. The authors argue that Israel is not merely a country but also a mentality, in contrast to the careful planning characteristic of Americans, in Israel venturesome business is rather common. At the geopolitical level, the authors show how the country's immigration, R&D, and military service policies contributed to its rise, and why more Israeli companies listed on NASDAQ than European, South Korean, Japanese, Singaporean, Chinese, and Indian firms combined. The book also demonstrates that Israel's example contains lessons that can be used by other countries, or even individuals seeking to establish thriving organizations. Therefore, the Israeli example may also help other countries to find the tools for jumpstarting growth inherent in new businesses.

Israel has always paid special attention to technological innovation. Data from the Organisation for Economic Co-operation and Development (OECD) shows that the country's R&D spending relative to GDP was twice the OECD average in 2008, surpassing Sweden, Japan, South Korea, and even the United States. The country's commitment to innovation is shown by the fact that as early as 1969, it created the role of chief scientist within the Ministry of Industry, Trade, and Labour. However, at the time when the chief scientist's office was created, socialist views dominated the Israeli economy, with extensive public ownership and limited foreign trade. The 1973 Yom Kippur War resulted in the 'lost decade', by the end of which government debt almost reached 300% of GDP. Israel only managed to get back on its feet after reining in hyperinflation in 1985 and managing the government debt. Nevertheless, the economy was truly straightened out only after the rise of the export-based high-tech sector in the 1990s, exhibiting annual GDP growth rates of at least 4%.[114] According to Peter Cohan, writing in *Forbes*, Israel made five key economic policy decisions that turned the country's economy based on state job creation into a thriving start-up nation.[115]

Choosing self-sufficiency

At the time of the country's founding in 1948, Israelis believed in big government, and their values were fundamentally determined by Kibbutzim (collective communities in Israel). This economic system satisfied the most basic needs, but did not provide incentives to those who would have worked harder than others. After the Six-Day War in 1967, this socialist approach started to erode. France formed new alliances with the Arab countries that lost the war, and therefore stopped supplying Israel with weapons, and in the 1970s, the country aimed to become self-sufficient in the areas of defence, food production, and intelligence. But the former socialist system did not provide the necessary economic footing for this.

The creation of a talent pool desperate for work

This was the time when the Israeli government started a huge project, the development of their own fighter jet. However, in the early 1980s Israel was ravaged by a banking crisis, which forced the government to spend US$7 billion on bailing out the banks, placing a heavy burden on the budget. The development of the Lavi fighter jet was continued for a few years, until the Israelis realized that using the American F-16s was cheaper. The Lavi project was cancelled, and as a result, 10,000 employees and 50,000 contractors involved in the project lost their job.

Israelis had already become distrustful of foreign governments, but this decision made them realize that when it comes to economic security, they could not trust their own economic policy decision-makers either.

Utilizing the demonstration effect

With their backs against the wall in an economic sense, the workers started establishing companies utilizing military technology in commercial products, and a few of them swiftly became successful. The failure of the government and these entrepreneurial successes brought about a cultural change in Israel. The Israelis grasped that they had been wrong to expect state assistance for their economic survival, but start-ups can make the world better, while individual wealth also accumulates considerably.

Establishing a stable investment environment

The 1977 Likud Party introduced several measures in Milton Friedman's vein, which led to smaller state interventions in business life. But as they did not halt government spending, inflation spiralled out of control (in 1984 it stood at 400%). In 1985, Israel implemented important measures for stabilizing the entrepreneurial investment environment: government debt was reduced, spending was cut, privatization was stepped up, and the role of the government on the capital markets was changed.

Making an offer to investors they could not refuse

The 1990s brought another change. After the collapse of the Soviet Union, millions of Russian immigrants entered the country, many of whom were highly skilled mathematicians, physicists, and engineers who needed jobs. Israel spent US$3 billion on building textile factories and similar investments to create jobs for the masses of immigrants, but the breakthrough came from a small project of US$2 million, the Yozma venture capital fund. This fund, financed by Israel and ten foreign venture capital investors, and now worth US$100 million, gives $2 of additional capital to every $1 provided by American venture capital investors on the condition that when investors sell their share in the established company, the $2 has to be paid back. Therefore the majority of the profits are pocketed by venture capital investors.

In addition, together with large enterprises such as Intel, Israel supported incubators that bought shares in start-ups to pay entrepreneurs for their R&D activities. These programmes boosted investments into Israeli start-ups, which generated handsome returns. In 2011–2012, 56 Israeli start-ups were bought by ten leading American companies such as IBM, Cisco, HP, or Apple for a total of US$15.2 billion, undoubtedly earning many times more with these deals. Cohan believes that it is impossible to copy what Israel did, but the five steps leading from socialism to the start-up paradise provide many lessons to the economies that strive to achieve similar results. The author's claim is definitely true in the sense that Israel's geopolitical situation has always been unique. The strategy employed in connection with new businesses is a natural response to the large masses of highly skilled immigrants with foreign language skills and often international connections, too. From the emergence of a start-up culture that is able to adapt to global markets no other country has similar resources. The case of the experts cut loose from military technology R&D is just as important. They possessed not only technical expertise, but most probably also the organizational and project management skills necessary for successful R&D activities, or the capacity to routinely use information technology that supports teamwork.

The most important lesson from Israel's example is that we cannot consider the above-mentioned five steps an intentional strategy. The Israeli government was reluctant to do what eventually led to success in all five cases; the shift toward the more efficient solution was always caused by the adverse circumstances. The country would not have abandoned the socialist, state-driven economic system, had the unfavourable change in the geopolitical environment not demanded better economic performance and self-sufficiency from it. Even then, the country chose costly public investments, which had to be cancelled in the wake of the banking crisis. The resulting unemployment was not solved by the government, but by the market, i.e. the people affected. Then Israel entered on a path of liberal reforms, but only half-heartedly, without curtailing government spending and reducing the size of the state, which led to inflation.

In the end, this and its mounting debt forced Israel to complete the reforms aimed at introducing the free market. The immigration wave of the 1990s was handled through building factories, even though once again a market-friendly project initiated with a fraction of the amount spent on this led to the eventual solution. The main lesson from the Israeli example is that if the government spearheaded the necessary changes instead of hindering them, the process of growth and job creation could have been even more rapid.

Chile's start-up programme

Chile was the first country that turned toward the free market in the mid-1970s to tackle its economic problems, even before United States President Reagan's and United Kingdom Prime Minister Thatcher's conservative economic revolution. In the end, this decision led Chile to sustained growth, and it also helped the country in the transition from a military dictatorship to a parliamentary democracy.

Chile launched its start-up programme in 2010, with a different attitude from Israel, and much more consciously. In the first phase of the originally small pilot project, 22 new businesses were attracted to Chile from 14 countries with an initial capital of US$40,000 without acquiring shares and with a one-year visa, to develop their projects in the country for six months. The participants were chosen from the applicants by Silicon Valley experts under the patronage of a Chilean innovation council, and the most important requirement was that applicants should think on a global scale, preferring openness to isolation on the road toward success.

The pilot project carried out in the first year ended in an application process started in 2011, which aimed to attract 300 new businesses to the country that year, and to have a total of 1,000 new start-ups in the programme by 2014. In the first application process, out of the 330 applicants 87 from 30 countries were accepted onto the programme, and in the second call for applications in July 2011, more than 650 applicants competed for 100 places.

The performance of the firms in the programme is measured continuously using several indicators, and the Start-up Chile programme has garnered great international acclaim. Similar programmes following the Chilean example were launched in the United States, the United Kingdom, Greece, and Italy. The programme is conducted under the aegis of the Chilean Economic Development Agency, CORFO.[116] The programme aims to make Chile Latin America's innovation and entrepreneurial hub, globalize the Chilean entrepreneurial culture, and establish a company worth US$1 billion.

Chile's examples hold many lessons, but before we start copying its solutions, let us not forget its individual situation. Chile is a Spanish-speaking country located on a continent that is dominated by Spanish speakers and Brazil, a country of Portuguese speakers close to the Spanish speakers both linguistically and culturally, and its economy is one of the most developed.[117] This provides a perfect opportunity for attracting companies from abroad.

An important goal was to promote start-ups in order to join the global economic structure. During this, the companies were not encouraged to punch above their weight, but to come up with technological and business solutions and develop them into marketable products that enable them to establish a symbiotic relationship with the leading global corporations. It is no coincidence that American venture capital investors took part in the selection of the applicants in the Chilean programme, and that in the case of Israel the new firms swiftly developed strong ties with the leading global enterprises of the given technologies. In the start-up culture, most of the small firms established to realize a special idea achieve success after the company enters the market with its product and it is acquired by a global corporation. The implementation of a successful start-up programme has to take this into account as well, as it is very rare that the small firm itself becomes a dominant player later on, because this requires not only creativity and innovation but also another type of knowledge and culture necessary for managing a large enterprise.

Nevertheless, the investment into the companies that are later acquired by larger corporations is not lost to the economy of the given country. These firms often integrate into the structure of the large enterprises by the latter establishing local development centres around the former small firm, or at least several of the acquired firm's old external partners can become regular suppliers for the global enterprises.

PART 6

CITIES: THE POWERHOUSES OF THE 21ST CENTURY

CHAPTER 21

LOCAL SPIRIT – *GENIUS LOCI*

Toronto University professor Richard Florida, a guru of the rise of the creative class and one of the most acknowledged thinkers in the world, has proved through his research that the most important factor of our life is the place where we live.

The landmark decisions of life – acquiring qualifications, job and career, relationships – are substantially determined by where we live, as it is easier to make good decisions in ambient conditions. The drivers of economic growth, i.e. talent, innovation, and creativity, are not distributed evenly in the world: they are concentrated in certain locations. In the past, they were clustered in cities and nation states, today they gather around super-regions and megaregions. Some 18% of the global population, 66% of global GDP, and 86% of global innovation is concentrated in the 40 largest integrated regions of the world economy. Out of the 12 megaregions in North America, the largest is the Boston–New York–Washington corridor stretching 500 miles, and even at the global level, only Greater Tokyo is able to outperform it in terms of economic power.

In Europe, the most powerful region is the Amsterdam–Brussels–Antwerp area with 60 million inhabitants and an economic output worth US$1,500 billion. It is followed by the British London –Birmingham megaregion, then the Milan–Rome axis, the Stuttgart–Frankfurt–Hamburg super-region and Greater Paris. The Vienna –Budapest zone, with its economic clout of US$180 billion, fares better than the region around Prague worth US$150 billion, the Greater Lisbon area's US$110 billion as well as the Scotland, Madrid, and Berlin megaregions. The global economy is divided into four parts in space: creative regions; regions utilizing imported innovation well; the hopeless megacities of the developing world; and agricultural areas.

Cities have their own 'personalities'. If we are looking for a place where people are open to new ideas, i.e. we wish to live in a creative and innovative environment, the author Richard Florida, citing Mihály Csíkszentmihályi, suggests that we should look for two things: the appreciation of beauty, and curiosity. Creative people are best characterized by these two traits: they love beauty, arts, beautiful environments and objects, and they are open to every novelty. We are headed toward a digital world where only two types of work will exist: highly paid creative and low-wage traditional service jobs. In developed countries, 35%–40% of jobs already call for creative work. In areas such as research and development, design, the media, and the knowledge industry, a rich imagination, creativity, intelligence, and the ability to think outside the box are the most important assets.

According to Florida, the creative class may or will have the opportunity to take part in shaping the world. Economic and social progress has to include three factors, which in *Who is your city*, Florida calls the 3Ts:

1. *Technological innovation*: the various institutions, universities, and businesses operating with the actual technological innovations need to have the capacity for innovation.
2. *Talent*: qualities and special skills should not only be produced or attracted but also retained.
3. *Tolerance and open thinking*: these are needed so that men, women, minority groups, immigrants, and people with different sexual orientations have the opportunity and the courage to join the process of innovation.

However, the main point is that most people can be creative, and our task is to unlock their potential. Factory workers work together in groups, as a living laboratory, and the creativity and intelligence of these people is what drives the economy forward. The economy is made great and prosperous not by technology but by the people who shape it.

Let us take a look at the service sector as an example. It constitutes well over 50% of developed countries' economic structure. For the businesses engaged in the service sector, performing even more creative work is important so that they know that they work better and that they can provide better services. The other great change in addition to the rise of the creative class is that the distances have not disappeared with the spread of technology. The world, and especially the world economy, clusters and culminates in 40 megaregions. The cities and the surrounding megaregions, where the 3Ts can be found together, are the places where the economy and the innovative stratum, the creative class, can truly prevail and thrive. Innovation will not come by locking ourselves up in ivory towers, but will emerge from the cohabitation of people, as individuals stimulate each other and as their city inspires them. Therefore, a fourth T can be added: *territory*. Its quality is significantly influenced by the degree of open-mindedness and receptiveness in its population. Its natural and local features and architectural environment are equally important, just like the population's ability to preserve everything that they create or receive ready-made.

Boundaries in a boundless world?

There are no confined or isolated units, yet humanity strives to keep and secure these,[118] even if only symbolically. Of course, everyone is aware of the phenomenon of spillover, i.e. that the results of every act or intervention in a process have effects outside their own sphere, or in other words, their impact can be felt in other places as well. This also holds true in fields such as the economy (global financial crisis, fluctuations on the stock exchange and the equity market, etc.), society (economic migration, migration motivated by war or politics, etc.) or the environment (the destruction of the rainforest, the Chernobyl disaster, or the accident at the Fukushima nuclear power plant, etc.).

We can see that the various effects spill over whatever we do, since the world functions as a complex closed system, and we cannot 'decouple' ourselves from its processes.[119] Nowadays, the intertwined economic and social systems have become so embedded due to globalization, that even the minutest change can considerably upset the system.

As a result of human action, processes emerge that cannot be 'locked up' or limited, not even with the help of the artificially determined and created borders as, more often than not, they are merely invisible, imaginary lines in geographical space.

There have always been and there will always be boundaries

Despite the fact that boundaries are just symbols, they have been of great importance in humanity's history. Just think of the traditional (historical) borders that emerged on account of basic differences such as religion, culture, or race.[120] We should also not forget about natural[121] and environmental[122] boundaries. For a long time, natural borders represented the greatest obstacle and hindrance to free movement in space,[123] and overcoming them helped humanity move without limits and boundaries. Later this freedom culminated thanks to modern communication technology, which eliminated the limiting factor of physical space, and every movement was transferred to virtual space.

Another similarly important group is power and economic boundaries, with numerous examples in history. Now we will mention a few examples from the past 100 years to demonstrate how boundaries disappeared (ceased to exist), and how new ones were created. The bipolar world gave rise to borders (boundaries) between the two opposing superpowers (the United States and the Soviet Union) and their allies. There was an imaginary power boundary between the two blocs, dividing the world in two, and eliminating the opportunity for both economic and social movement between the them.[124] One of the emblematic symbols of this was the Iron Curtain in Europe, which represented the boundary between the two sides in all senses (ideological, economic, political, etc.). The bipolar world existed for almost 50 years. However, due to the arms race between the two superpowers during the Cold War and the untenable economic and social processes of the communist system, the Soviet Union gradually weakened and then dissolved for good in 1991, and the world became unipolar. The dominance of the United States became official in the early 1990s, but has now started to wane, and slowly but surely, a multipolar world is emerging once again.[125]

In the unipolar world, the economic system and social model represented by the 'winner' started to take hold, i.e. capitalism replaced the communist economic model, and the undiminished supremacy of the welfare state and consumer society could be observed. The functioning and the processes of the world started to point in one direction, which did not hinder the emergence of the globalized world in any way, and which is (or was) completely determined by economic clout, money, capital, and knowledge.

Although a sort of 'uniformity' developed, new boundaries were established, albeit not geographical, but economic. In the end, these economic boundaries led to the differentiation and separation of the countries (on a financial and economic basis). Nevertheless, globalization slowly ushered in a contrary process as well, which started to enhance the value of the unique and special qualities of places, i.e. globalization was born. Globalization entailed a robust (economic) centralization, which ultimately had a deep impact on the established roles and positions of power. Countries with prosperous economies (e.g. China) wish to have an ever greater say in controlling the developments of the world. Due to the economic rifts (boundaries) created by globalization,[126] the status quo has been upset, i.e. power has started to become decentralized. This means that more and more actors in world politics have started to re-evaluate their clout in light of their economic power. Partly on account of this, they started to establish their own economic or political alliances of interest[127] to present a united front and promote their own goals and interests or those – purportedly – shared with the other members of the group.

The best example for one of the most advanced alliances forged by countries (international alliances) is the European Union, wich was conceived by Western European countries and which currently has 28 Member States, although at the time of writing the United Kingdom was negotiating its exit. With the symbolic abolition of the borders between the countries,[128] the European Union exemplifies the idea of the free flow of goods, capital, labour, and knowledge.[129] Nevertheless, the European Union is under great pressure due to the migration flows from Syria and Africa, and the different national responses and countries' varying willingness to take part in managing the issue have sparked serious internal conflicts.

Boundaries are ubiquitous, and they are constantly abolished and revived. We can see boundaries in several places,[130] however, it is not always possible to pinpoint or draw them with complete certainty, whatever we might first think. Perhaps the following statement is the best summary about the situation of boundaries and connections without boundaries: 'boundlessness always creates new boundaries, and boundaries entail the abolition of boundaries'.

The global significance of cities and urban processes

The urban concentration of global social and economic processes is attested by the following figures:[131]

- 55% of the world's population (3.6 billion people) live in cities, which will increase to 67.7% (6.3 billion people) by 2050
- 75% of natural resources are used in urban areas
- 50% of global waste is produced in cities
- 80% of global GDP is generated in cities
- 60%–80% of the global greenhouse effect can be attributed to cities
- cities cover merely 3% of the Earth's surface.

Cities are also important scenes for growth, paradigm shifts, and recoveries from crises. Their local partnerships and social organizing capacity may bolster national governments' objectives and measures in the face of global challenges.

Cities are the drivers of economic development

In its project, "The role, specific situation and potentials of urban areas as nodes in a polycentric development" (1999), ESPON identified the greatest European concentration of urban areas as the pentagon outlined by London, Hamburg, Paris, Munich, and Milan.

This is where 30% of the population and 42% of the European Union's combined GDP is concentrated, even though this region covers only 13% of Europe. The researchers divided the cities into five categories:

1. *Global nodes*: the largest, most competitive urban systems with highly advanced transport and communication networks (London, Paris).
2. *European engines*: very competitive metropolises with substantial human resources and good transport and communication links

(Munich, Frankfurt, Milan, Hamburg, Brussels, Stuttgart, Zürich, Amsterdam, Düsseldorf, Cologne; Madrid, Rome, Copenhagen, Berlin, Barcelona, Stockholm, Vienna).

3. *Strong centres*: competitive metropolises, often with strong human resources (Helsinki, Manchester, Athens, Dublin, Gothenburg, Turin, Geneva, Oslo).
4. *Potential centres*: smaller, less competitive, peripheral metropolises, often with less favourable human resources than in the previous group (Warsaw, Budapest, Prague, Lisbon; as well as Lyon, Antwerp, Rotterdam, Malmö, Marseille, Nice, Naples, Bremen, Toulouse, Lille, Bergen, Glasgow, Edinburgh, Birmingham, Luxembourg, Palma de Mallorca, Bologna, Valencia, Bilbao, Aarhus, Bern).
5. *Weak centres*: peripheral cities smaller and less competitive than the potential centres, with weaker human resources (Bordeaux, Le Havre, Genova, Bucharest, Tallinn, Sofia, Seville, Porto, Ljubljana, Katowice, Vilnius, Krakow, Riga, Gdańsk-Gdynia, Wrocław, Bratislava, Poznań, Łódz, Szczecin, Timișoara, Valetta, Turku, Cork, Southampton-Eastleigh).

New global urban hierarchy

The research bulletins published by the Globalization and World Cities Research Network (GaWC),[132] on regional corporate centres, world cities, and the competitiveness of cities presents the latest research about the topic.

In the age of globalization, not only national economies but also metropolises wage fierce fights with each other to establish regional corporate centres. In the globalizing world economy, a new global urban hierarchy is emerging, mainly driven by the international flow of capital, information, and services. The metropolises that can attract international corporations' regional or global centres can claim the top spots in this hierarchy.

Strategic business services play a key role in achieving a strong competitive position, as corporations set up their regional centres where there are a large number of firms operating in this field.

The 223rd GaWC study summarizing the latest research determines a four- or, when taking into account variables other than population, five-step ranking for cities. The urban hierarchy includes alpha cities (with at least 5 million inhabitants, and a vicinity of 20 million), beta and gamma cities (1 million to 5 million inhabitants and a vicinity of 10 million), regional cities (between 250,000 and 1 million inhabitants), and provincial cities (with a population of 100,000–200,000). In this hierarchy, the first three levels are reserved for world cities. When determining the ranking among the world cities, the analyses take into account not only the demographic factor, but also the cities' ability to attract and secure strategic business services. Population is merely a potential opportunity for becoming a true world city and to be listed as a global city in the business world.

The analysis takes into consideration the world's 46 largest international corporations engaged in strategic business services (accounting, financial services, advisory services, advertising). European rivals in this 35-member global group include Amsterdam, Barcelona, Berlin, Düsseldorf, Geneva, Hamburg, Copenhagen, Munich, Prague, Rome, Stockholm, and Warsaw. In Europe, more advanced strategic business services can be found in beta or major world cities such as Brussels, Madrid, Moscow, or Zürich. In contrast, London, Paris, and Frankfurt – the alpha or full-service world cities – offer the whole spectrum of global strategic business services.

CHAPTER 22

HUBS IN THE NETWORK: HUB CITIES

In a geographic sense, hubs are the most active centres of various economic, commercial, transportation, and innovation networks that also play a pivotal role at a global and/or regional level. Their influence strongly shapes the processes of the surrounding areas or even the global economy, therefore they are also important from the perspective of polycentric development.

In the global urban race, economic processes exert a major impact on the role of cities in the network. A striking example for this is the explosive growth of East Asian metropolises. Depending on countries' socioeconomic system and geopolitical situation, the economic crisis catalysed the transformation of the cities with global significance.

In contrast to the previous stages of urbanization, the power centres spearheading globalization are no longer found in the most developed countries, but in the international metropolitan areas that have the greatest sway over global economic and financial processes and that host several transnational corporate centres. On account of this process, the fourth stage of modern urbanization that has now completely unfolded is referred to in the literature as the urbanization of globalization.[133] The top spot in the global urban hierarchy is occupied by global metropolitan regions that differ in terms of their size, structure, and functioning from earlier metropolises and metropolitan agglomerations.

One of the new results of economic globalization is that global metropolitan regions not only emerge in the most developed countries but also in emerging economies, sometimes even in the least-developed countries.

The 'developed world' used to mean the Euro-Atlantic region, as each new stage of urbanization has followed the European and North American principles of urban management, urban policy, and governance. However, global metropolitan regions have also cropped up in Asian countries that have very different traditions, and where city dwellers demand different rights, needs, and behavioural rules than their European peers. In general, global metropolitan regions emerged outside the developed world in regions where urban culture had a long history stretching back thousands of years. In addition to their economic clout, hub cities often fill the role of a node in the global network of cities in other respects as well.

The typology of hubs, when not taking into account economic features, usually includes three groups:

1. *transport hubs* (accessible by road, rail, sea, and air): the nodes of European and global transportation networks;
2. *knowledge/innovation/creative hubs*: leading innovation centres in the European innovation/knowledge networks;
3. *energy hubs*: e.g. the nodes of the gas pipeline network.

With respect to transport, the literature mostly stresses the importance of air traffic nodes. Transport hubs can mainly be found where air traffic is the most intense, and where geographical location facilitates interaction with the other continents. The latter are the so-called gateway cities. The major economic/control centres are outlined by the network of overnight business trips that are often linked to transport hubs. Knowledge hubs are centres that play a pivotal role in global and local innovation networks with regard to knowledge-intensive activities and knowledge sharing. This type of hub typically has three chief functions: the creation or production of knowledge (information), the application of knowledge to practical problems, mediating knowledge between the various actors (researchers, practical professionals, clusters), and education.

Global Innovation Index: the knowledge economy, social capital, and technological innovation

One of the most widely known rankings about the cities fostering innovation was prepared by the Australian 2thinknow. The ranking was created in 2007 with the aim of providing global guidelines for the establishment of urban development strategies fostering innovation. Initially, the ranking examined 22 cities, but in 2013 it looked at 445 cities and by 2018 it covered 500 cities. The cities to be reviewed were carefully filtered. The chief criteria were the health, income, and demographic data of the urban population and that the list should cover all continents.

The cities are studied using a complex, multivariable analysis including 162 indicators, and evaluated in three main subject areas based on various indicators:

1. *Cultural assets*: the quantifiable sources of ideas and inspiration (designers, art galleries, opportunities for sport, museums, natural conditions);
2. *Infrastructure*: the hard and the so-called soft infrastructure (transport, universities, business infrastructure, venture capital opportunities, office space, governance, and technological conditions and features) supporting innovation;
3. *The degree of the market's interconnection*: the basic conditions and connections for innovation (geographical location, the interconnection of the market elements concerned).

These three factors measure the preconditions of successful innovation from a basic idea at the global or regional level. At the end of the analysis, all cities are assigned a value and a confidence factor. Based on the values, the cities are grouped into four (previously five) categories:

1. *Nexus*: a city in a transistor role that ensures dynamic knowledge flows between social and economic actors;
2. *Hub*: a city capable of communicating the latest trends to key figures in society and the economy;

3. *Node*: a city that delivers a relatively strong performance in several social and economic segments;
4. *Upstart*: a city that has potential strong future performance, with some further improvement.

The European cities under review are traditionally in the Nexus category, and usually this continent hosts half of the top 30.

Global Financial Centres Index[134]

In the Global Financial Centres Index (GFCI) model, there are a total of 102 instrumental factors, which are divided into five major groups and various subgroups. Being a composite index, the GFCI draws on several sources and many objective and subjective indicators, which are ultimately condensed into one indicator or rather the ranking based on that.

CHAPTER 23

LIVEABLE AND COMPETITIVE CITIES

Urban quality of life: we need new indicators

The density, quality, and dynamism of social, economic, and scientific ties and networks are essential for successful development and progress: these are more important factors than physical distance, administrative legal barriers, or the so-called hard indicators. In addition to economic development, it is vital for balanced progress to ensure the development of social and environmental subsystems as well as the operation of these spheres and the coordination of their cycles. The indicators measuring economic output should be taken into account together with social and environmental considerations. When measuring development, the factors to be taken into consideration should include the welfare of the public, the degree of the social and territorial distribution of income, i.e. its inequalities, healthy environmental conditions, and the method of utilizing resources.

If we interpret social and economic development and progress broadly, and analyse them together as a system of interactions, we should examine the following factors: the actual performance of the economy (e.g. actual costs), social progress (e.g. with respect to social capital or social inequalities), and environmental sustainability. Social progress can be measured more accurately if we evaluate the development processes with a regional set of indicators as well as with a national set. The majority of these indicators identify and measure quality of life as the paramount component of the liveable environment. They represent the development of public services, the quality of the environment, social stability, and the security of livelihood. The indicators help local decision-makers in preparing developments and determining the strategic directions of future progress and growth.

In a liveable and competitive city innovation potential and the creative class is concentrated

- People-centred and safe: it supports the community by establishing connections, being healthy and receptive, and by creating social capacities.
- Affordable: it is economically viable and prosperous.
- Smart: it builds bridges between economic development and social progress with the help of IT tools. An efficient city communicates with the people using IT (operates a technical system coordinated on a territorial basis, organizes social capacity, and builds a regional economic network).
- Environmentally conscious, fair: it manages its natural resources and cultural heritage well, preserves its assets, strengthens the local economy together with its rural environment, and promotes the sense of identity, the conservation of special features, identity, and uniqueness.
- Sustainable: its development policy uses a systemic approach, finding a balance between social, environmental, and economic interests on a territorial basis.
- Successful urban development as it prioritizes and measures the so-called soft factors:
  - › creativity;
  - › innovation capacity;
  - › the creation of new knowledge;
  - › knowledge transfer;
  - › the capacity for cooperation;
  - › trust and collective competencies.

New soft power competitiveness

The notion and concept of 'soft power' was coined by American political analyst Joseph Nye, a former dean of Harvard University, to describe a new approach to the capacity for persuasion, in which acceptance and attraction trump power, money, and oppression. The expression was first used in his book *Bound to Lead* (1990); after refining the concept, he published *Soft Power* in 2004. The concept has become internationally recognized in the scientific sphere, and it is also used by national leaders. In an address at the 17th congress of the Communist Party of China in 2007, Hu Jintao, the general secretary of the Party declared that China should increase its 'soft power'. American Secretary of Defence Robert Gates also argued that soft power should be enhanced, and more should be spent on supporting national security diplomacy, strategic communication, foreign assistance, civic initiatives, and economic reconstruction and development projects. The concept of soft power is becoming ever more closely tied to foreign policy, and international relations and investment decisions.

Soft power or soft dominance is the third way of achieving desired results. Hard power has played a more central role in history, and it can be realistically measured with national performance and various quantitative indicators (e.g. population, military equipment, or the gross domestic product of the nation). However, these indicators and resources do not always produce the desired results, which the United States experienced for the first time during the Vietnam War. The degree of attractiveness is also shaped by subjective factors that can be measured through opinion polls, one-on-one interviews, and case studies.

Nowadays, depending on the various political systems in the countries and the forms of exercising power, different types of power dominate. In advanced democracies, force is less marked in power, while in several African countries with pre-industrial economies, an autocratic power dominates over a weak institutional system.

The three forms of power

The three forms of power – military, economic, and soft – are always in flux (*Table 1*).

Table 1 – The three forms of power

	Functioning	Primary tools	Government policies
Military power	Restriction Deterrence Protection	Threats Violence	Coercive and restrictive diplomacy War Alliance
Economic power	Motivation Restriction	Payments Sanctions Punishments	Aid Bribes Sanctions Punishments
Soft power	Attraction Programming	Intellectual values Culture Policies Institutions	Open diplomacy Bilateral or multilateral diplomacy

The information revolution and globalization processes transform and shrink the world. If these social and economic processes intensify, analysts predict that soft power will become more dominant.

In the information society, the networks spanning across the populations and communities of nation states create international communities. As a result, in addition to the state actors, civic and other, international, organizations are central in governing communities and influencing human judgment. These organizations also contribute to the increasing dominance of soft power. The capacity for sharing information is one of the crucial factors of power and attraction. In order to be successful in developing soft power, countries need to have multichannel, complex communication, implement global norms (free flows), their domestic and international values should exude reliability, and their domestic and foreign policy relations should be credible.

Measuring soft power

In 2010, the development of the concept reached a milestone when, moving away from its definition, its exact characteristics, quality, and measurability began to be examined. The development of the first complex soft power index based on several indicators can be attributed to Jonathan McClory, the senior researcher at the British Institute for Government (IfG). IfG is a charity controlled by the parties and the government with the aim of increasing the efficiency of governance through its research. McClory's field of expertise covers the examination of diplomacy and foreign policy strategies as well as the areas of cultural relations, creative industries, and territorial branding and territorial marketing. The index combines statistical measures with data based on subjective surveys, assessing 50 indicators in all, to provide a ranking of the countries. The indicators are classified into five sub-index groups based on statistical data and seven groups based on subjective data. These describe the quality of governance, the diplomatic infrastructure, cultural output, education capacities, and the territories' innovation or business attractiveness. When determining the final value of the index, the share of objective and subjective sub-indices is 70% and 30%, respectively. The index presents the top 30 countries.

The cultural sub-index contains indicators that reflect individual countries' attractiveness and are therefore also connected to tourism (e.g. the number of foreign tourists and visitors), and that measure the output of countries' cultural sectors (e.g. the presence of a given country's inhabitants in the global music industry or the achievements at international sporting events). The sub-index linked to governance assesses the availability of public services, the share of the grey economy as well as other indices and values used for describing governance (e.g. the United Nations' Human Development Index, World Bank Good Governance Index, The Economist Freedom Index). The diplomatic sub-index seeks to measure the resources and global impact of diplomacy. It analyses to what extent countries are able to shape the positive image the world has about them and to address an international audience. The sub-index also measures how much the country is connected to the global economy and international flows, examining for example the diplomatic structure or the number of diplomatic missions and memberships in international organizations. The education sub-index looks at the attractiveness of the country's higher education in the eyes of students (number of foreign students), the number of educational and knowledge exchanges and the relative quality of universities (the number of institutions ranked among the top 200 of the world). The business/innovation sub-index aims to highlight the attractiveness of the given country's economic model, which is determined by examining the economy's openness and innovation capacities and the quality of regulation.

Liveable cities

Alternative urban growth indicators

Cities' ranking in the global competition is increasingly determined by complex analyses, taking into account not only economic development but also alternative environmental and social data. A city's place in liveability rankings is often a separate factor in multinational corporations' decisions when choosing a location for their headquarters or formulating their geo-strategy and the direction of their geographic expansion. Therefore, to cities, the ranking based on these indicators represents an alternative force shaping their growth policies, and it is used in branding in the form of urban metaphors.

Monocle's Quality of Life Survey

The London-based *Monocle* magazine has been publishing its city ranking measuring liveability every year since 2007, listing the 25 top cities on a global scale (*Table 2*). It is among the few indices that take into account subjective factors based on opinion polls in addition to statistical indicators. Its aim is to shift away from the world of work, and expand the traditional environmental approach, consequently recreation and cultural life also heavily influence its ranking. This list is often used for choosing travel destinations.

Table 2 – *Monocle*'s Quality of Life Survey Ranking 2014

1. Copenhagen	10. Fukuoka	19. Amsterdam
2. Tokyo	11. Sydney	20. Hamburg
3. Melbourne	12. Auckland	21. Barcelona
4. Stockholm	13. Hong Kong	22. Lisbon
5. Helsinki	14. Berlin	23. Portland, Oregon
6. Vienna	15. Vancouver	24. Oslo
7. Zürich	16. Singapore	25. Brisbane
8. Munich	17. Madrid	
9. Kyoto	18. Paris	

Source: *Monocle*: https://bit.ly/2DyVZQ4.

The cities in *Monocle*'s ranking perform well in the following areas:

- international ties spanning great distances and a well-controlled and carefully designed airport (hub);
- crime rate – the number of murders and burglaries;
- education and healthcare;
- number of hours of sunshine and average temperatures;
- communication and contact ties;
- social tolerance, including the welcoming atmosphere of ethnic diversity;
- female employment rate and gay rights;
- the ease of getting a drink after 1am;
- the cost and quality of public transport;
- the power and availability of the media; and
- the availability and quantity of green areas and the main urban planning interventions aimed at improving the environment.

The Economist Intelligence Unit's (EIU) Global Liveability Index
With the development of the latest quality-of-life index, the EIU sought to enhance its previously used liveability index, by expanding it with an assessment of cities' unique territorial characteristics.

This was achieved by reducing the weight of the existing five categories in the index (stability, healthcare, environment and culture, education, infrastructure) equally to total 75%, and by introducing a sixth dimension about territorial features with a weight of 25%.

The indicator provides a picture about the territorial character of urban life determining social welfare and quality of life: a city's green areas, its resources and connections, the cultural assets of the region as well as the degree of pollution. The significance of the indicators describing the territorial dimension lies in their so-called democratic character.

They mainly represent natural assets or the phenomena and trends that affect almost everyone, such as air pollution. The indicator is published by *The Economist* every year, and the calculations are based on EIU's own database, which draws on the data sets of several international organizations, including statistical data from the World Bank and the United Nations. The EIU evaluates the index for 70 metropolitan regions based on the population and geographical distribution of the cities. The advantage of using this index is that it interprets the quality of life and liveability broadly, and presents it in a complex manner, using an extensive set of indicators, therefore it is able to appropriately demonstrate the integrated nature of alternative growth (including factors pertaining to culture, heritage conservation, and the situation of education and healthcare). However, its drawback is, like any alternative system measuring growth and social progress, that the availability of the data is limited. Thus, expanding the coverage of the database is essential.

Table 3 – The ranking based on the EIU's index adjusted for territorial characteristics

1. Hong Kong	6. Stockholm
2. Amsterdam	7. Berlin
3. Osaka	8. Toronto
4. Paris	9. Munich
5. Sydney	10. Tokyo

UN-Habitat's City Prosperity Index (CPI)

The index aims to measure city prosperity in a comprehensive manner, complementing the traditional welfare economic indicators with social and environmental dimensions (*Table 4*). The index uses the indicators relevant in an urban setting that promote growth-oriented urban development policies as a form of decision-support.

Table 4 – The ranking based on UN-Habitat's City Prosperity Index

1. Vienna	6. Tokyo
2. Helsinki	7. London
3. Oslo	8. Melbourne
4. Dublin	9. Stockholm
5. Copenhagen	10. Paris

Therefore, the choice of indicators used in the index was heavily influenced by the following considerations:

- the policy tools and development policy decisions should have a direct impact on the indicators' development,
- they should be adjustable through policy measures, thereby enabling the index to outline opportunities for action for decision-makers, and
- providing a picture based on a complex analysis on an international scale.

Its elements are made up of five sub-indices: productivity, quality of life, the development of infrastructure, environmental sustainability, and equality and social inclusion.

The official data are compiled based on UN members' reporting and using UN-Habitat's Global Urban Observatory Database. The index is published by the United Nations Human Settlements Programme and examines and ranks 72 cities at a global level.

The advantage of the index is that it provides a global assessment and comparison about rapid urbanization developments, and it has a development policy focus of facilitating decision-support. Furthermore, it examines economic development in a complex manner, appropriately complementing it with social, environmental quality, and technical and infrastructural factors.

Siemens Green City Index (GCI)

Commissioned by Siemens, it was prepared by EIU in 2009, and it has not only a European version but also ones with a macroregional and continental character (United States and Canada; Germany; Asia; Australia and New Zealand; Africa; and Latin America). The indicator examines cities along eight dimensions (carbon dioxide emissions, energy use, buildings, transport, water, waste and land use, air quality, environmental policy), and it aims to raise awareness in cities about environmental sustainability.

CHAPTER 24

THE RISE OF CREATIVE CITIES

Members of this new social class can best unlock their potential at one of the start-ups; their ideal work environment is best exemplified by the freedom and multicoloured furniture in Google's offices. Their work is their way of life, and they are remunerated handsomely for this, as their skills are up-to-date and they develop themselves. Perhaps this is the best way to characterize the members of the creative class, whose increasing role is examined by American urbanist professor Richard Florida in his book, *The Rise of the Creative Class.*

Richard Florida's work published in 2012 is the revised version of the original 2002 edition. During the long years spent with social and urban policy and other research and presentations, Florida has always analysed the situation and opportunities of a new group shaping the economy and society, i.e. the creative class. This class, just like any other, can be distinguished on an economic basis, but no common identity has emerged that would mould it into a strong community. The book aims to pinpoint why and how this class has gained prominence, and what effect this will have on society as a whole.

Creativity, to employ the words of Keith Simonton, is determined by the interconnection of "novelty, utility and surprise".[135] Creativity is necessary for today's lifestyle and it can be used in all areas; however, it is sometimes difficult to reconcile with an organized system. The creative personality is not a novelty anymore, it has become the mainstream in the United States. According to Florida, the major economic, cultural, and geographical changes since the 1990s have been principally shaped by creative professionals.

The creative class has been produced by the creative economy, therefore its identity may also arise out of economic change. This tallies with the statistical findings that show that the share of the creative class in the labour market has not declined in the aftermath of the 2008 global financial crisis, in fact, it mostly increased. There are two basic types of workers within this group: first, the 'super-creative' who are the active drivers of innovation, and second, the creative professionals who get an opportunity to unlock their talent. They comprise one third of active workers, and Florida argues that it should be one of our future goals to utilize the creativity of the other two thirds.

The geography of the creative class

Geographical location plays a key role in exploiting the creative personality, and one of the main themes of the book is taking advantage of the favourable parameters. Florida conducted his studies in the United States, so he concentrates on the territorial and demographic make-up of that country from the perspective of the creative class. The analysis of the United States may also be important as it is the country where the creative class has the largest share of the labour market, and the rest of the world lags behind the United States in this respect. In his global outlook, Florida only mentions developed countries, because they host metropolises that creative people may find attractive.

One of the main topics of the book is the definition of the successful city. What makes a city successful, and why does the creative class move into specific cities? The answer is determined by the people. According to the human capital theory, the widespread hypothesis about regional growth, development is guaranteed by the abundance of highly qualified labour. Florida believes that this thought should be supplemented, and argues that the development of a city hinges on the combination of three factors: technology, talent, and tolerance. At first sight, only tolerance calls for further clarification, and that may be difficult to define in geographical terms. For creative people, the choice of residence is mainly influenced by the openness of the environment, that is why there are large homosexual and immigrant communities in the cities creatives prefer. They always look for diversity, since that fosters the encounters between innovative ideas.

The keys to the success of top-performing cities

Singapore

The island state with a population of 5.7 million is not only an industrial and innovation centre but also one of the world's most liveable cities. In the 1960s, however, Singapore faced an acute concentration of urban problems. It was plagued by everyday traffic jams, air pollution, profound urban deviance, and crime, while its population stood at merely 2 million. Yet in 40 years, the city managed to tackle almost all of its issues, creating an environment ensuring a high quality of life, now for close to 6 million people. Smart-city planning is driven by the strategic balance between innovative policy solutions, a practical, people-centred approach, and environmental sustainability.

What are the cornerstones and implications of Singapore's rise?

1. *User-friendly city with smart simplicity: e-Symphony card*
   Singapore may be the first country where cash will not be necessary in a decade. Instead, city dwellers will pay with a single card. The e-Symphony card can be used on all forms of public transport. Parking fees, road tolls, and taxi fares are all deducted from the same card, and it can also be used for paying in most shops. City dwellers used public transport for 59% of their travel in 2008. The city wishes to raise this share to 70% by 2020.
2. *Housing policy: people-centred construction policy with community areas*
   The housing policy is one of the prime factors in the city's success, as 83% of the population lives in state-built or state-subsidized homes. This high proportion is due to the fact that everyone is entitled to a state-subsidized home, which can later be purchased. As the inhabitants know that they can become owners, they take care of their surroundings, which help keep rental fees and maintenance costs low. The state-controlled home distribution can also

prevent social segregation, and with the quota system, the city seeks to maintain society's diverse composition from a territorial perspective as well. The main goal is to avoid the territorial separation of families' dwellings based on income. In the housing project, community areas were considered a priority: the ground floor of residential buildings is dominated by open, integrated spaces where residents can meet. And at apartment blocks, community gardening has become highly popular.

3. *Strategic planning supported by geo-informatics*
   ForCity, a smart-city consultancy based in France, uses maps, 3-D graphics, and tables to simulate the impact of the decisions made in the fields of energy, transport, the expansion of green areas, and waste collection. Singapore benefited early, as one of ForCity's pilot sites.
4. *Advanced green space planning*
   Green space is increased in line with population growth. The City Biodiversity Index (CBI) – also called Singapore Index – measuring the biodiversity of green spaces and waters was developed in Singapore. On a large portion of the city's roofs, we can now find small gardens, and climbing plants adorn walls, bridges, and concrete surfaces.

Copenhagen

People-centred, useful public spaces give back the city to its people, and its bicycle-friendly developments have become something of a brand for the city. Public space planning in Copenhagen (spearheaded by Jan Gehl, CEO of Gehl Architects) is based on the idea that modern urban space is versatile and changes easily. Modern urban space is never finished, as it always has to reflect city dwellers' changing lifestyle and space-use habits.

The five most important components of Copenhagen's success are:

1. bold reforms, reasonable alternatives;
2. the precise assessment of local needs before planning (the Public Life Survey method), and one of the basic principles of its philosophy is that design serves the people and not the other way around;
3. the creation of useful, multipurpose, and integrated spaces;

4. placing reasonable restrictions on car traffic;
5. high-standard public spaces around public transport stations (that encourage people to use public transport).

In the complex renewal of brownfield sites – previously in industrial use – Copenhagen managed to achieve a breakthrough due to two factors:

1. Mixed functions and space use: the new neighbourhoods can only become vibrant public spaces if they do not fulfil merely one function (e.g. residential, business, or recreational area), but instead offer a variety of services and mixed space use. Varied functions also guarantee that diverse people will populate the given space. The revitalization of the Carlsberg brewery complex is a good example of this, as in that case the primary goal was to make the restored industrial complex an integral part of the city, where people can not only live but also work and do sports, and where the conditions for a lively cultural and social life are in place. This was sought while preserving much of the 150-year-old red-brick brewery.
2. It was also considered crucial that the new neighbourhood should be easily accessible (affordable) and traversable for city dwellers, and that it should be connected (transport links) to the other parts of the city, forming an integral part of urban life.

Barcelona

Barcelona's city council and town hall was substantially transformed after the new mayor, Xavier Trias, took office following the 2011 elections. The city's economic development strategy entered on a new path, mainly driven by the stimulation of innovation activities. This urban development initiative was called 'Smart City'. The innovation-based strategy can also be traced in the city authorities' institutional structure and the relationship between local politicians and the private sector. One of the five deputy mayors, Antoni Vives, was put in charge of urban development based on information and communication technologies, and sustainability.

Public institutions, private entrepreneurs, and NGOs all take part in the city's Smart City project. The relationship between public institutions and private entities is managed and administered by special bodies (e.g. Barcelona Activa), forging harmonious ties with several employers' and employees' organizations, universities, and research institutes. The city also established a technological quarter by restoring industrial buildings.

What sets this city apart from the several others that employ a smart-city concept is that Barcelona relies the most on the relationship with the private sector. CISCO, one of the world's largest technological enterprises, has established strong ties with the city, for example by becoming a partner in founding the Barcelona Institute of Technology (BIT), where it now functions as both a sponsor and an active project manager. The institution is engaged in education and research, and offers services to companies in the information and communication sector.

Another interesting fact about Barcelona is that it places special emphasis on the optimal balance between the small and large enterprise sector in the ties to the private sector. The city encourages both the promotion of the entrepreneurial spirit and the establishment of relationships with large enterprises. This is true not only of the ties between the city's leaders and the companies, but also of the connections between the small and large firms operating in the city. The diverse relationships between the city (municipal sector) and the private sector, as well as between companies and scientific institutions are maintained by the following tools:

- The city hosts several international-level events and conferences, for example the world's largest smart-city conference (Smart City World Congress).
- One of the chief tools of the city's human capital development is the attraction of foreign, talented, and highly qualified labour employed in the technology industry by building personal relationships and bridges.
- Institutional and management framework: the relationship between the public and the private sector in the context of economic development measures is managed by Barcelona Activa. The organization is also in charge of the '22@Barcelona' technology quarter.

- The city has an advanced information and communication infrastructure, which ensures rapid information flows across the internet.
- Linking innovation and the entrepreneurial spirit: Barcelona's incubators host more than 110 companies with combined sales revenues of over €450 million annually and 650 new jobs are created every year in this field.
- Technology quarters: 22@Barcelona and Barcelona Nord Technology Park.
- The alliances between the city authorities and the large enterprises (partnership agreements).

The city's main goals are to promote innovation activities and knowledge-intensive industries, and to utilize the achievements in information and communication technology in the city's operation and development by using the city's ties to large enterprises. The agreements also seek to strengthen the ties between these large enterprises and the small start-up firms of the city. The prime example for this is CISCO, which cooperates with the city's authorities and plays a pivotal role in education. In order to improve the quality of life in the city and to lay the foundations of economic development, the city's leaders also signed agreements with companies outside the knowledge-intensive industries as a supplemental measure. In 2014, the city's leadership concluded a cooperation agreement with ENDESA, the largest energy provider in the city, to coordinate the payments of municipal subsidies and benefits to those that have been rolling over their electricity and gas debt.[136]

Also in 2014, Barcelona's leaders entered into an agreement with the retail outlets in certain tourist quarters of the city enabling them to open on 19 public holidays determined in the agreement and some Sundays, albeit with shorter opening times.[137]

Finally, Barcelona's mayor and Carlos Giménez, the mayor of Miami-Dade County, signed an agreement in the spring of 2014 aimed at a cooperation in developing the shipping and maritime industry, as the city founded a maritime and shipping cluster in 2012.

City and culture

In his Aspen Review 2015 article, Krzysztof Czyzewski, the director of the 'deep culture' programme in the framework of the European Capital of Culture 2016 in Wrocław, attempts to establish whether culture is merely a burden on cities' budget or if it assists them in their recovery. In parallel with Europe's urbanization, during which an ever-larger portion of its population – currently two thirds – clusters in cities, we can also see that in the central areas, gentrification and the expansion of the spaces of consumption deprive the inhabitants of the opportunity to develop ties in the city. As a result, several urban movements have emerged that seek to revive social capital, revitalize urban spaces, and put common property and shared common responsibility at the forefront.

Reinterpreting the cities

The modern and postmodern city afflicted by the transformation of its demographic and economic structure has to face the restoration of physically run-down districts. From a social perspective, it has to find answers to challenges such as defining its new identity, social integration and cohesion (reducing inequalities), sustainable development (responsibility toward future generations), and ensuring a better quality of life (for today's generations). According to Czyzewski, culture and arts, if they can exert a profound impact on society, are useful tools for managing cities' challenges during their transformation, and they contribute significantly to the prosperity of the people in the new economic environment.

The practical approach to art's capacity for shaping society

According to Czyzewski, a new era of culture has dawned, and we can only hope that it will not completely wipe out and replace the old order or those that think differently, but will rather lead to the integration of various social groups in a wise transformation process. For Wrocław, the European Capital of Culture (ECC) project means the extension of culture's positive effect on society. If the project can engender organic development, it will mean more for the city than a simple one-year event in which culture is an ad hoc, extravagant, and superficial phenomenon. This is because in ECC projects, cities often make hastily conceived, costly prestige investments and developments concentrating on physical infrastructure that only shape their external image.

Therefore, Wrocław not only developed the venues of the European Capital of Culture, but also involved locals to jumpstart creative processes and foster creativity. To this end, the city cooperated with several festivals, cultural institutions, civil society organizations, and workshops during the multiyear preparatory cycle.

The following proposals are necessary if we want to develop the future's cities

1. Association, coordination, and cooperation

- In order to achieve sustainability, it is vital that we strengthen the participation-based approaches built on partnership, so that we can offer all-encompassing urban development processes.

2. Governance – Structures, consciousness

- The World Urban Forum supports national urban policy as the tool for enhancing the quality of urbanization, and stands by projects that facilitate appropriate urban planning and the establishment of functions within the city, thereby preparing the city for the challenges of the future.
- We need to reinterpret, strengthen, and transform the ties between the organizations representing the poor in the city and local authorities. In this regard, local authorities need to allocate more funds at all levels, and utilize their existing and new opportunities, putting them at the service of the population.
- The participants at the World Urban Forum call for the more active use of information and communication systems and social networks (such as the internet, Twitter, Facebook, world news, or movies), so that the activities of UN-Habitat can reach even more people in the future, not only helping in orientation but also in common participation and cooperation between partners.

3. Urban management

- We need to recognize the strong positive link between urbanization and development.
- We have to pay particular attention to urban management, especially job creation. We have to empower women and young people in this respect, so that they can make proposals at any time.

4. Social integration

- The forum has shown that planning has to cover everything: it has to involve the different cultures, people on the periphery, and the various elements that increasingly characterize the communities of the 21st century on the road to prosperity.
- Public spaces have to enjoy priority in urban planning so that they can enhance the quality of life in the given community.

5. Future plans and the way ahead

- We need a new approach to provide adequate and affordable housing.
- The City Prosperity Index has to be used by partner cities to extend better quality of life to all inhabitants. The City Prosperity Index includes the five dimensions of welfare: productivity, infrastructure, quality of life, equity, and environmental sustainability.

PART 7

GEOMANIFESTO

EPILOGUE

"If geopolitics caused your life to hit rock bottom, then geopolitics will also pull you back up." In this century, George Friedman's famous quote[138] will become a guiding maxim for all leaders. The decision makers of the 21st century will be those able to view the world through a geopolitical lens, those daring to redraw maps.

Philip Zimbardo, the creator of the Stanford prison experiment, said that "if one man takes a stand against the world, he is insane, but if three or four do the same thing, it becomes an opinion". If one map is flawed, useless, or perhaps misleading, it does not signal an intrinsic defect in the system, but if three or four exhibit the same features, it is the first sign of a paradigm change. Leaders of the fastest-growing multinational corporations, professors from leading universities, and politicians boasting extensive relationship networks have already thrown away their flawed maps and are drawing their own sets of interpretation and objectives on a clean page. The world's leading corporations are forming increasingly tighter networks with Eastern Europe, India, and South-East Asia to inject the creativity of small start-ups into their portfolios. Meanwhile, China is building a modern Silk Road traversing the Asian continent from the east. The leaders of technological corporate giants are focusing more and more on global social issues, putting pressure on international political decisions such as the space race, global warming, and migration. Science has also turned toward geopolitics. In 2015, Stanford University launched a US$700 million global leadership programme to explore socioeconomic issues and seek answers to globalization and technological challenges.

The National University of Singapore, Asia's top university, has complemented the economics course offered at its faculty of social sciences with geography, communication theory, psychology, and political studies. The world's leading economic, political, and knowledge centres are trying to redraw global maps, adding their own definitions and legends. These metropolises and regions (Boston, San Francisco, Bangalore, Singapore, etc.) are striving to become vital hubs within the data, knowledge, and innovation networks shaping global decisions.

At the end of the day, geopolitical events are always driven by people and human decisions. The decision makers and economic, political, scientific, and technological leaders of the 21st century will be those who are able to see global correlations and attract hubs of creativity and information flow; those who are brave, curious, and creative enough to draw power from crises and to rethink the role of territoriality within global decision-making; those who seek fusion and new boundary areas, whether physical, natural, or scientific; those who build personal networks with other creative hubs and gain strength from the exchange of experiences between cultures. They are the authentic explorers, global leaders, the migrants of dynamic maps, who will reshape the world equipped with a geopolitical perspective.

1. Redraw the map

Some Tibetan sand mandalas cannot be shown because they are more than mere images, constituting entire stories. The mandalas are the result of weeks of work, grain of sand by grain of sand, and, once completed, the beautiful creations are destroyed with a couple of motions and released into a river. These religious maps gain meaning not in a static state, but in the series of moments leading up to their creation, telling the story of the cosmos of creation and destruction as well as the Buddhist philosophy. Sand mandalas remind us of the dynamic and ever-changing world, one in which we are not merely observers, but of which we are also a part of. Tibetan sand mandalas have now conquered the West, which explains the recent popularity of adult colouring and mandala books, a trend that was launched by *Secret Garden*, a book by Scottish illustrator Johanna Basford. The popularity of

In order to understand the 21st century, we must redraw our obsolete personal and professional maps. An own map is also a set of objectives, and redesigning a map always begins with a question, followed by another one…

the genre stems from the resolution of the static state between a static artist and the audience, and from a personal, intimate, and interactive recreation. The era of static maps has ended. We are part of an exceptional geo-moment where human values and technological innovations are redrawing the map. Geography has not disappeared, and has now, early in the 21st century, become more relevant than ever. Navigation has become a dynamic part of our everyday lives, with optimal routes changing to adapt to current traffic conditions.

We also make maps of our acquaintances and relationship networks. Emotional maps are born, and we use time maps and infographics to explain the events in our world and to better understand correlations. The world's leading firms, from Google to Alibaba, have reached their level of success by reinterpreting customized network maps and by 'guiding' their users. The most important political decisions are once again shaped by the price of oil. The creative migrants of the brain drain, i.e. the migration of talent, are creating new colonies from the Silicon Valley through Bangalore to Zhongguancun. Development has not rendered geographical location irrelevant, but has instead made it a part of our day-to-day lives: the world is once again reading maps as it tries to understand history, culture, religion, and ethnicity, not to mention the fight for natural resources and routes of commerce.

We are living in an era of dynamic maps. Behind the century of dynamic and personal maps lies a dynamic and personal world that is made up of various forces and interest networks, and various idea and knowledge hubs. Accordingly, we, the explorers and geostrategists of the 21st century, no longer rely on the North Star for guidance but instead on innovation clusters. We draw university hotspot globes in lieu of traditional globes,and, in addition to geomorphology, explore the arcs of local cultures and the projections of global trends. Wherever we look, dynamic social and economic geography dominates. If we want to understand the events and processes around us, we need to recolour our old maps, read from them, look at them more closely, turn them upside down, and turn them inside out to grasp the true correlations of the 21st century.

2. Learn how to ask

Why have we kicked the habit of asking questions? The questions that children ask can be a source of honest and creative inspiration, as their thinking has not been dogmatized by the rigid paradigms of adulthood. Children see things from an entirely different perspective: they are treading a unique and inimitable path of exploration whenever they draw, think, and link their words together, drawing their own map of interpretation of the world. For this reason, it is more important than ever to spend quality time with our children in order to learn the art of asking and curiosity from them. Average four-year-olds ask 390 questions every single day.[139] How many do we ask?

I believe that we have lost our curiosity and our appetite for discovery because we hold the misconception that we have long discovered our surroundings. Likewise, science also used to believe that there was no need for geography, and global politics used to believe that there was no need for geopolitics. The safety afforded by our customary rules, usual environment, and old maps has simply made us lose our appetite for questions and curiosity, which are the foundations of creativity.

In his 2007 TED talk, the founder of the popular Tinkering School, Gever Tulley,[140] identifies five dangerous things that you should let your children do. These are: playing with fire, owning a pocket knife, using a spear, deconstructing appliances, and breaking the Digital Millennium Copyright Act. Tulley argues that we need to create an environment for future generations that allows them to become explorers.

One of the most captivating museums that I have ever been to is San Francisco's Exploratorium, a sort of centre of wonders, or more precisely a harbour of miracles in Silicon Valley. The Exploratorium encourages children to be creative: take apart your washing machine

> *Learn curiosity from your children: do not be afraid to ask questions. Build your own world where you are not afraid of fire. Build your personal space, a workshop, or a laboratory where you can freely experiment.*

and your DVD player and use the parts to build robots that light up. Build cities from cardboard, and cars from recycled Coca-Cola cans. In the steps of Tulley and the Exploratorium, let us build DIY workshops and laboratories for our children to keep the flame of curiosity alive in them. We must also find our own laboratories, our toolbox, and scientific instruments to explore the world once again. The important thing is to try to create something.

3. Shape your environment instead of letting your environment shape you

The 21st century is the century of knowledge and creativity, and creativity is very much a spatial thing. Creative individuals are generally outsiders and deviants who operate outside the mainstream, and this feature is a key element of discovery. External or internal migrants are able to view the world from a different perspective. At the same time, creativity does not happen in an isolated environment, in a vacuum. We often decontextualize creativity, while in fact the environment should be incorporated into the incentivization and support of creativity, as well as into its definition and assessment.

Mihály Csíkszentmihályi, perhaps the greatest living researcher of creativity, recommends creating an environment that is cosy but motivating and without too many encumbrances, which occupies some of our attention while leaving the rest of it free so the subconscious can continue working on thoughts and create possible links between them. The best environment for this is found in cities or other places

The citizens of a perfect creative city are curious migrants who identify with and personify the local spirit, even though they come from afar. They are irreplaceable drivers of development and creativity.

where cultures meet and people are exposed to a plethora of impulses and ideas. These are the centres of creative creation, i.e. hubs. They are the most active centres of various economic, commercial, transportation, and innovation networks that also play a pivotal role at a global and regional level. Their impact and influence strongly shape the surrounding areas or even global economic processes, innovation, and development. In Csíkszentmihályi's interpretation, these places give rise to a creative process of global significance that has the capacity to change a symbolic area within the given culture forever.

Meanwhile, world-famous network researcher Albert-László Barabási argues that the success or failure of a network depends on such hubs. For this reason, places play a pivotal role, and one of the most important decisions in anybody's life is where to live.

Richard Florida posits that every city has its own personality, which is why we also notice the tiny, everyday character traits of hubs. The se are the small, beautiful details that are not about the big questions of life but rather about its minutiae such as urban gardening or urban knitting (decorating drab lamp posts or bicycle storage racks), community terraces where people sit around with friends, corner health-food delis, bookstores, spaces, and meeting points, i.e. unique places.

4. Choose your battleground

Many wars are being waged worldwide, but the most important battleground is now the economy. Military action has been replaced by economic sanctions, and military alliances have been replaced by competing trade frameworks. The likelihood of a currency war

Those who are able to make most of their economic, geographic, political, and diplomatic know-how and their unique creative traits will be the ones to benefit from the positional advantages of this era of geo-economics.

is far greater today than that of annexation, and manipulating the price of certain raw materials (such as oil) is a far more powerful weapon than the conventional arms race. We are witnessing the rise of geo-economics.

Geo-economics is simultaneously the antithesis and the greatest triumph of globalization. The mutual dependency and interconnection between countries has become so strong that exclusion from this system is considered as great a tragedy as war. Multipolar force dynamics are emerging among the major regional powers.

States now compete for markets rather than resources. Resources are becoming increasingly cheaper as technology progresses and new supplies are discovered, which decreases dependence on traditional sources.

Meanwhile, the demographic and economic rise of developing countries is generating significant global demand and relatively cheap qualified labour. Competition thus has a dual objective: there is competition for outsourcing on the one hand, and for accessing new consumers on the other hand.

The World Economic Forum has asked global leaders to create a regulatory framework for economic warfare. A balanced role of the state within the economy must also be found. Small states must unite their powers, concentrating on regional players and sub-global politics instead of international institutions.

In the early 21st century, a rushed effort has started for securing good positions as local leaders. This global repositioning not only reshapes political, diplomatic, and economic interests, but also pits them against each other. This means that successful leaders (whichever area they come from) must also be well-versed in each of the other disciplines.

5. Become irreplaceable

Wired editor David Rowan's favourite sentence is that start-ups in China talk of being '9-9-6' companies: that is working 9 a.m.–9 p.m., six days a week. One key attribute of the new technology-based global 24/7 economy is that talent cannot be kept at bay or curbed: if people are talented, diligent, and not afraid of work, nothing will stand in the way of their success. Our Western geographic position provides waning protection against the talented and ambitious East, and an ever-growing crowd is forming at the world's gates. We are headed toward a digital dystopia where only two types of work will exist: highly paid creative jobs or low-wage traditional service jobs.

In developed countries, 35%–40% of jobs already call for creative work. In areas such as research and development, planning, design, the media, and the knowledge industry, a rich imagination, creativity, intelligence, and the ability to think outside the box are the most important assets. From driving cars to accounting, everything will become replaceable over time. We have arrived at this point on a long but straight road. After the post-Fordist change in economic structure and industrialization, services gained significance, and with the progress of the information revolution, the value added by human resources and knowledge is increasingly becoming the driver of economic growth.

Many researchers have shown that creativity is what defines the true utility and value of knowledge and information. The change is not only economic, but can also be felt in the restructuring of society, the labour market, and education. The importance of cultural and creative industries is apparent from their R&D spending, the rise in registered patents and their increasing contribution to GDP. The rhythm of the future will be dictated by the dynamics of creativity (creating new things) and data processing (structuring existing ones).

An original idea, a bespoke service, and data will be the raw materials of the future, and the fight for these elements will be the battleground that shapes the new world order. The countries, corporations, and decision makers that fail to create unique knowledge will have no choice but to buy it, thus getting left behind in international competition and pushed to the periphery, which will entail a solidification of their vulnerability. Those who only consume innovation will be

> *Data and talent will push the 21st century into an unforgiving race. In this drag race, creative ideas will serve as the fuel, and relationship and knowledge networks will be the safety belts.*

crowded out from the market. However, creativity as a quality category is not directly proportionate to the size of a country or the market weight of a company. The map of creativity is far more complicated, consisting of personal networks in which even a single small country or a single person may constitute a hub. The diplomatic, economic, and knowledge networks of smaller players can compete with bigger ones thanks to their creative capital, just like garage companies (start-ups) can compete with multinational enterprises, the athletes of a small country can compete with the entire Olympic field of players, or the discovery of a talented scientist can compete with the entire world.

Just think of Chris Anderson's Long Tail theory: he was the first to demonstrate that varied, diverse, and unique supply can create similar demand as mass production. These small-industry, artisan, and start-up products are generally geared toward a clearly defined audience: although they cannot be separated from their environment, they are inimitable. Those who are unable to conquer large industry can become irreplaceable by drawing on their own local strengths and individual solutions.

6. Test first, think afterwards

While in the past only winning theories were tested in practice following long academic debates, nowadays Big Data and the associated calculation capacity have enabled the reversal of the process. In essence, every idea, question and microprocess can be demonstrated immediately in a test environment or even in reality. Google is conducting many such experiments; few will remember the Google Wave program, and a similar fate may be in store for the Google Glass a couple of years down the road. In the 21st century, failure is no longer something to be ashamed of, but merely the ruling out of a flawed solution that brings us closer to the right one.

Opportunities missed yesterday will never return, and somebody else will turn the ideas of tomorrow into reality. We can overstep our own boundaries by building on local resources and using the momentum of the moment. Beyond these boundaries lie new relationships.

The era of armchair designers is over; the world cannot be changed from behind a desk. The world's leading universities and professors are trying their hand in more and more boundary areas, with economists searching for opportunities for fusion, from psychology to artificial intelligence, in order to find a radically new approach to achieve even greater success, and to potentially implement these opportunities in practice soon afterwards. What other choice do they have? In the past, a path to discovery was a huge, costly, and dangerous undertaking. Today, anyone can become an entrepreneur in 24 hours. The continuous evolution of globalization, digital copying, and IT is creating a surplus that opens the door for experimenting with basically no risk involved.

There is less and less time to adapt: firms are striving to converge with or surpass their competitors in leaps and bounds rather than through continuous transition. In this race, instantaneous and local resources and existing partial results have greater value. The same holds true for relationships.

Noah Raford, advisor on futures, foresight, and innovation at the United Arab Emirates prime minister's office and curator of Dubai's Museum of the Future, essentially founded Dubai's drone programme at an exhibition. An audience member asked what these flying devices could be used for. Raford and his staff shot a short film right there, which was wrapped up by the end of the conference and which showcased local entrepreneurs demonstrating parcel shipping and other services that drones could be used for. The video became a huge hit and the government called for the launch of a drone programme. So much for market research.

7. Seek opportunities for fusion

We draw maps because of itineraries. They represent the links between different points in the world, how these points can be reached or conversely, what separates them from each other. When using a map, we select a possible itinerary from the numerous ones available, whether we are seeking the best, the most scenic or the quickest route to reach our destination or to discover what others are seeking.

We live in an era of networks, webs of trajectories and airways, and the relationship, interest, and decision networks between rivers and gas pipelines, and between companies and people. Albert-László Barabási claims that anyone familiar with the hubs of a network is also familiar with its binding force and greatest weaknesses. The unknown suddenly shrinks and becomes apparent, the most distant point of the internet can be accessed in merely six clicks, we can find out which of our acquaintances can connect us to the person able to help us, or which person is not forwarding information within a company. In this network economy and in network-structured geopolitics, we are all close to each other. That said, if we do not have the right map to the network, if we do not know what to look for, we will be constrained to a miniaturized world. By contrast, those in possession of the right map will suddenly find themselves within arm's reach of every important decision and piece of new information.

A key trait of networks is that they not only describe the world but also influence it. The first maps of the New World paved the way for colonization, while human genome mapping has reformed medicine. Something greater emerges from the relations between familiar

We are living in an era of fusion within science, gastronomy, architecture, and music. But the advantages of this era can only benefit those who are familiar with the network map of their own communities and environment, and foster creative and active meetings.

elements (in a worst-case scenario, the fact of being bound together), and downright surprising things such as scientific, technological, economic, artistic, cultural, or diplomatic breakthroughs can emerge from chance encounters and boundary areas; I refer to these as synergies or fusions.

8. Spread positive examples

Harvard and MIT, two prestigious universities, have created a US$60 million online programme that may redraw the current structure of higher education. Interactive courses held by world-famous Harvard and MIT professors will be available to the general public (for the time being) through the edX platform created for this purpose, without any application criteria and free of charge. Likewise, Stanford and Princeton have created another online course programme called Coursera, which has been a huge success.

The most important feature of creativity is to love beauty and share it with others when we find it. Plato said that what is beautiful is good; along this (perhaps not fully sound) analogy, I want creativity to be something positive, constructive, and likeable. Let us be positivists and have a positive approach to the environment and people surrounding us. Let us notice positive examples and initiatives, and let sharing be our first thought when we discover something new. Creativity should be spread instead of being locked away, because we never know where a stroke of brilliance might come from.

I firmly believe that good examples inspire and generate further creativity and ideas, and often, this is enough to connect the missing links and to create a viable initiative.

Many of us believe in diplomacy that builds upon talent, knowledge, and culture, and in the mutually positive impact of cooperation.

9. Build your own Silk Road

The world-famous Silk Road that stretched from China to the Roman Empire more than 2,000 years ago played a pivotal role in the trade, and cultural and political dialogue between the countries in Asia, Europe, and Africa. The Silk Road was not a clearly outlined, paved ancient superhighway, but rather a continuously shifting multifunctional network that essentially existed only on the parallel maps of caravan leaders, soldiers, and explorers, and in their personal relationships.

In the early 21st century, the Silk Road is undergoing a revival. Railways and maritime routes, gas pipelines, diplomatic routes, and cultural tours form a web across the Asian continent to Europe and North Africa. China's diplomatic priority in 2015 was clearly to implement its 'One Belt, One Road' strategy, in other words to build a New Silk Road economic zone.

China is responding not to the world's questions, but to its own: more railways, more ships, more pipelines, more Silk Roads instead of tactical games. The Great Game between the British and Russian empires was a political and diplomatic confrontation over Inner Asia; China is able to draw on its economic, cultural, and knowledge networks to circumvent the classic domination war over Central Asia. The flow of labour, capital, and technology is boosting the efficiency and competitiveness of the New Silk Road's countries. The best strategy for new entrants is to join existing active hubs, which reinforces these hubs and accelerates the creation of new centres.

The Chinese Silk Road could be an illuminating example, tempting smaller states to join and great regional powers to build their own networks. The modern Silk Road is based on long-term investments, infrastructure and knowledge-sharing, multilevel and parallel network systems, and mutual trust, all linked by a comprehensive global strategy focused on local issues.

The Silk Road model can be applied not only to political decisions, but may also be useful in the corporate world, in state affairs and in business-to-business relations, or even personal networks.

It is neither international trade nor online retail that makes the economy great and prosperous, but local talents with a global perspective and an ability to shape and transform the world through their environment.

10. Think global, start local

Thomas Friedman's famous declaration that "the world is flat" spread like wildfire across the globe, announcing the victory of globalization. Friedman's main message in his book is that everyone has equal chances of rising to success, therefore everybody needs to participate in globalization's competition devoid of preconditions, historic traditions, or geographical binds. The world is flat and we can easily fall off.

However, recent decades have shown that those living at the perimeter of the world are in danger. The world has not become flat, especially not the global economy, which is concentrated in 40 megaregions. Richard Florida has demonstrated that cities and the surrounding megaregions, the ones that host talent, technology, and tolerance, are where the economy and the innovative stratum, the creative class, can truly prevail and thrive. The various urban regions fill our particularly complex world with mountains, hills, and valleys.

Renewal will not come by locking ourselves up in ivory towers, but will emerge from the cohabitation of people, where individuals stimulate each other and where the urban environment stimulates and inspires them. So even if we live in a global village, our fate is decided in our microenvironment. Florida's 3Ts – talent, technology, and tolerance – are thus supplemented with territory as a defining feature.

In his book *Future Files*, Richard Watson analyses 200 trends to demonstrate that localization, urbanization, and sustainability will feature on the maps of the future alongside globalization.

City-building start-ups account for the lion's share of a new movement. Emerging new types of businesses inject cultural diversity and creative competition into the new global capitals. This is how Silicon Valley has reshaped San Francisco and how the city centres of Berlin, Boulder, London, Bangalore, Amman, and Tel Aviv have been transformed. The meeting of the city, young talent, and entrepreneurial world travellers has a beneficial impact on the development of every stakeholder.

11. Follow your inner compass

"A smooth sea never made a skilled sailor" goes the old English adage, and this also holds true for leaders. Harvard professor Bill George argues that leadership programmes do not teach this to global leaders, teaching them theories instead about throwing them in at the deep end. But not even the best simulation is capable of substituting for the real world.

A leader's role is not to protect his position or job, but to navigate the ship out of the storm and to protect the entire crew. To put it differently, one must not only climb the mountain, but one must also be able to come down. We need solution-oriented leaders instead of task-oriented ones: those who think in terms of systems, who are willing to take risks, who are socially sensitive, intuitive, and not turned off by getting their hands dirty.

Year-end bonuses, earnings per share (EPS), and exits are only results, not a strategy. When the latest global economic crisis was already unfolding, most leaders tried to conceal the issue (while others tried to sell it). Many were merely trying to survive rather than using this period for enacting change or restructuring. They had no strategy and forgot about the people behind the product. They forgot that a true leader must take into consideration a company's long-term objectives, the interests of workers and consumers, as well as global trends.

Opening up is always a daring decision that requires a huge amount of trust from both employees and the public. A common flawed mentality compels corporate leaders to try to resolve everything alone, cut off from the world and doing business as usual. This generally spawns inbreeding, emptiness, and the concealment of issues. In the 21st century, the world cannot be excluded from decision-making, and there is nowhere to hide from the results of peripheries.

Leaders equipped with a geopolitical perspective know themselves very well, are open to the unknown, and know what the next step will be once they reach their objective. They follow their own internal compass.

World-famous anthropologist Arjun Appadurai wrote that nobody is able to turn back the hands of time, but we can change how the hands move forward. Perhaps the dynamics of globalization, the structure of nation states, and what are currently considered unquestionable alliances will all change. We must entrust our future to the strategists designing the distant future to come up with stable and competitive ideas for any situation, whether in a crisis or in prosperity.

We are part of an exceptional 'geo-moment' where unsurpassable human values and technological innovations are redrawing the map. The inextricably intertwined global world seeks new inspiration in individual creativity and new partners in local networks, transforming the frontiers of the past into the new hubs of the future. Geography has once again become valuable. The greatest modern explorers will be the ones capable of interpreting global trends and brave enough to redraw the map of the 21st century to create lasting value for the world.

ACKNOWLEDGMENTS

Life is a journey, a journey is music, music is energy, and energy is life, as the Tuareg saying goes. My first childhood memories are about a backpack. I remember how glad I was when I saw the backpack on the back of my father, as to me it symbolized hiking and exploration. I was about six years old when I decided that I would become a geographer-explorer. Since then, I have been to several exciting places in the world, I was engaged in geographic issues as a minister of state for the Hungarian government and as an executive director at the Magyar Nemzeti Bank. I had the opportunity to assist in the implementation of numerous economic development programmes, and we launched a geopolitical foundation as well as the geopolitical journal *HUG*.

The preparation and writing of this book started exactly one year ago. György Matolcsy encouraged me to distil the thoughts from the recent analyses and research from my favourite fields, i.e. to write a book about geostrategy, geo-economics, and the new, creative, and intriguing initiatives of the 21st century. In the summer of 2015, thousands of pages of documents, studies, and analyses were collected, then we started organizing, refining, and constructing the outlines of the book week by week, and I used this as a basis when I began arranging the material into a coherent whole to describe our shared geo-moment. As for every book, this is also the result of the work of many people. I would like to take this opportunity to express my gratitude to György Matolcsy, with whom I have been working for more than a decade, whom I can constantly learn from, and who lets me pursue my passion in my career, providing me with countless new ideas through his insights. I am grateful to my colleagues who have been helping me for over five years in processing the studies by the world's leading strategic thinkers, scientific workshops, and think tanks. I am indebted to Anton Bendarzsevszkij, Tamás Bánkuty, Ráhel Czirják, Viktor Eszterhai, Sára Farkas, Zsolt Gál, László Gere, Júlia Gutpintér, Péter Klemensits, László Körtvélyesi, Tamás Rózsás, Géza Salamin, and Ákos Vajas for helping me with their ideas, suggestions, and work in shaping my book into its final form.

I also owe thanks to Zoltán Cséfalvay who has been teaching me since 2000 how wide-ranging thorough research can be and that our world presents its new and colourful side to us when we examine it through the lens of geography. In recent years, several exciting geopolitical and strategic thinkers have been invited to Hungary, and there have been several great personal meetings and professional cooperations organized by PAIGEO, and I would like to take the opportunity and thank the following magnificant thinkers: Parag Khanna, George Friedman, Noah Raford, Bruno Giussani, David Rowan, Tina Saaby, Richard Florida, Sugarta Mitra, Simon Anholt, Arjun Apparudai, Leonard Brody, Yukon Huang, Abishur Prakash, László Albert Barabási, and Mihály Csíkszentmihályi.

Thank you for LID Publishing staff's attentiveness, for their competent and careful work, attention, and the professionalism of the editors and associates of the company: Sara Taheri, Martin Liu, Caroline Li, Susan Furber, María Cid Chouciño, and Sue Littleford. I would also like to thank Bence Gáspár, Kata Paulin, and Catherine Feurverger for translating the book into English.

I am immensely grateful to Professor Zoltán Baracskai and Professor István Tózsa for reviewing my book with expert eyes, and for helping me in its finalization with their different approaches and observations.

I am much obliged to everyone, including our professional partners, the universities, institutions, and think tanks with whom I have had the privilege of working, for the mutual inspiration we provide to each other in our work, and for joining me in the exploration of new ideas, memes, domains, and research, and the building of this special geo-moment of the 21st century in which we live.

I thank my wife and my children for their support and their endless love. They teach me so much every day, they never cease to inspire me, and they show me completely new approaches. I am grateful to my parents for trusting me and spurring me on to constantly explore and seek to understand the world.

NOTES AND LINKS

1. O'BRIEN, Richard (1992): *Global Financial Integration: The End of Geography*. New York: Council on Foreign Relations Press.
2. GLAESER, Edward (2012): *Triumph of the City: How Our Greatest Invention Makes Us Richer, Smarter, Greener, Healthier, and Happier*. London: Pan.
3. KRUGMAN, Paul (2000): *The Return of Depression Economics*. London: Penguin; KRUGMAN, Paul (2003): *The Great Unraveling*, New York: W.W. Norton.
4. KRUGMAN, Paul (1994): Competitiveness. A Dangerous Obsession. *Foreign Affairs*, 73(2): 28–42.
5. PORTER, Michael E. (2008): The Five Competitive Forces that Shape Strategy. *Harvard Business Review*, 86(1): 78–93.
6. CAPELLO, Roberta (2007). *Regional Economics*. Abingdon: Routledge.
7. PARRILLI, Mario David, FITJAR, Rune Dahl, and Rodríguez-Pose, Andrés (2013): *Innovations Drivers and Regional Innovation Strategies*. New York: Routledge.
8. GLAESER, Edward (2012): *Triumph of the City: How Our Greatest Invention Makes Us Richer, Smarter, Greener, Healthier, and Happier*. London: Pan.
9. LOROT, Pascal (1999): *Introduction á la géoéconomie*. Paris: Economica; SOLOMON, Richard H. (1992): America and Asia in an Era of Geoeconomics. *Dispatch*, 3: 410; DU CASTEL, Viviane (2001): *La Géoéconomie et les Organisations Internationales*. Paris: L'Harmattan; BÁRDOS-FÉLTORONYI, Nicolas (2002): *Géoéconomie*. Amsterdam: De Boeck; DE CASTRO, Renato Cruz (2000): Whither Geoeconomics? Bureaucratic Inertia in U.S. Post-Cold War Foreign Policy Toward East Asia. *Asian Affairs: An American Review*, 26(4): 201–221; SØILEN, Klaus Sobel (2012): *Geoeconomics*. Bookboon.com.
10. PIRISI, Gábor and TRÓCSÁNYI, András (n.d.): *Általános társadalom- és gazdaságföldrajz (General social and economic geography)*. Online: https://bit.ly/2xXzPRx.
11. European Commission (Wine). Online: https://bit.ly/2xXAr9N.
12. European Commission (Wine statistics and data). Online: https://bit.ly/2zC3CRM.
13. BURKE, Marshall, HSIANG, Solomon M., and MIGUEL, Edward (2015): Global non-linear effect of temperature on economic production. *Nature* (12 November) 527: 235–239.

14. Putting Goldilocks to work: *The Economist*, 24 October 2015. Online: https://econ.st/2xUN31r.

15. *The Little Prince* was published in 1943. At that time, the world's population was 2.3 billion.

16. https://bit.ly/2OTv3f5.

17. Plate Tectonics. Online: https://bit.ly/2JjtveW.

18. https://bit.ly/2OiM71b.

19. MASON, Betsy (2009): *Erupting Volcanoes on Earth as Seen from Space. Wired*, 24 August. Online: https://bit.ly/2Q8Yn1o.

20. Minden képzelet felülmúlt a Krakatau kitörése (Krakatoa's Eruption Was Beyond Imagination). *Múlt-kor*, 27 August 2013. Online: https://bit.ly/2NJB01I.

21. https://bit.ly/2OTv3f5.

22. https://bit.ly/2pdhnAn.

23. Ibid.

24. Ibid.

25. JHA, Alok (2015): Wasting Water Is a Luxury We Can No Longer Afford. *The Guardian*, 29 May. https://bit.ly/2xH7EH9.

26. 100 Amazing Water Facts You Should Know. Seametrics Blog, 28 April 2014. Online: https://bit.ly/2J4FsoB.

27. Virtual Water: Online: https://bit.ly/2xVCBGW.

28. https://bit.ly/1DehQPx.

29. PEARSON, D.G. et al. (2014): Hydrous Mantle Transition Zone Indicated by Ringwoodite Included Within Diamond. *Nature*, 507: 221–224.

30. https://bit.ly/1DehQPx.

31. KISS Ádám (ed.) (2012): *A környezettan alapjai (Introduction to ecology)*. Budapest: ELTE TTK, Typotex Kiadó.

32. SMITH, Craig (2016): By the Numbers: 100 Amazing Google Statistics and Facts. *DMR*, 25 February. Online: https://bit.ly/2Dzp663.

33. ALBANESIUS, Chloe (2011): How Much Electricity Does Google Consume Each Year? *PC*, 8 September. Online: https://bit.ly/2OiNsFf.

34. Key World Energy Statistics 2018, International Energy Agency (IEA). Online: https://bit.ly/2xWzHSr.

35. PEEK, Katie (2013): The Energy Fix: How Geography Drives Energy Development. *Popular Science*, 12 June. Online: https://bit.ly/2Q7QKYY.

36. SMITH, Tierney (2015): 5 Countries Leading the Way Toward 100% Renewable Energy. *EcoWatch*, 9 January. Online: https://bit.ly/2IqMwcF.

37. US Energy Information Administration: Frequently Asked Questions. Online: https://bit.ly/2QDv5wG.

38. US Energy Information Agency: China – International Energy Data and Analysis (Overview) 14 May 2015. Online: https://bit.ly/28NmW12.

39. https://bit.ly/1DehQPx.

40. Ibid.

41. Deforestation Facts. Online: https://bit.ly/2zGir6e.

42. https://bit.ly/2pdhnAn.

43. https://bit.ly/2tai6HE.

44. Living Planet Report 2014 – Species and Spaces, People and Places. WWF. Online: https://bit.ly/2xQTbc3.

45. Ecological Wealth of Nations. Online: https://bit.ly/2ImgHl8.

46. HENNIG, Benjamin (2015): Ecological Footprint. *Geographical*, 30 October. Online: https://bit.ly/1VjnPRr.

47. http://www.worldometers.info/world-population

48. Statistics and Facts on Population. Online: https://bit.ly/2MCZFAi.

49. Ibid.

50. World Urbanization Prospects: United Nations, New York. Online: https://bit.ly/2zBCOkF.

51. MEADOWS, Donella H. (1997): Who Lives in the 'Global Village?'. Online: https://bit.ly/2QZuEJw.

52. *Global Strategic Trends – Out to 2045*, Ministry of Defence, UK. Online: https://bit.ly/1Hu0y3O.

53. World Airline Map. *SquidHammer*, 5 March 2009. Online: https://bit.ly/2zC4yWe.

54. KOTKIN, Joel (2010): The New World Order: Tribal ties – Race, Ethnicity, and Religion – Are Becoming More Important than Borders. *Newsweek*, 26 September. Online: https://bit.ly/2OUdCel.

55. WATSON, Richard (2009): *Future Files: A Brief History of the Next 50 Years*. London: Nicholas Brealey Publishing.

56. World Economic Forum (2014): *Outlook on the Global Agenda 2015*. Online: https://bit.ly/1wfO4Ht.

57. Ibid.

58. The 2014 list: 1. Rising social tensions in the Middle East and North America; 2. Widening income disparities; 3. Persistent structural unemployment; 4. Intensifying cyber threats; 5. Inaction on climate change; 6. Diminishing confidence in economic policies; 7. A lack of values in leadership; 8. The expanding middle class in Asia; 9. The growing importance of megacities; 10. The rapid spread of misinformation online.

59. A German loanword. It means a policy or diplomacy that relies on the use of force and practical and materialistic considerations rather than on explicit ideologies or moral or ethical principles. It is often used in a negative sense to describe coercive, amoral, Machiavellian politics.

60. PRISLAN, Nika (2011): The Changing International Landscape for the European Union's External Energy Security Policy. In: José María Beneyto (ed.), *La Unión Europea como actor global: las nuevas dimensiones de la política exterior europea*. Madrid: Biblioteca Nueva, Instituto Universitario de Estudios Europeos de la Universidad CEU San Pablo.

61. The Economist Intelligence Unit: *Long-term macroeconomic forecast – Key trends to 2050*, 2015. Online: https://bit.ly/2OmITJS.

62. Mexico (from 16th to 8th place); Indonesia (from 15th to 4th).

63. Angola (from 9 million to 28 million); Nigeria (from 56 million to 161 million); Kenya (from 18 million to 48 million).

64. Greece (from 4.8 million to 3.8 million); Portugal (from 5.2 million to 4.2 million); Germany (from 45 million to 35 million).

65. Goldman Sachs's definition of the middle class: those with an annual income between US$6,000 and US$30,000 at purchasing power parity.

66. NEXT 11: Bangladesh, Turkey, Mexico, South Korea, Iran, Indonesia, Philippines, Egypt, Nigeria, Pakistan, Vietnam.

67. Asian Development Bank (2011): *Asia 2050: Realizing the Asian Century*. Online: https://bit.ly/2NQsuyd.

68. FRIEDMAN, George (2009): *The Next 100 Years: A Forecast for the 21st Century.* New York: Doubleday.

69. FRIEDMAN, George (2011): *The Next Decade: Where We've Been … And Where We're Going.* New York: Doubleday.

70. KAGAN, Robert (2012): *The World America Made.* New York: Knopf.

71. BRZEZINSKI, Zbigniew (2012): *Strategic Vision: America and the Crisis of Global Power.* New York: Basic Books.

72. MAULDIN, John and TEPPER, Jonathan (2011): *Endgame: The End of the Debt Supercycle and How It Changes Everything.* Hoboken, NJ: John Wiley.

73. KURZWEIL, Ray (2006): *The Singularity is Near: When Humans Transcend Biology.* New York: Penguin Putnam.

74. GHEMAWAT, Pankaj (2011): *World 3.0: Global Prosperity and How to Achieve It.* Boston, MA: Harvard Business Review Press.

75. NYE, Joseph (2013): The World in 2030. *Project Syndicate*, 9 January. Online: https://bit.ly/2ORghFS.

76. Pivot is a frequent military term in the US.

77. HAASS, Richard N. (2014): The New Thirty Years' War, *Project Syndicate*, 21 July. Online: https://bit.ly/2OguKxY.

78. The Economist (2014): Wars and Rumours of Wars. *The Economist*, 14 September. Online: https://econ.st/1vn7Wy4.

79. ROGERS, Paul (2003): A Thirty-Year War. *OpenDemocracy*, 4 April. Online: https://bit.ly/2ImGf1u.

80. OGERS, Paul (2014): The Thirty-Year War, Continued. *OpenDemocracy*, 11 September. Online: https://bit.ly/2Oh7DDv.

81. KLARE, Michael T. (2011): Energy: The New Thirty Years' War. *The Guardian*, 29 June. https://bit.ly/2R2wDwN.

82. The Economist (2015): The infrastructure gap. *The Economist*, 19 March. Online: https://econ.st/1CBNyuX.

83. BARABÁSI Albert-László (2003): *Behálózva – a hálózatok új tudománya (Linked: How Everything Is Connected to Everything Else and What It Means).* Budapest, Magyar Könyvklub.

84. HAUSMANN, Ricardo, BUSTOS, Sebastián, COSCIA, Michele, CHUNG, Sarah, JIMENEZ, Juan, SIMOES, Alexander, YILDIRIM, Muhammed A., and HIDALGO, César (2013): The Atlas of Economic Complexity – Mapping Paths to Prosperity. Cambridge, MA: Center for International Development, Harvard University.

85. The Economist (2014): Creative capitalism. *The Economist*, 30 October. Online: https://econ.st/2P2YY4s.

86. One of the largest retail firms in the world, and a leader in terms of sales revenue.

87. Here we have to think of Generation Y (those born between 1980 and 1994), but mostly Generation Z (those born between 1995 and 2010) as well as the representatives of Generation Alpha (those born after 2010).

88. Several humanistic psychologists such as Mihály Csíkszentmihályi or Abraham Maslow achieved significant results in researching the social dimension of experience, and they underlined the importance of experience, although they expressed this differently.

89. Of course, the experience economy had historical precedents in the form of the so-called traditional experience industries

(e.g. culture, theatre, circus, cinema, music, literature etc.), where 'experience' could be bought for money.

90. There is a considerable duality in several Central and Eastern European countries, because the 'experience society', i.e. those that can afford these services, and the 'scarcity society' who do not have the opportunity and/or the means to enjoy this live side by side.

91. According to Rolf Jensen, a more complex experience can be created if a well-constructed 'story' about the product itself or its production is developed or formulated in a way that is relivable. Non-tangible aspects can increase the 'experience' sought to be conveyed, i.e. they can strengthen its impact.

92. UNCTAD (2008): *Creative Economy Report.* Online: https://bit.ly/2qmzMwr.

93. KERESNYEI, Krisztina (2012): *Kulturálisan kreatív? A kulturális és kreatív iparágak közötti különbségek (Culturally creative? – Differences between the cultural and the creative industries).* In: László Weinreich (ed.), *Kultúra és kreativitás: kulturális klaszterek Magyarországon.* Pécs: Pannon Klassz Közösség Kulturális Klaszter.

94. Aspen Review, Central Europe. No. 2. 2013. Online: https://bit.ly/2xXSixc.

95. GEORGE, Bill (2009): *7 Lessons for Leading in Crisis.* San Francisco: Jossey-Bass.

96. SUSSKIND, Lawrence (2014): *Great for You, Great for Me: Finding the Trading Zone and winning at Win-Win Negotiation.* New York: PublicAffairs.

97. HARFORD, Tim (2011): *Why Success Always Starts With Failure.* New York: Picador.

98. For example: visualization, journey mapping, value chain analysis, mind mapping, brainstorming, concept development, assumption testing, road prototyping, costumer co-creation, learning launch (Source: LIEDTKA, Jeanne M., KING, Andrew, and BENNETT, Kevin (2013): Solving Problem with Design Thinking. New York: Columbia University Press).

99. LIEDTKA, Jeanne M., KING, Andrew, and BENNETT, Kevin (2013): *Solving Problem with Design Thinking.* New York: Columbia University Press.

100. DRUCKER, Peter F. (2008): *Managing Oneself.* Boston, MA: Harvard Business Press.

101. GEORGE, Bill (2009): *7 Lessons for Leading in Crisis.* San Francisco: Jossey-Bass.

102. The Earth's story stretches back approximately 4.567 billion years from the Big Bang to today. The term 'Cambrian' is derived from Wales' Roman name. The period (542 million to 488 million years ago) is sometimes referred to as the Cambrian explosion, due to the rapid evolution of the biosphere. The largest climatic change, which also meant a change in the life conditions on Earth was that the cold early Cambrian period was followed by warming, and the Cambrian period as a whole was typically warm, which contributed substantially to the emergence and spread of living organisms. Therefore the Cambrian period is one of the most important eras of fossilization, both in terms of the number and significance of the fossils (proof for the lush vegetation is for example the large amount of black coal that developed from it in this age).

103. The term 'start-up accelerator' comes from the United States and means a complex support mechanism in which the given new company receives not only knowledge and advice with respect to business and technological development but also capital from investors.

104. JOHNSON, Steven (2014): How We Got to Now: Six Innovations that Made the Modern World. London: Particular Books.

105. LISA Project (NASA). Online: https://go.nasa.gov/2vGn6mE.

106. https://www.topuniversities.com/university-rankings/world-university-rankings/2015.

107. https://www.class-central.com/report/mooc-stats-2017.

108. BENKO, Georges (1953–2009) was an internationally renowned researcher of economic geography who was born in Hungary and raised in Germany, later settling in France. One of his main research areas was the geography of technology parks and technopolises. In his work and basic tenets, Benko did not accept the neutral space concept of classic spatial economics: "Human, regional, economic or ecological geography considers space as the material dimension of social relations. They are human activity, human relations of any kind, which constitute the very substance of space".

109. www.bridgebudapest.hu

110. http://www.aiwfonline.com/home.aspx

111. ROBINSON, Joe (2014): The 7 Traits of Successful Entrepreneurs, *Entrepreneur*, 10 January. Online: https://bit.ly/1TSVpgf.

112. SENOR, Dan and SINGER, Saul (n.d.): Start-Up Nation. The Story of Israel's Economic Miracle. *Council on Foreign Relations*. Online: https://on.cfr.org/2xH183m.

113. COHAN, Peter (2013): 5 Steps that Turned Israel from Socialism to Startup Haven. *Forbes*, 23 March. Online: https://bit.ly/2OUddZA.

114. MOSS, Ilan (2011): Start-Up Nation: An Innovation Story. *OECD Observer* No 285, Q2. Online: https://bit.ly/2DzIX4N.

115. COHAN, Peter (2013): 5 Steps that Turned Israel from Socialism to Startup Haven. *Forbes*, 23 March. Online: https://bit.ly/2OUddZA.

116. CORFO (Chilean Economic Development Agency) (2013): The Program. 18 April. *Start-Up Chile*. Online: http://startupchile.org.

117. The neighboring Argentina's GDP per capita (US$18,205) is somewhat more than in Chile (US$17,380), but the other countries in the region are less developed (for example Brazil's GDP per capita is US$12,075).

118. Of course, everyone acts in their own interest, which can lead to various economic, social and environmental problems and foreign policy or armed conflicts.

119. From an environmental perspective, this has always been the case. Just think of global issues such as ozone depletion or global warming, which are due to the combined effect of significant interventions, despite the fact that these interventions are far from each other in geographical terms (e.g. the destruction of the rainforest – South America; high pollution – China), yet they influence the lives of everyone.

120. Of course, these boundaries have become completely blurred and lost their significance. Just think of today's multicultural society and communities.

121. For example seas, oceans, mountains, deserts.

122. Natural boundaries hindered the spread of plants and animals species. They needed the help of humankind to establish themselves in other suitable territories as well. These are the so-called invasive species.

123. For humanity, overcoming the obstacles posed by these natural boundaries is not an issue anymore, therefore we can say that they have been rendered insignificant.

124. Of course, the isolation was not perfect, but the extent of actual movements was truly negligible.

125. When observing the current developments, we can see that a multipolar world has started to emerge, in which the US gradually loses its advantage but is still a dominant power. China converges rapidly and Russia attempts to regain its old splendour and influence.

126. Just think of the Asian Infrastructure Investment Bank (AIIB) established by China, which basically attempts to act as a counterweight to the IMF and the World Bank that are in the sphere of influence of the Western world.

127. For example: Union of South American Nations, Association of Southeast Asian Nations, OPEC etc.

128. In a physical sense (the abolishment of border controls), and this is only true between the Member States of the European Union.

129. This can be felt in the European Union as well, which is under great pressure due to the migration flows from Syria, and the different national responses and countries' varying willingness to take part in managing the issue have sparked serious internal conflicts.

130. For example the boundaries between the different scientific domains. Initially, the knowledge available to humanity could be surveyed by one person (polymaths); however, as knowledge expanded, science started to break up into parts, and even within one sphere, separate but closely related areas developed without clear-cut boundaries between them (disputes between the different scientific domains), since they inherently belonged together.

131. World Urbanization Prospects: United Nations, New York. Online: https://bit.ly/2zBCOkF.

132. http://www.lboro.ac.uk/gawc/publicat.html.

133. ENYEDI, György (2011): A városnövekedés szakaszai – újragondolva (The Stages of Urban Growth – Revisited). Tér és Társadalom, 25(1). Online: https://bit.ly/2DzgvA1.

134. Global Financial Centres Index, the competitiveness index of the Qatar Financial Centre Authority and the Z/Yen Group assessing cities functioning as financial centres.

135. https://www.tandfonline.com/doi/abs/10.1080/10400419.2012.676974?journalCode=hcrj20

136. Endesa, Barcelona City Council Sign Cooperation Agreement. *Energy Business Review*. 31 March 2014. Online: https://bit.ly/2DBuoOm.

137. Shops are to open on 11 more public holidays during the year. *Barcelona News* (BCN) (14 March 2014).

138. HUG magazine 2016/1

139. https://www.telegraph.co.uk/news/uknews/9959026/Mothers-asked-nearly-300-questions-a-day-study-finds.html

140. https://www.ted.com/talks/gever_tulley_on_5_dangerous_things_for_kids

REFERENCES AND FURTHER READING

BOOKS, ARTICLES, ONLINE NEWS

ABDALLAH, Saamah, THOMPSON, Sam, MICHAELSON, Juliet, MARKS, Nick, and STEUER, Nicola (2009): *The Happy Planet Index 2.0. The (un)Happy Planet Index 2.0. Why Good Lives Don't Have to Cost the Earth.* London, The New Economics Foundation.

ABRAHAM, Saji (2015): *China's Role in the Indian Ocean: Its Implications on India's National Security.* New Delhi, Vij Books India.

AHMAD, Khurshid (2011): Global Economic Crisis Need for a Paradigm Shift. *Policy Perspectives*, 8(2): 1–17.

ALBANESIUS, Chloe (2011): How Much Electricity Does Google Consume Each Year? *PC*, 8 September. Online: https://bit.ly/2OiNsFf.

ALCALÁ, María José et al. (ed.) (2006): *UNFPA State of World Population 2006. A Passage to Hope. Women and International Migration.* New York: United Nations Population Fund.

ALEXANDER, Samuel (2014): Post-Growth Economics: A Paradigm Shift in Progress, *The Simplicity Collective*, 2 March. https://bit.ly/2N2Hbsp.

ANDERSON, Chris (2006): *The Long Tail: Why the Future of Business Is Selling Less of More.* New York: Hyperion.

ANDERSON, Chris (2009): *Ingyen! A radikális árképzés jövője (Free: The Future of a Radical Price).* Budapest: HVG Kiadói Rt.

ARNOTT, Sarah (2010): China's Geely Buys Volvo for $1.5bn. *The Independent*, 3 August. https://ind.pn/2IjTwYF.

BAJARI, Patrick, BENKARD, C. Lanier, and KRAINER John (2003): House Prices and Consumer Welfare. NBER Working Paper No. 9783. Cambridge, MA: National Bureau of Economic Research.

BAKRÓ-NAGY Marianne et al. (2014): Hány nyelv van a világon? (How Many Languages Are There in the World?) Online: https://bit.ly/2QcQubb.

BALDWIN, Natylie (2015): Ukraine: Zbig's Grand Chessboard & How the West Was Checkmated. San Francisco: Next Revelation Press.

BARABÁSI Albert-László (2003): *Behálózva – a hálózatok új tudománya (Linked: How Everything Is Connected to Everything Else and What It Means).* Budapest, Magyar Könyvklub.

BARABÁSI Albert-László (2010): *Villanások – a jövő kiszámítható (Flashes – The Future Is Predictable).* Budapest, Nyitott Könyvműhely.

BARCA, Fabrizio (2009): An Agenda for a Reformed Cohesion Policy. A Place-based Approach to Meeting European Union Challenges and Expectations. Independent report. European Commission, Brussels. April 2009.

BÁRDOS-FÉLTORONYI, Nicolas (2002): *Géoéconomie.* Amsterdam: De Boeck.

BARU, Sanjaya (2012): Geo-economics and Strategy. *Survival,* 54(3): 47–58.

BASFORD, Johanna (2013): *Secret Garden: An Inky Treasure Hunt and Colouring Book.* London: Lawrence King.

BÉKÉSI László (2004): *A politika földrajza (The Geography of Politics).* Budapest: AULA kiadó.

BENKO, Georges (1992): *Technológiai parkok és technopoliszok földrajza (The geography of technology parks and technopolises).* Budapest, MTA Regionális Kutatások Központja.

BENKO, Georges (2002): *Regionális tudomány (Regional science).* Budapest, Dialóg Campus.

BERNEK Ágnes (ed.) (2002): *A globális világpolitikai földrajza (Geopolitics in the global world*). Budapest: Nemzeti Tankönyvkiadó.

BERNEK Ágnes (2010): Geopolitika és/vagy geoökonómia – A 21. század világgazdasági és világpolitikai folyamatainak összefüggései (Geopolitics and/or Geo-economics – The Correlations Between Global Economic and Political Developments). *Geopolitika a 21. században,* 1(1): 31–64.

BERNEK Ágnes (2010): A 21. századi „Kínai Birodalom" – Kína külföldi működőtőke-befektetéseinek területi szerveződése (The 21st Century 'Chinese Empire' – The territorial Structure of Chinese FDI). *Geopolitika a 21. században,* 1(2): 47–65.

BESZTERI, Béla and MAJOROS, Pál (2011): *A huszonegyedik század kihívásai és Magyarország jövőképe (21st Century Challenges and Hungary's Vision).* Veszprém: MTA VEAB.

BHONSLE, Rahul K. (2007): China's 100 Year Vision of Greatness. *News Blaze,* 5 April. Online: https://bit.ly/2xJUqJN.

BLASCOVICH, Jim and BAILENSON, Jeremy (2011): *Infinite Reality: Avatars, Eternal Life, New Worlds, and the Dawn of the Virtual Revolution.* New York: Harper Collins.

BOLT, Jutta and ZANDEN, Jan Luiten van (2014): *The First Update of the Maddison Project; Re-Estimating Growth Before 1820.* Maddison Project Working Paper 4. https://bit.ly/2IlsZtU.

BORAVIA, Judy (1994): *Silk Road: From Xian to Kashgar.* Lincolnwood, IL: NTC Publishing.

BÖRNER, Katy (2015): *Atlas of Knowledge.* Cambridge, MA: The MIT Press.

BORSI Balázs – VISZT Erzsébet (2010): *A kreatív és kulturális ágazatok (CCI) szerepe és növekedési lehetőségei a Budapest Metropolisz Régió gazdaságában (Kutatási jelentés) (The role and growth opportunities of creative and cultural industries (CCI) in the economy of the Budapest Metropolitan Region (Research report)),* 5 December. Budapest GKI Gazdaságkutató Zrt.

BRAUTIGAM, Deborah (2015): *Will Africa Feed China?* Oxford: Oxford University Press.

BREMMER, Ian (2015): *Superpower: Three Choices for America's Role in the World.* London: Portfolio.

BRITO, Rosa M. (2012): The Bipolar World and the Art Expressions of the Consumers Society – Second Part, 2 August. Online: https://bit.ly/2zA8MOc.

BROOKS, Karen (2014): Six Markets to Watch: Indonesia and the Philippines. A Tale of Two Archipelagoes. *Foreign Affairs,* Jan-Feb.: 37–44.

BRZEZINSKI, Zbigniew (1999): *A nagy sakktábla (The Grand Chessboard).* Budapest, Európa Kiadó.

BRZEZINSKI, Zbigniew (2012): *Strategic Vision: America and the Crisis of Global Power.* New York: Basic Books.

BUCHANAN, Leigh (2010): Decoding the New Consumer. *Inc.*, 32(7): 159–60.

BUCHANAN, Leigh (2013): Between Venus and Mars. *Inc.*, 35(5): 64–130.

BUCSKY Péter and SZIRMAI S. (2014): Bezzeg Budapest – Versenyképcsségi rangsorok (But Budapest – Competitiveness rankings). *Figyelő* 2014/12, 20 March. Online: https://bit.ly/2NLcygy.

BURKE, Edmund (2009): *Reflections on the Revolution in France.* Oxford: Oxford University Press.

BURKE, Marshall, HSIANG, Solomon M., and MIGUEL, Edward (2015): Global non-linear effect of temperature on economic production. *Nature* (12 November) 527: 235–239.

BURKE, Sara and PUTY, Claudio (2004): In the Belly of the Beast. A Perspective on the Global Justice Movement in the United States: Its Roots and Emergence. *Gloves Off*, June. Online: https://bit.ly/2QciQCq.

CAPELLO, Roberta (2007). *Regional Economics.* Abingdon: Routledge.

CARMICHAEL, Kevin (2012): Federal Reserve Pledges Low Interest Rate Until Jobless Level Eases to 6.5%. *The Globe and Mail*, 13 December. Online: https://tgam.ca/2zAcBD5.

CARMICHAEL, Kevin (2012): Why Central Banks Are Approaching the Policy Wall. *The Globe and Mail.* 14 December. Online: https://tgam.ca/2xHzIKs.

CARR, Nicholas (2014): *Hogyan változtatja meg agyunkat az internet? – A sekélyesek kora (How our brain changes the Internet – The age of the shallow).* Budapest: HVG Kiadói Rt.

CASTELLS, Manuel (1994): *The Rise of the Network Society.* Oxford: Blackwell.

CASTELLS, Manuel (2002): *Cities and Social Theories*, ed. Ida Susser. Oxford: Blackwell.

CASTELLS, Manuel (2005): *A hálózati társadalom kialakulása (The Emergence of the Network Society).* Budapest: Gondolat-Infonia.

CATMULL, Ed and WALLACE, Amy (2014): *Creativity Inc.: Overcoming the Unseen Forces That Stand in the Way of True Inspiration.* New York: Random House.

CLARK, Wesley K. (2007): *A Time to Lead: For Duty, Honor and Country.* New York: St. Martin's Press.

CLARK, Wesley K. (2014): *Don't Wait for the Next War: A Strategy for American Growth and Global Leadership.* New York: PublicAffairs.

CLEMENTI, Fabio, GALLEGATI, Mauro, and PALESTRINI, Antonio (2012): A Big Mac Test of Price Dynamics and Dispersion Across Euro Area. *Economic Bulletin*, 30(3): 2037–2053.

COCKBURN, Andrew (2015): *Kill Chain: The Rise of the high-Tech Assassins.* New York: Henry Holt.

COHAN, Peter (2013): 5 Steps that Turned Israel from Socialism to Startup Haven. *Forbes*, 23 March. Online: https://bit.ly/2OUddZA.

COHEN, Saul Bernard (1999): *Geopolitics: The Geography of International Relations.* New York: Rowman & Littlefield.

COLLIGNON, Stefan, ESPOSITO, Piero, and CUI, Yuming (2012): Unconventional Monetary Policy Measures: A Comparison of the ECB, FED, and BoE. Directorate General for Internal Policies Note, Brussels: European Parliament.

CORFO (Chilean Economic Development Agency) (2013): The Program. 18 April. *Start-Up Chile.* Online: http://startupchile.org.

COUR-THIMANN, Philippine, ROUGEMONT, Philippe de, and Winkler, Bernhard (2012): The ECB's Monetary Policy Response to the Crisis: The Role of Institutional Factors and Financial Structure. Preliminary Draft.

CSÁKI, György (ed.) (2009): *A látható kéz: A fejlesztő állam a globalizációban (The visible hand: The developmental state in globalization).* Budapest: Napvilág Kiadó.

CSÉFALVAY, Zoltán (1994): *A modern társadalom-földrajz kézikönyve (Handbook to Modern Social Geography).* Budapest: Ikva Kiadó.

CSÉFALVAY, Zoltán (2004): *Globalizáció 1.0 (Globalization 1.0).* Budapest: Nemzeti Tankönyvkiadó.

CSÉFALVAY, Zoltán (2004): *Globalizáció 2.0 (Globalization 2.0).* Budapest: Nemzeti Tankönyvkiadó.

CSÍKSZENTMIHÁLYI, Mihály (1990): *Flow: The Psychology of Optimal Experience.* New York: Harper and Row.

CSÍKSZENTMIHÁLYI, Mihály (2004): *Good Business Leadership, Flow, and the Making of Meaning.* New York: Penguin.

CSÍKSZENTMIHÁLYI, Mihály (2014): *Kreativitás – A flow és a felfedezés, avagy a találékonyság pszichológiája (Creativity – Flow and the Psychology of Discovery and Invention).* Budapest: Akadémiai Kiadó.

CSÍKSZENTMIHÁLYI, Mihály (2015): *Flow – Az áramlat: A tökéletes élmény pszichológiája (Flow: The Psychology of Optimal Experience).* Budapest: Akadémiai Kiadó.

CSIZMADIA, Sándor, MOLNÁR, Gusztáv, and PATAKI, Gábor (1999): *Geopolitikai Szöveggyűjtemény (Geopolitical Reader).* Budapest: Stratégiai és Védelmi Kutatóintézet.

CSURGAI, Gyula (1998): *Geopolitics, Geoeconomics and Economic Intelligence.* Toronto: Canadian Institute of Strategic Studies.

DA CUNHA, I.V. and SELADA, C. (2009): Creative Urban Regeneration: The Case of Innovation Hubs. *International Journal of Innovation and Regional Development*, 1(4): 371–386.

DE CASTRO, Renato Cruz (2000): Whither Geoeconomics? Bureaucratic Inertia in U.S. Post-Cold War Foreign Policy Toward East Asia. *Asian Affairs: An American Review*, 26(4): 201–221.

DEHESA, Guillermo (2012): Monetary Policy Responses to the Crisis by ECB, FED, and BoE. Directorate General for Internal Policies Note, Brussels, European Parliament.

DRUCKER, Peter F. (1998): The Discipline of Innovation. *Harvard Business Review*, 76(6): 149–157.

DRUCKER, Peter F. (2002): The Discipline of Innovation. *Harvard Business Review*, 80(8): 95–100.

DRUCKER, Peter F. (2008): *Managing Oneself.* Boston, MA: Harvard Business Press.

DU CASTEL, Viviane (2001): *La Géoéconomie et les Organisations Internationales.* Paris: L'Harmattan.

DUGIN, Alexandr (2004): A geopolitika alapjai. Oroszország geopolitikai jövője. Térségben gondolkodni (The Fundamentals of Geopolitics. Russia's Future. Think Regional). In: *Oroszország és Európa – Orosz geopolitikai szöveggyűjtemény.* Budapest: Zrínyi Kiadó, 333–376.

DYKSTRA, Peter (2014): Analysis: 35 Years Later, Jimmy Carter's Energy Warning. *Daily Climate*, 27 July. https://bit.ly/2NL0Nqb.

ÉBER, Márk Áron (2007): *Élménytársadalom. Gerhardt Schulze koncepciójának tudás- és társadalomelméleti összefüggéseiről (Experience Society: On the Knowledge and Social Theory Implications of Gerhardt Schulze's Concept).* Budapest: ELTE Társadalomtudományi Kar.

EDWARDS, Stevens (2015): 10 Things You Didn't Know About the World's Population. *UNFPA*, 13 April. Online: https://bit.ly/2xV8Q9m.

EHRLICH, Paul (2000): *Human Natures: Genes, Cultures and the Human Prospect.* Washington, DC: Shearwater.

ELIADE, Mircea (2010): *Vallási hiedelmek és eszmék története I (The History of Religious Beliefs and Ideas).* Budapest, Osiris Kiadó.

ELLIOTT, Larry, TEATHER, David, and TREANOR, Jill (2010): Credit Crunch Consequences: Three Years After the Crisis, What's Changed? *The Guardian*, 8 August. https://bit.ly/2DAcETk.

ENYEDI, György (2011): A városnövekedés szakaszai – újragondolva (The Stages of Urban Growth – Revisited). *Tér és Társadalom*, 25(1). Online: https://bit.ly/2DzgvA1.

FERGUSON, Niall (2003): *Empire. How Britain Made the Modern World.* London: Penguin.

FERGUSON, Niall (2004): *Colosseum: The Price of America's Empire.* London: Allen Lane.

FERGUSON, Niall (2011). *Civilization: The West and the Rest.* London: Penguin.

FERGUSON, Niall (2013). *The Great Degeneration.* New York: Penguin.

FERGUSON, Niall (2015): *Kissinger: 1923–1968: The Idealist.* New York, Penguin.

FERRIE, Joseph P. and HATTON, Timothy J. (2013): Two Centuries of International Migration. IZA Discussion Paper No. 7866.

FISCHER Ferenc (2005): *A kétpólusú világ 1945–1989: Tankönyv és atlasz (The Bipolar World 1945–1989: Coursebook and Atlas).* Pécs: Dialóg Campus.

FLEMING-WILLIAMS, Mark (2015): China's New Investment Bank: A Premature Prophecy, *Stratfor*, 22 April. https://bit.ly/2nxk5xw.

FLINT, Colin (2007): *Introduction to Geopolitics.* Abingdon: Routledge.

FLORIDA, Richard (2002, 2012): *The Rise of the Creative Class … and How It's Transforming Work, Leisure and Everyday Life.* New York: Basic Books.

FLORIDA, Richard (2008): *Who's Your City? How the Creative Economy Is Making Where to Live the Most Important Decision of Your Life.* New York: Basic Books.

FLORIDA, Richard (2010): *The Great Reset: How New Ways of Living and Working Drive Post-Crash Prosperity*, New York: HarperCollins.

FLORIDA, Richard (2014): *The Rise of the Creative Class – Revisited.* New York: Basic Books.

FOLTZ, Richard (2010): *Religions of the Silk Road: Premodern Patterns of Globalization.* New York: Palgrave Macmillan.

FORSBERG, Kevin, MOOZ, Hal, and COTTERMAN, Howard (2005): *Visualizing Project Management: Models and Frameworks for Mastering Complex Systems.* Hoboken, NJ: John Wiley.

FOX, Justin (2014): Will Economics Finally Get Its Paradigm Shift? *Harvard Business Review*,
28 April. Online: https://bit.ly/2OnKiAd.

FRANCK, Irene M. and BROWNSTONE, David M. (1986): *Silk Road: A History.* New York: Facts on File.

FRIEDMAN, George (2004): *America's Secret War: Inside the Hidden Worldwide Struggle Between the United States and Its Enemies.* New York: Doubleday.

FRIEDMAN, George (2009): *The Next 100 Years: A Forecast for the 21st Century.* New York: Doubleday.

FRIEDMAN, George (2011): *The Next Decade: Where We've Been … And Where We're Going.* New York: Doubleday.

FRIEDMAN, George (2015): *Flashpoints.* Melbourne: Scribe.

FRIEDMAN, George and FRIEDMAN, Meredith (1996): *The Future of War: Power, Technology and American World Dominance in the Twenty-First Century.* New York: Crown Publishers.

FRIEDMAN, George and LEBARD, Meredith (1991): *The Coming War With Japan.* New York: St. Martin's Press.

FRIEDMAN, George, FRIEDMAN, Meredith, CHAPMAN, Colin, and BAKER, John (1997): *The Intelligence Edge: How to Profit in the Information Age.* New York: Crown Publishers.

FRIEDMAN, Thomas L. (2005): *The World Is Flat: The Globalized World in the Twenty-First Century.* London: Penguin.

FUKUYAMA, Francis (2014): *Political Order and Political Decay: From the Industrial Revolution to the Globalization of Democracy.* New York: Farrar, Straus and Giroux.

FUKUYAMA, Francis (2014): *A történelem vége és az utolsó ember (The End of History and the Last Man).* Budapest: Európa Könyvkadó.

FULLWILER, Scott T (2008): Modern Central Bank Operations – The General Principles. *Social Science Research Network*, June. https://bit.ly/2OglozL.

FUNG, Brian (2013): The Head of Google X Thinks We're All too Risk-Averse. *Washington Post*, 13 November. https://wapo.st/2QZ7rqS.

GEHL, Jan (2010): *Cities for People.* Washington, DC: Island Press.

GEORGE, Bill (2003): *Authentic Leadership: Rediscovering the Secrets to Creating Lasting Value.* San Francisco: Jossey-Bass.

GEORGE, Bill (2009): *7 Lessons for Leading in Crisis.* San Francisco: Jossey-Bass.

GERZEMA, John (2009): The Brand Bubble. *Marketing Research*, 21(1): 7–11.

GERZEMA, John (2013): Athena Doctrine. *Leadership Excellence*, 30(4): 19.

GERZEMA, John (2013): The Athena Doctrine: Female Values Are the Future. *Market Leader*, Q2: 36–39.

GERZEMA, John (2015): About John Gerzema. https://bit.ly/2DCn8BJ.

GERZEMA, John and D'ANTONIO, Michael (2011): *Spend Shift: How the Post-Crisis Values Revolution is Changing the Way We Buy, Sell, and Live.* San Francisco: Jossey-Bass.

GERZEMA, John and D'ANTONIO, Michael (2013): *The Athena Doctrine: How Women (and the Men Who Think Like Them) Will Rule the Future.* San Francisco: Jossey-Bass.

GHEMAWAT, Pankaj (2011): *World 3.0: Global Prosperity and How to Achieve It.* Boston, MA: Harvard Business Review Press.

GIUDICE, Maria and IRELAND, Christopher (2013): *Rise of the DEO: Leadership by Design.* San Francisco: New Riders.

GLAESER, Edward (2008): *Cities, Agglomeration, and Spatial Equilibrium.* New York: Oxford University Press.

GLAESER, Edward (2012): *Triumph of the City: How Our Greatest Invention Makes Us Richer, Smarter, Greener, Healthier*, and Happier. London: Pan.

GLEDHILL, John (2015): *The New War on the Poor: The Production of Insecurity in Latin America.* London: Zed Books.

GONZALEZ, Mike (2015): *The Last Drop: The Politics of War.* London: Pluto Press.

GOODMAN, Marc and KHANNA, Parag (2013): The Power of Moore's Law in a World of Geotechnology. *The National Interest.* 123: 64–73.

GRAY, Colin S. and SLOAN, Geoffrey (eds) (1999): *Geopolitics, Geography and Strategy.* London: Routledge.

GRAZIANI, Tiberio (2013): The Globalisation of the Crisis and the Political Shift. *World Public Forum*, 28 June. https://bit.ly/2NHjzPn.

GROS, Daniel, ALCIDI, Cinzia, and GIOVANNI, Alessandro (2012): Central Banks in Times of Crises: The FED versus the ECB. Directorate General for Internal Policies Note, Brussels, European Parliament.

GWARTNEY, James D. and STROUP, Richard L. (1995): *Economics: Private and Public Choice.* Fort Worth, TX: Dryden Press.

HAASS, Richard N. (1999): *The Bureaucratic Entrepreneur: How to Be Effective in Any Unruly Organization.* Washington, DC: Brookings Institution. https://brook.gs/2OfNEoC.

HAGGETT, Peter (1996): *The Geographer's Art.* Oxford: Wiley-Blackwell.

HAGGETT, Peter (2001): *Geography: A Global Synthesis.* Harlow: Pearson.

HALL, Peter (2001): *Cities in Civilization.* New York: Fromm International.

HAMEL, Jean-Yves (2009): Information and Communication Technologies and Migration. UNDP Human Development Research Paper 2009/39.

HANDEL, Michael I. (1996): *Masters of War: Classical Strategic Thought.* London: Frank Cass.

HARFORD, Tim (2011): *Why Success Always Starts With Failure.* New York: Picador.

HAUSMANN, Ricardo, BUSTOS, Sebastián, COSCIA, Michele, CHUNG, Sarah, JIMENEZ, Juan, SIMOES, Alexander, YILDIRIM, Muhammed A., and HIDALGO, César (2013): *The Atlas of Economic Complexity – Mapping Paths to Prosperity.* Cambridge, MA: Center for International Development, Harvard University.

HESMONDHALGH, David (2002): *The Cultural Industries.* London: Sage.

HEDIN, Sven Anders (1938): *The Silk Road.* London: Routledge.

HELLERSTEIN, Joseph M. and STONEBRAKER, Michael (2005): *Readings in Database Systems.* Cambridge, MA: MIT Press.

HENDERSON, David R. (ed.) (2013): *The Concise Encyclopedia of Economics.* Carmel, IN: Liberty Fund.

HENDERSON, David. R. and HOOPER, Charles L. (2007): *Making Great Decisions in Business and Life.* Chicago: Chicago Park Press.

HENDERSON, David R (1993): Japan and the Myth of MITI. In: David R Henderson (ed.), *The Fortune Encyclopedia of Economics,* 743–746. New York: Warner Books.

HENDRICK-WONG, Yuwa and CHOONG, Desmond (2015): *MasterCard Global Destination Cities Index: Tracking Global Growth: 2009–2015.* Online: https://mstr.cd/2OjW6Dl.

HENNIG, Benjamin (2015): Ecological Footprint. *Geographical,* 30 October. Online: https://bit.ly/1VjnPRr.

HENNIG, Benjamin (2015): World Religions. *Geographical,* 7 June. Online: https://bit.ly/1SKV62c.

HIDALGO, Cesar A. (2015): *Why Information Grows: The Evolution of Order from Atoms to Economies.* New York: Basic Books.

HINGE, Daniel (2013): Former BoE MPC Members Divided on 'Maxed Out' Easing. *Central Banking,* 4 February. Online: https://bit.ly/2OVsF7w.

HUNTINGTON, Samuel P. (1999): A civilizációk összecsapása és a világrend átalakulása (The Clash of Civilizations and the Remaking of World Order). Budapest, Európa Kiadó, 646.

HUNTINGTON, Samuel P. (2004): *Who Are We? America's Great Debate.* London: Simon and Schuster.

JHA, Alok (2015): Wasting Water Is a Luxury We Can No Longer Afford. *The Guardian,* 29 May. https://bit.ly/2xH7EH9.

JOHNSON, Hugh and Robinson, Jancis (2013): *The World Atlas of Wine,* 7th ed. London: Mitchell Beazley.

JOHNSON, Steven (2014): *How We Got to Now: Six Innovations that Made the Modern World.* London: Particular Books.

JONES, Med (2006): *The American Pursuit of Happiness: Gross National Happiness (GNH) – A New Economic Metric.* Las Vegas, NV: International Institute of Management. https://bit.ly/2OSBzCN.

JUHOS, Andrea (2015): "Akikből a jövő sikeres vezetői lesznek" (The successful leaders of the future) Presentation, FLOW A siker evolúciója c. konferencia (FLOW, The Evolution of Success conference), 9 November.

KAGAN, Robert (2004): *Of Paradise and Power: America and Europe in the New World Order.* New York: Vintage.

KAGAN, Robert (2008): *The Return of History and the End of Dreams.* New York: Knopf.

KAGAN, Robert (2012): *The World America Made.* New York: Knopf.

KAPLAN, Robert D. (2009): Center Stage for the Twenty-first Century. *American Diplomacy,* 16 March. Online: https://unc.live/2zzPrge.

KAPLAN, Robert D. (2010): The Geography of Chinese Power. *Foreign Affairs,* 89(3): 22–41.

KAPLAN, Robert D. (2013): *The Revenge of Geography: What the Map Tells Us About Coming Conflicts and the Battle Against Fate.* New York: Random House.

KAPLAN, Robert D. (2015): *Asia's Cauldron: The South China Sea and the End of a Stable Pacific.* New York: Random House.

KASAHARA, Shigehisa (2004): The Flying Geese Paradigm: A Critical Study of Its Application to East Asian Regional Development. Discussion Paper No. 169, Budapest: United Nations Conference on Trade and Development.

KAUZ, Ralph (ed.) (2010): *Aspects of the Maritime Silk Road: From the Persian Gulf to the East China Sea.* Wiesbaden: Harrassowitz.

KELLEY, Donna J., BRUSH, Candida G., GREENE, Patricia G., LITOVSTKY, Yana, and Global Entrepreneurship Research Association (2013): *Global Entrepreneurship Monitor 2012 Women's Report.* Babson Park, MA: Babson College.

KERESNYEI, Krisztina (2012): *Kulturálisan kreatív? A kulturális és kreatív iparágak közötti különbségek (Culturally creative? – Differences between the cultural and the creative industries).* In: László Weinreich (ed.), *Kultúra és kreativitás: kulturális klaszterek Magyarországon.* Pécs: Pannon Klassz Közösség Kulturális Klaszter.

KERESNYEI Krisztina and EGEDY Tamás (2015): Adalékok a kreatív gazdaság elméletéhez (Additional data to the theory of creative economy). *Földrajzi Közlemények,* 139(1): 30– 42.

KHANNA, Parag (2008): *The Second World: Empires and Influence in the New Global Order.* New York: Random House.

KHANNA, Parag (2011): *How to Run the World: Charting a Course to the Next Renaissance.* New York, Random House.

KHANNA, Parag (2014): A World Reimagined. *The American Interest,* 6 June. Online: https://bit.ly/2N5rReH.

KHANNA, Parag and KHANNA, Ayesha (2012): *Hybrid Reality: Thriving in the Emerging Human-Technology Civilization.* New York: TED.

KINNANDER, Ola (2012): Saab Auto Sold to China-Japan Group in Electric-Car Push. *Bloomberg,* 13 June. Online: https://bloom.bg/2Oh4iUL.

KIRSHNER, Jonathan (2014): Geopolitics After the Global Financial Crisis. *ISN,* 9 March. Online: https://bit.ly/2zALKXH.

KISS Ádám (ed.) (2012): *A környezettan alapjai (Introduction to ecology).* Budapest: ELTE TTK, Typotex Kiadó.

KISSINGER, Henry (1979): *The White House Years.* Boston, MA: Little Brown.

KISSINGER, Henry (2002): *Korszakváltás az amerikai külpolitikában. A 21. századi Amerika diplomáciai kérdései (Does America Need a Foreign Policy? Toward a Diplomacy for the 21st Century).* Budapest: Panemex Kiadó.

KISSINGER, Henry (2008): *Diplomácia (Diplomacy).* Budapest: Panem Kiadó.

KLARE, Michael T. (2008): *Rising Powers, Shrinking Planet: The New Geopolitics of Energy.* New York: Metropolitan Books.

KLARE, Michael T. (2011): Energy: The New Thirty Years' War. *The Guardian*, 29 June. https://bit.ly/2R2wDwN.

KLARE, Michael T. (2012): *The Race for What's Left: The Global Scramble for the World's Last Resources.* New York: Metropolitan Books.

KOLLÁNYI Bence (2007): *Térhasználat az információs társadalom korában.* Az Európai Bizottság és a NETIS támogatásával készült tananyag (Space Use in the Age of the Information Society. Course material produced with the support of the European Commission and NETIS). Formerly available at: http://www.ittk.hu/netis/doc/ISCB_hun/05_Kollanyi_ter.pdf.

KOPP, Mária and MARTOS, Tamás (2011): *A magyarországi gazdasági növekedés és a társadalmi jóllét, életminőség viszonya (The Relationship Between the Hungarian Economic Growth and Social Welfare, i.e. the Quality of Life).* Budapest: Magyar Pszicho-fiziológiai és Egészséglélektani Társaság.

KOPP, Wendy (2011): *A Chance to Make History: What Works and What Doesn't in Providing an Excellent Education for All.* New York: PublicAffairs.

KOROMPAI, A. (1995): *Regionális stratégiák jövőkutatási megalapozása (Establishing the Foundations of the Futurology of Regional Strategies).* Budapest: Eötvös Loránd Tudományegyetem.

KOTKIN, Joel (1994): *Tribes: How Race, Religion and Identity Determine Success in the New Global Economy.* New York: Random House.

KOTKIN, Joel (2002): *The New Geography: How the Digital Revolution Is Reshaping the American Landscape.* New York: Random House.

KOTKIN, Joel (2006): *The City: A Global History.* New York: Modern Library.

KOTKIN, Joel (2010): *The Next Hundred Million: America in 2050.* New York: Penguin.

KOTKIN, Joel (2010): The New World Order: Tribal ties – Race, Ethnicity, and Religion – Are Becoming More Important than Borders. *Newsweek*, 26 September. Online: https://bit.ly/2OUdCel.

KOTKIN, Joel (2014): *The New Class Conflict. Candor,* NY: Telos Press Publishing.

KOTLER, Philip and KELLER, Kevin Lane (2006): *Marketing management*, 12th edn. Upper Saddle River, NJ: Pearson Education.

KOVÁCS, Dezső (2011): *Az élménygazdaságig és tovább? Magyarország-Horvátország Határmenti Együttműködési Program 2007–2013 UNIREG IMPULSE projekt tanulmánya (To the Experience Economy and Beyond? The Study by the Hungary–Croatia Cross-Border Co-operation Programme 2007–2013 UNIREG IMPULSE project).* Online: https://bit.ly/2IjpWSV.

KOVÁCS, Dezső (2014): Élmény, élménygazdaság, élménytársadalom és turizmus (Experience, experience economy, experience society and tourism). *Turizmus Bulletin*, 16(3/4): 40–48.

KRUGMAN, Paul (1994): Competitiveness. A Dangerous Obsession. *Foreign Affairs*, 73(2): 28–42.

KRUGMAN, Paul (1996): *The Self-Degrading Economy.* Malden, MA: Blackwell.

KRUGMAN, Paul (2000): *The Return of Depression Economics.* London: Penguin.

KRUGMAN, Paul (2003): *The Great Unraveling*, New York: W.W. Norton.

KRUGMAN, Paul (2007): *The Conscience of a Liberal.* New York: W.W. Norton.

KRUGMAN, Paul (2008): *The Return of Depression Economics and the Crisis of 2008.* New York: W.W. Norton.

KRUGMAN, Paul (2012): *End This Depression Now!* New York: W.W. Norton.

KUHN, Thomas S. (2012): *The Structure of Scientific Revolutions.* Chicago: University of Chicago Press.

KUNDNANI, Hans (2011): Germany as a Geo-Economic Power. *The Washington Quarterly*, 34(3): 31–45.

KURZWEIL, Ray (2006): *The Singularity is Near: When Humans Transcend Biology*. New York: Penguin Putnam.

KURZWEIL, Ray (2013): *How to Create a Mind: The Secret of Human Thought Revealed.* New York: Penguin.

LAAR, Mart (2007): The Estonian Economic Miracle. Backgrounder #2060 on Democracy and Human Rights. *The Heritage Foundation*, 7 August. Online: https://herit.ag/2NL6FzR.

LANDSBURG, Steven (2010): *Price Theory and Applications*, 8th edn. Boston, MA: Cengage Learning.

LENGYEL Balázs and SZANYI Miklós (2011): Agglomerációs előnyök és regionális növekedés fel-zárkózó régiókban – a magyar átmenet esete (Agglomeration Advantages and Regional Growth in Converging Regions – The Hungarian Transition). *Közgazdasági szemle*, 58(Oct.): 858–876. https://bit.ly/2xPktzx.

LENGYEL, Imre: (2015). A gazdasági növekedés regionális alapjai – kézirat. (The Regional Fundamentals of Economic Growth – manuscript).

LEONARD, Mark (2015): Geo-economics in an Age of Risk. *Brink News*, 29 January. Online: https://bit.ly/2y3q9VV.

LEWIS, David W. (2012): Inevitability of Open Access – Summary. *College & Research Libraries*, 73(5): 493–506.

LIBERMAN, Vadim (2014): The Value of Values. *The Conference Board Review*. Online: https://bit.ly/2N52DNG.

LIEDTKA, Jeanne M., KING, Andrew, and BENNETT, Kevin (2013): *Solving Problem with Design Thinking*. New York: Columbia University Press.

LIU, Xinru (1998): *The Silk Road: Overland Trade and Cultural Interactions in Eurasia*. Washington, DC: American Historical Association.

LIU, Xinru (2010): *The Silk Road in World History*. New York: Oxford University Press.

LOROT, Pascal (1999): *Introduction á la géoéconomie*. Paris: Economica.

LUBART, Todd I. (1998): Creativity Across Cultures. In: Robert J. Sternberg (ed.) *Handbook of Creativity*, 339–350. Cambridge: Cambridge University Press.

LUCAS, Robert (2009): In Defence of the Dismal Science. *The Economist*, 6 August. https://econ.st/2IosBLq.

LUTTWAK, N. Edward (1990): From Geopolitics to Geo-Economics: Logic of Conflict, Grammar of Commerce. *The National Interest*, 20: 17–23.

MACKINDER, Halford (1919): *Democratic Ideals and Reality: A Study in the Politics of Reconstruction*. New York: H. Holt.

MALCEKI, Edward J. (2004): Jockeying for Position: What It Means and Why It Matters to Regional Development Policy When Places Compete. *Regional Studies*, 38(9): 1101–1120.

MARSHALL, Tim (2015): *Prisoners of Geography: Ten Maps That Explain Everything About the World*. New York: Scribner.

MASON, Betsy (2009): *Erupting Volcanoes on Earth as Seen from Space. Wired*, 24 August. Online: https://bit.ly/2Q8Yn1o.

MATOLCSY György (2008): *Éllovasból sereghajtók – Elveszett évek krónikája (From the Vanguard to Bringing Up the Rear: A Chronicle of Lost Years)*. Budapest: Éghajlat Könyvkiadó Kft.

MATOLCSY György (2015): *Egyensúly és növekedés (Economic Balance and Growth)*. Budapest: Kairosz Könyvkiadó Kft.

MATOLCSY György (2015): *Amerikai birodalom – A jövő forgatókönyvei (American empire – Scenarios for the future)*. Budapest: Pallas Athéné Geopolitikai Alapítvány.

MATURA Tamás (2015): Új fejezet a globális hatalmi játszmában – magyar részvétellel. (A New Chapter in the Global Power Struggle – With the Participation of Hungary). *Kitekintő*, 8 April. Online: https://bit.ly/2N6DWAv.

MAULDIN, John and TEPPER, Jonathan (2011): *Endgame: The End of the Debt Supercycle and How It Changes Everything*. Hoboken, NJ: John Wiley.

MAZZUCATO, Marianna (2015): *The Entrepreneurial State: Debunking Public vs. Private Sector Myths*. New York: Perseus.

MEADOWS, Donella H. (1997): Who Lives in the 'Global Village?'. Online: https://bit.ly/2QZuEJw.

MENINO, Thomas M. (2014): *Mayor for a New America*. New York: Houghton Mifflin.

MEZŐ, Ferenc (2003): *A politikai földrajz alapjai (The Geographical Foundations of Politics)*. Debrecen: Debreceni Egyetem.

MISZLIVETZ, Ferenc and MÁRKUS, Eszter (2013): A KRAFT-Index – Kreatív városok – Fenntartható vidék (The KRAFT Index – Creative Cities – Sustainable Rural Areas). *Vezetéstudomány*, 44(9): 2–21. https://bit.ly/2IjxuFf.

MOHOR, Jenő (2013): A nyílt hozzáférés elkerülhetetlen. *Könyvtári Figyelő*, 28 December. Online: https://bit.ly/2R5Ijiu.

MOSS, Ilan (2011): Start-Up Nation: An Innovation Story. *OECD Observer* No 285, Q2. Online: https://bit.ly/2DzIX4N.

NAGY, Gabriella (2012): Az üzleti felhőszolgáltatások bevezetése Magyarországon (The Introduction of Business Cloud Services in Hungary). Budapest: Budapesti Gazdasági Főiskola. Online: https://bit.ly/2zzmn8n.

NARAY, Rai (2005): *The Geopolitics of Globalization: The Consequences of Development*. Oxford: Oxford University Press.

NELSON, Elizabeth (2013): The Athena Doctrine: How Women (and the Men Who Think Like Them) Will Rule the Future. *Library Journal*, 138(9): 85.

NOLAND, Marcus (2014): Six Markets to Watch: South Korea – the Backwater that Boomed. *Foreign Affairs*, 93(1): 17–22.

NYE, Joseph (1990): *Bound to Lead: T he Changing Nature of America*. New York: Basic Books.

NYE, Joseph (2004): *Soft Power: The Means to Success in World Politics*. New York: PublicAffairs.

NYE, Joseph (2012): *The Future of Power*. New York, The Perseus Books Group.

NYE, Joseph (2013): The World in 2030. *Project Syndicate*, 9 January. Online: https://bit.ly/2ORghFS.

NYE, Joseph (2015): *Is the American Century Over (Global Futures)*. Cambridge: Polity Press.

Ó TUATHAIL, Gearóid, DALBY, Simon, and ROUTLEDGE, Paul (eds) (2007): *The Geopolitics Reader*. Abingdon: Routledge.

O'BRIEN, Richard (1992): *Global Financial Integration: The End of Geography*. New York: Council on Foreign Relations Press.

ORENSTEIN, Mitchell A. (2014): Six Markets to Watch: Poland – From Tragedy to Triumph. *Foreign Affairs*, 93(1): 23–27.

OWEN, Deborah and GRIFFITHS, Robin (2006): *Mapping the Markets: A Guide to Stockmarket Analysis*. London: Profile Books.

PACHAURI, Rajendra K., Meyer, Leo, and The Core Writing Team (eds) (2014): *Climate Change 2014: Synthesis Report. Contribution of Working Groups I, II and III to the Fifth Assessment Report of IPCC*. IPCC. Online: https://bit.ly/1DeDVUN.

PARKER, Geoffrey (1998): *Geopolitics: Past, Present and Future*. London: Pinter.

PARKIN, Michael and BADE, Robin (1992): *Macroeconomics*, 2nd edn. Englewood Cliffs, NJ: Prentice-Hall.

PARRILLI, Mario David, FITJAR, Rune Dahl, and Rodríguez-Pose, Andrés (2013): *Innovations Drivers and Regional Innovation Strategies*. New York: Routledge.

PATRICK, Stewart (2014): The Unruled World: The Case for Good Enough Global Governance. *Foreign Affairs*, 93(1): 58–73.

PEARSON, D.G. et al. (2014): Hydrous Mantle Transition Zone Indicated by Ringwoodite Included Within Diamond. *Nature*, 507: 221–224.

PEEK, Katie (2013): The Energy Fix: How Geography Drives Energy Development. *Popular Science*, 12 June. Online: https://bit.ly/2Q7QKYY.

PERKINS, Dwight H., RADELET, Stephen, LINDAUER, David L., and BLOCK, Steven A. (2013): *Economics of Development*, 7th edn. New York, W.W. Norton.

PIKETTY, Thomas (2014): *Capital in the Twenty-First Century*, trans. Arthur Goldhammer. Cambridge, MA: Harvard University Press.

PILKINGTON, John (1990): *An Adventure on the Old Silk Road: From Venice to the Yellow Sea*. North Pomfret, VT: Trafalgar Square.

PINE, II., Joseph B. and GILMORE, James H. (1999): *The Experience Economy: Work Is Theatre & Every Business a Stage*. Boston, MA: Harvard Business Review Press.

PINE II., Joseph B. and GILMORE, James H. (2007): *Authenticity: What Consumers Really Want*. Boston, MA: Harvard Business Review Press.

PINTER, Vanessa (2015): Overview and Analysis of the Performance of Spin-offs at the Swiss Federal Institute of Technology Zurich and Their Effect on the Swiss Economy. *ETH Zürich*, January. Online: https://bit.ly/2Ik1CjO.

PIRISI, Gábor and TRÓCSÁNYI, András (n.d.): *Általános társadalom- és gazdaságföldrajz (General social and economic geography)*. Online: https://bit.ly/2xXzPRx.

POLENSKE, Karen R. (2004): Competition, Collaboration and Cooperation: An Uneasy Triangle in Networks of Firms and Regions, *Regional Studies*, 38(9): 1029–1043.

PONGSUDHIRAK, Thinitinan (2014): Six Markets to Watch – the Mekong Region. *Foreign Affairs*, 93(1): 45–50.

POPPER, Karl (1998): *Szüntelen keresés – Intellektuális önéletrajz (Unended Quest: An Intellectual Autobiography)*. Budapest: Áron Kiadó.

PORTER, Michael E. (2008): The Five Competitive Forces that Shape Strategy. *Harvard Business Review*, 86(1): 78–93.

PRISLAN, Nika (2011): The Changing International Landscape for the European Union's External Energy Security Policy. In: José María Beneyto (ed.), *La Unión Europea como actor global: las nuevas dimensiones de la política exterior europea*. Madrid: Biblioteca Nueva, Instituto Universitario de Estudios Europeos de la Universidad CEU San Pablo.

RAFORD, Noah and TRABULSI, Andrew (2015): *Warlords, Inc.: Black Markets, Broken States, and the Rise of the Warlord Entrepreneur.* Berkeley, CA: North Atlantic Books.

RAFORD, Noah, GUPTA, Vinay, and LUPTON, Cat (2012): *The Future We Deserve*. Mainz: Pedia Press.

RECINE, Fabio and TEIXEIRA, Pedro Gustavo (2009): The New Financial Stability Architecture in the EU. Paolo Baffi Centre Research Paper No. 2009-62.

RECKLIES, Oliver (2001): *Managing Change: Definition and Phases in Change Processes*. Recklies Management Project GmbH. Online: https://bit.ly/2NLC1Xe.

RICE, Gillian (2013): Book Review: Conscious Capitalism Reflects the Ascendancy of the Athena Doctrine. *Global Business & Organizational Excellence*, 32(4): 83–87.

ROBINSON, Jancis (2015): *The Oxford Companion to Wine*. Oxford: Oxford University Press.

ROBINSON, Joe (2014): The 7 Traits of Successful Entrepreneurs, *Entrepreneur*, 10 January. Online: https://bit.ly/1TSVpgf.

RODIN, Judith (2014): *The Most Important Job You Haven't Heard Of (Yet): The Resilience Dividend.* The Rockefeller Foundation, 11 November. Online: https://bit.ly/2OVBzlN.

ROGERS, Paul (2003): A Thirty-Year War. *OpenDemocracy*, 4 April. Online: https://bit.ly/2ImGf1u.

ROGERS, Paul (2007): *Why We're Losing the War on Terror.* Cambridge: Polity Press.

ROGERS, Paul (2010): *Losing Control: Global Security in the 21st Century.* London: Pluto.

ROGERS, Paul (2014): The Thirty-Year War, Continued. *OpenDemocracy*, 11 September. Online: https://bit.ly/2Oh7DDv.

ROSE, Gideon (2013): Google's X-Man: A Conversation with Sebastian Thurn. *Foreign Affairs*, 92(6): 2–8.

ROSE, Gideon and TEPPERMAN, Jonathan (2014): The Shape of Things to Come. *Foreign Affairs*, 93(1): 2–3.

RÓZSÁS Tamás (2014): Sokkhullámok: a világ átalakulásának előterében (Shock Waves: On the Verge of the World's Transformation). *Polgári Szemle*, 10(1/2). Online: https://bit.ly/2N5FwlZ.

RUDD, Kevin (2010): *Building on ASEAN's Success: Towards an Asia Pacific Community.* Singapore: Institute of Southeast Asian Studies.

SÁGVÁRI Bence (2005): *A Kreatív Gazdaság elméletéről (On the Theory of the Creative Economy).* Budapest: ELTE – ITHAKA.

SAIN, Márton (1986): *Nincs királyi út! Matematikatörténet (No Easy Way! A History of Mathematics).* Budapest: Gondolat Kiadó.

SCHAWBEL, Dan (2013): John Gerzema: How Women Will Rule the Future of Work. *Forbes*, 16 April. Online: https://bit.ly/2zAvl5A.

SCHROEDER, Christopher M. (2012): Parag and Ayesha Khanna Foresee a Hybrid Future, and It's Great. *Washington Post*, 2 July. https://wapo.st/2NNctJ0.

SCHROVER, Marlou (2008): Consequences of Migration. In: *History of International Migration.* University of Leiden. Online: https://wapo.st/2NNctJ0.

SCHULZINGER, Robert D. (1998): *U.S. Diplomacy Since 1900*, 4th edn. New York: Oxford University Press.

SCHUMPETER, Joseph (2014): Second wind. *The Economist*, 14 June. Online: http://www.economist.com/news/business/21604156-some-traditional-businesses-are-thriving-age-disruptive-innovation-second-wind.

SCHWAB, Klaus (ed.) (2013): *The Global Competitiveness Report 2013–2014.* Geneva: World Economic Forum.

SCOTT, Karen (n.d.): *Rural Culture Economies.* Newcastle upon Tyne: Centre for Rural Economy Newcastle University. Online: https://bit.ly/2OgprPa.

SEN, Amartya (2009): Capitalism Beyond the Crisis. *The New York Review of Books,* 26 March. https://bit.ly/2N7couL.

SENOR, Dan and SINGER, Saul (2009): *Start-Up Nation: The Story of Israel's Economic Miracle.* New York: Hachette.

SENOR, Dan and SINGER, Saul (n.d.): Start-Up Nation. The Story of Israel's Economic Miracle. *Council on Foreign Relations.* Online: https://on.cfr.org/2xH183m.

SILVERSTEIN, Ken (2015): *The Secret World of Oil.* London: Verso.

SIMON, Julian Lincoln (1998): *The Ultimate Resource 2.* Princeton, NJ: Princeton University Press.

SMITH, Craig (2016): By the Numbers: 100 Amazing Google Statistics and Facts. *DMR*, 25 February. Online: https://bit.ly/2Dzp663.

SMITH, Tierney (2015): 5 Countries Leading the Way Toward 100% Renewable Energy. *EcoWatch*, 9 January. Online: https://bit.ly/2IqMwcF.

SØILEN, Klaus Sobel (2012): *Geoeconomics*. Bookboon.com.

SOLOMON, Richard H. (1992): America and Asia in an Era of Geoeconomics. *Dispatch*, 3: 410.

SPEICHER, Sandy (2013): Design Thinking for Educators. *IDEO*.

STEPHENS, Philip (2008): Crisis Marks Out a New Geopolitical Order. *Financial Times*, 9 October. https://on.ft.com/2NLPv5g.

STIGLITZ, Joseph E., SEN, Amartya, and FITOUSSI, Jean Paul (n.d.): *Report by the Commission on the Measurement of Economic Performance and Social Progress*. Online: https://bit.ly/2sq0MvV.

SUN Tzu (1971): *The Art of War*, trans. Samuel B. Griffith. London: Oxford University Press.

SUSSKIND, Daniel and SUSSKIND, Richard E. (2015): *The Future of the Professions: How Technology Will Transform the Work of Human Experts*. Oxford: Oxford University Press.

SUSSKIND, Lawrence (2014): *Great for You, Great for Me: Finding the Trading Zone and winning at Win-Win Negotiation*. New York: PublicAffairs.

SZABO, Stephen F. (2015): *Germany, Russia, and the Rise of Geo-economics*. London: Bloomsbury Academic.

SZILÁGYI, István (2009): *Európa és a mediterrán világ (Europe and the Mediterranean World)*. Budapest: Áron Kiadó.

SZILÁGYI, István (2011): A földrajz a történelem kulcsa. Százötven éve született Sir J. Halford Mackinder a földrajztudomány és a geopolitika klasszikusa (Geography Is the Key to History: Sir J. Halford Mackinder, a Classic Figure in Geography and Geopolitics Was Born 150 Years Ago). *Magyar Tudomány*, 11: 1362–1373.

SZILÁGYI István (2013): *Geopolitika (Geopolitics)*. Pécs: Publikon.

TADELIS, Steven (2013): *Game Theory: An Introduction*. Princeton, NJ: Princeton University Press.

TAPSCOTT, Don and WILLIAMS, Anthony D. (2007): *Wikinómia – Hogyan változtat meg mindent a tömeges együttműködés (Wikinomics: How Mass Collaboration Changes Everything)*. Budapest, HVG Kiadói Rt.

TAYLOR, Peter J. and Derudder, Ben (2015): *World City Network: A Global Urban Analysis*. London: Taylor & Francis.

TERDIMAN, Daniel (2013): Mystery Google Barge Will Be Invite-Only Google X Showroom, Says Report. *CNet*, 31 October. Online: https://cnet.co/2R1ATwF.

THRUN, Sebastian, BURGARD, Wolfram, and FOX, Dieter (2005): *Probabilistic Robotics*. Cambridge, MA: MIT Press.

TOCQUEVILLE, de Alexis (1864): *Democracy in America*. Cambridge, MA: Sever and Francis.

TOFFLER, Alvin (1970): *Future Shock*. London: Bantam.

TOFFLER, Alvin (1980): *The Third Wave*. New York: William and Morrow.

TOFFLER, Alvin (1990): *Powershift: Knowledge, Wealth and Violence at the Edge of the 21st Century*. New York: Bantam Books.

TOFFLER, Alvin (1999): *The Third Wave*. New York: Bantam Books.

TOFFLER, Alvin and TOFFLER, Heidi (1995): *Creating a New Civilization*. Nashville, TN: Turner Publishing.

TOFFLER, Alvin and TOFFLER, Heidi (2007) *Revolutionary Wealth: How it Will be Created and How it Will Change Our Lives*. New York: Bantam Doubleday Dell.

TRANOS, Emmanouil and NIJKAMP, Peter (2013): A távolság halálának új vizsgálata: kiberhely, földrajzi és kapcsolati közelség (A New Study of the Death of the Distance: Cyber Place, Geographical and Connection Proximity). *Tér és Társadalom*, 27(3): 3–27.

TSOULFIDIS, Lefteris (2009): *Competing Schools of Economic Thought.* Berlin: Springer.

UNITED NATIONS Department of Economic and Social Affairs (2015): *The World Population Prospects: 2015 Revision.* New York: UNDESA.

VERCSEG, Ilona (2012): A helyi közösség elmélete és gyakorlata c. előadás (The Theory and Practice of Local Community – Presentation).

VIGVÁRI, Gábor (2009): Változó szerepek: Ágazati politikák a fejhlesztő állam tevékenységében (Changing Roles: Sectoral Policies in the Activity of the Developmental State). In: Csáki György (ed.): *A látható kéz: A fejlesztő állam a globalizációban (The vVsible Hand: Developing the State in Globalization),* 127–160, Budapest, Napvilág Kiadó.

VIGVÁRI, Gábor (2012): Globalizáció és fejlesztő állam: A nemzetközi rezsimek változásának hatása a fejlesztő államra (Globalization and the developmental state: The impact of the change of international regimes on the developmental state). PhD dissertation, Budapest: Budapesti Corvinus Egyetem Nemzetközi Kapcsolatok Multidiszciplináris Doktori Iskola.

VINE, David (2015): *Base Nation: How U.S. Military Bases Abroad Harm America and the World* (American Empire Project). New York: Metropolitan Books.

WALL, Larry D (2012): Central Banking for Financial Stability: Some Lessons from the Recent Instability in the United States and Euro Area. *ABDI Working Paper* No. 379, Asian Development Bank Institute.

WALTON, C. Dale (2007): *Geopolitics and the Great Powers in the 21st Century: Multipolarity and the Revolution in Strategic Perspective.* New York: Routledge.

WATSON, Richard (2009): *Future Files: A Brief History of the Next 50 Years.* London: Nicholas Brealey Publishing.

WEINREICH László (ed.) (2012): *Kultúra és kreativitás: kulturális klaszterek Magyarországon (Culture and Creativity: Cultural Clusters in Hungary).* Pécs: Pannon Klassz Közösség Kulturális Klaszter.

WEN, Jiabao (2007): Our Historical Tasks at the Primary Stage of Socialism and Several Issues Concerning China's Foreign Policy. *Embassy of the People's Republic of China in the United Kingdom,* 6 March. Online: https://bit.ly/2Dzw7DV.

WESLEY, Michael (2015): *Restless Continent: Wealth, Rivalry and Asia's New Geopolitics.* New York: Overlook Duckworth.

WILSON, Paul and HADNAGY, Christopher (2010): *Social Engineering: The Art of Human Hacking.* Chichester: John Wiley.

WOOLLASTON, Victoria (2013): China Lifts Ban on Facebook – But Only for People Living in a 17 Square Mile Area of Shanghai. *Daily Mail,* 25 September. Online: https://dailym.ai/2R7wJ6v.

WORLAND, Justin (2015): Climate Change Could Wreck the Global Economy. *Time,* 22 October. Online: https://ti.me/1i09WWY.

WRIGHT, Gilly (2015): The Best Cities To Live in the World 2015. *Global Finance,* 2 November. https://bit.ly/XaTEAC.

YERGIN, Daniel and STANISLAW, Joseph (2002): *The Commanding Heights: The Battle for the World Economy.* New York: Free Press.

ZUBER, Corine and LEBRET, Hervé (2014): *Support to Innovation Around EPFL.* École Polytechnique Fédérale de Lausanne, May. Online: https://bit.ly/2OfmcY3.

ANALYSES, STUDIES, WEBSITES, VIDEOS

100 Amazing Water Facts You Should Know. Seametrics Blog, 28 April 2014. Online: https://bit.ly/2J4FsoB.

100 Resilient Cities. City of New Orleans. Online: https://bit.ly/2NPn1HW.

2014: By the Numbers. A snapshot of what 2014 Looked Like on Kickstarter. *Kickstarter.com*. Online: https://bit.ly/2zAPtnP.

2015 Quality of Living in Cities Global Survey. *Mercer*. Online: https://bit.ly/1Sj7Qz2.

A Cambrian Moment. Special Report: Tech Startups. *The Economist*, 18 January 2014. Online: https://bit.ly/1goUQ7z.

A diszruptív innovációk kék óceánja – Könyvszemle Kim, W. Chan – Mauborgne, Renée Kék óceán stratégia. A verseny nélküli piaci tér című kötetéről (The Blue Ocean of Disruptive Innovations – Book Review of Kim, W. Chan – Mauborgne, Renée: Blue Ocean Strategy: How to Create Uncontested Market Space and Make the Competition Irrelevant). Online: https://bit.ly/2OURr81.

A Summary of the Liveability Ranking and Overview. August 2014. The Economist Intelligence Unit's Liveability Survey. Online: https://bit.ly/1IJnajd.

Aalto FabLab. Online: https://bit.ly/2Qfep9V.

About Richard Florida. *Martin Prosperity Institute*. Online: https://bit.ly/2NIy5Gy.

ASEAN Member States. The Official Website of the Association of Southeast Asian Nations. Online: https://bit.ly/2OV8uqr.

Aspen Review, Central Europe. No. 2. 2013. Online: https://bit.ly/2xXSixc.

Atlas of Prejudice. Online: https://bit.ly/2Dzjrwv.

BBC News: Samsung Overtakes Nokia in Mobile Phone Shipments. *BBC News*, 27 April 2012. Online: https://bbc.in/2N7vp07.

Best Cities Ranking and Report: A Special Report from the Economist Intelligence Unit, August 2013. Online: https://bit.ly/2xVj5dT.

Big Mac Index Data, 28 July 2011. Online: https://bit.ly/2xFPTIo.

Board of Governors of the Federal Reserve System: 98th Annual Report. Washington, DC: Fed, 2011. Online: https://bit.ly/2NOrLgT.

BUD – Budapest Vízió (Pallas Athéné Geopolitikai Alapítvány) (Budapest Vision [Pallas Athéné Geopolitical Foundation]). Online: https://bit.ly/2xUKpIZ.

Budapest Runaway 2.0 2.0: A Start-up Credo. 2013. Nemzetgazdasági Minisztérium, Parlamenti és Gazdaságstratégiáért Felelős Államtitkárság. Online: https://bit.ly/2xHipJK.

CASE – Center for Social and Economic Research. About us. Online: https://bit.ly/2Ir7A2J.

Central Banking Newsdesk: Krugman Adds Lustre to $1 Trillion Coin Plan. *Central Banking*, 8 January 2013. Online: https://bit.ly/2OUVIs6.

City Resilience Framework. The Rockefeller Foundation, ARUP, April 2014. Online: https://bit.ly/2xQah8M.

Climate Vulnerability Monitor. 2nd Edition. A Guide to the Cold Calculus of a Hot Planet. DARA & Climate Vulnerability Forum. Online: https://bit.ly/2Q9Q0me.

Copenhagenizing Vancouverism, 25 June 2012. The Blog by Copenhagenize Design Co. Online: https://bit.ly/2RaC254.

Cost of Living City Rankings. *Mercer*. Online: https://bit.ly/2Imi2bw.

Creative City Berlin. Online: https://bit.ly/2OjANli.

Creative Class Group. Online: https://bit.ly/1uxXErU.

Creative Economy Report 2013, Special Edition: Widening Local Development Pathways. New York, UNESCO – UNDP. Online: https://bit.ly/1gmNLaR.

Early Support Pays Off – Press Release. *ETH Zürich*, 5 January 2016. Online: https://bit.ly/1kHAuNY.

Endesa, Barcelona City Council Sign Cooperation Agreement. *Energy Business Review*. 31 March 2014. Online: https://bit.ly/2DBuoOm.

EPFL Innovation Park: Company List. Online: https://bit.ly/2Ongq6G.

EPFL Startups, 2016. VPIV – Technology Transfer Office TTO. École Polytechnique Fédérale de Lausanne. Online: https://bit.ly/2OU02Yz.

EPFL Resources for Entrepreneurs. Vice Presidency for Innovation and Technology Transfer VPIV. École Polytechnique Fédérale de Lausanne. https://bit.ly/2N6I1Vk.

Eurostat: Forestry in the EU and the World: A Statistical Portrait. Luxembourg: Publications Office of the European Union, 2011. Online: https://bit.ly/2OUJsry.

Fab Foundation. Online: https://bit.ly/1PUPLaM.

FabLab Budapest. Online: https://bit.ly/2zB2MoA.

FDI in Figures, OECD. October 2015. Online: https://bit.ly/2OkSwZF.

FED: Board of Governors of the Federal Reserve System website. Online: https://bit.ly/2nn8ZMo.

Federal Reserve Bank of Richmond: The Federal Reserve Today (16th edn). Richmond, VA, Federal Reserve Bank of Richmond, 2012.

Gartner's 2014 Hype Cycle for Emerging Technologies Maps the Journey to Digital Business. Press Release, Stamford, CT, Gartner. 11 August 2014. Online: https://gtnr.it/1vGSVXn.

Global Strategic Trends – Out to 2045, Ministry of Defence, UK. Online: https://bit.ly/1Hu0y3O.

Globalization (cartoon). Online: https://bit.ly/2OUVmBL.

Google's Locations. Online: https://bit.ly/2xIQyIU.

Google's Management Team. Online: https://bit.ly/2xIQyIU.

Green IT Strategy for the City of Stockholm. Online: https://bit.ly/2ORGS5G.

Gross National Happiness. Online: https://bit.ly/1JaEUZk.

Hot Spots 2025 – Benchmarking the Future Competitiveness of Cities. The Economist Intelligence Unit, 2013. Online: http://citi.us/1kHCAbU.

In defence of dismal science. *The Economist*, 8 June 2018. Online: https://econ.st/2IosBLq.

Innovation Cities Index 2014: Global City Innovation Economy Classifications and Rankings, 2014. *Innovation Cities Program*. Global Innovation Agency. Online: https://bit.ly/2OWChiw.

Intelligence Debates: Look West not East: South America will be the 21st century's superpower, IQ2 debate (speech) 22 March 2011. Online: https://bit.ly/2NI2zIG.

International Institute of Management: Global Gross National Happiness / Well-being Index Survey 2005–2015. Online: https://bit.ly/2Offul3.

Key World Energy Statistics 2018, International Energy Agency (IEA). Online: https://bit.ly/2xWzHSr.

Knowledge Economy Index (KEI) 2012 Rankings. World Bank, 2012. Online: https://bit.ly/2Qe7aPK.

Kreatív Iparágak Platformja: Megvalósítási Terv (Creative Industry Platform: Implementation Plan). Budapest, November 2010.

Legatum Prosperity Index, Legatum Institute, 2015. Online: https://bit.ly/2dSzMug.

List of ETH spin-offs. ETH Zürich. Online: https://bit.ly/2QdV3l.

Living Planet Report 2014 – Species and Spaces, People and Places. WWF. Online: https://bit.ly/2xQTbc3.

Loffice Coworking+. Online: https://bit.ly/2R6U7B1.

Made to measure. In: *The Economist* (The Technology Quarterly, Q2). 30 May 2015. Online: https://econ.st/2OWJIq7.

Map depicting Communist Takeovers in Eastern Europe, 1945–1955. *Pinterest.* Online: https://bit.ly/2zARDnv.

Methodology: The Economist Intelligence Unit's liveability survey. Online: https://bit.ly/2Qfdlmv.

Migration and Globalization. SUNY LEVIN Institute. Online: https://bit.ly/2ImD89T.

Minden képzelet felülmúlt a Krakatau kitörése (Krakatoa's Eruption Was Beyond Imagination). *Múlt-kor*, 27 August 2013. Online: https://bit.ly/2NJB01I.

Nation Master: Broadband Access (most recent) by Country. *Nation Master*, 2012. Online: https://bit.ly/2Ohzd3j.

Nation Master: Telephones > Mobile Cellular (Most Recent) by Country. *Nation Master*, 2012. Online: https://bit.ly/1z8MEpU.

National Intelligence Council: *Global Trends 2030: Alternative Worlds.* National Intelligence Council, 2012.

Növekedési Jelentés, 2015 (Growth Report 2015). Magyar Nemzeti Bank. Online: https://bit.ly/2DACaYP.

OECD (2008): *Handbook on Constructing Composite Indicators: Methodology and User Guide.* Online: https://bit.ly/1rmUeYZ.

OECD Better Life Index: Iceland. Online: https://bit.ly/1RDFyOt.

OECD (2011): OECD Better Life Index: Better Life Online: https://bit.ly/2Okvty4.

OECD (2011): Country statistical profiles 2010: China, Hungary, United States. In: OECD. StatExtracts. Online: https://bit.ly/2Qgqwn9.

Professor Dr Robot QC. In: *The Economist.* 17 November 2015. Online: https://econ.st/2xKGOhw.

RePEc. Top 10% Authors. *IDEAS.* Online: https://bit.ly/2DDzrxQ.

RePEc. Top 10% Institutions and Economists in the Field of Monetary Economics, as of August 2013. *IDEAS.* Online: https://bit.ly/2RbNBce.

RePEc. Top 25% Institutions and Economists in Hungary. *IDEAS.* Online: https://bit.ly/2DEiK5d.

RePEc. Top Countries and States IDEAS. Online: https://bit.ly/2DzAu1O.

Richard Florida – CityLab. Online: https://bit.ly/2Oog53E.

Richard Florida – Rotman School of Management. Online: https://bit.ly/2xVzleG.

Smart Cities: Smart City Wien. Online: https://bit.ly/2OWQlsa.

State of the World's Cities 2012/2013. Prosperity of Cities. UN-Habitat, 2012. Online: https://bit.ly/2jwErFL.

Stratfor: *Annual Forecast 2012.* Online: https://bit.ly/2DzGwQ0.

Stratfor: *Forecast 2015-2025.* Online: https://bit.ly/2hy6ipf.

TED: The post-crisis consumer, August 2009. John Gerzema. Online: https://bit.ly/2DNym6L.

TEDxWOMEN Talk: The Athena Doctrine. 2012. Online: https://bit.ly/2NJwyjA.

Területfejlesztési füzetek 1. Segédlet a közösségi tervezéshez (Territorial Development Booklets 1 – Guide to Community Planning). Budapest, 2010. Online: https://bit.ly/2xWjxZn.

Területfejlesztési füzetek 2. Helyi gazdaság-fejlesztés: Ötletadó megoldások, jó gyakorlatok (Territorial Development Booklets 2 – Local Economic Development: Inspiring Solutions, Best Practices). Budapest, 2010. Online: https://bit.ly/2Il6G7D.

The Creative Economy Report 2010: Creative Economy – A Feasible Development Option. ENSZ–UNCTAD, United Nations Conference on Trade and Development. Online: https://bit.ly/1pJwcav.

The Economy of Culture in Europe. KEA European Affairs, October 2006. Online: https://bit.ly/2R34YvP.

The Global Financial Centres Index 21. Qatar Financial Centre, March 2017. Online: https://bit.ly/2xIxtXB.

The Green City Index – A Summary of the Green City Index Research Series. The Economist Intelligence Unit, Siemens, 2012. Online: https://sie.ag/122XX2Z.

The Monocle Quality of Life Survey 2015. *Monocle.* Online: https://bit.ly/1S800Z2.

Tokyo Rated the World's Best City to Live In. *Daily Mail Online*, 16 June 2015. Online: https://dailym.ai/2zCoJn4.

The Index of Economic Freedom. The Heritage Foundation, *The Wall Street Journal.* Online: https://herit.ag/2kdRNJc.

TOP 100 – The Best Swiss Startups 2017. Online: https://bit.ly/2R4ol7z.

Udacity. *Udacity, Inc.* Online: https://bit.ly/2r7jmHN.

Új Széchenyi Terv: A talpraállás, megújulás és felemelkedés fejlesztéspolitikai programja (New Széchenyi Plan: The Development Policy Programme of Recovery, Renewal, and Rising). Nemzetgazdasági Minisztérium, Budapest, 2011.

UNDP: *Human Development Report 2013.* New York, United Nations Development Programme, 2013.

United Nations Development Programme (2010): *Human Development Report 2010.* 20th Anniversary Edition. New York: Palgrave Macmillan, 2010.

United Nations Development Programme: The Human Development Index (HDI). Online: https://bit.ly/1kkByXA.

US Energy Information Agency: China – International Energy Data and Analysis (Overview) 14 May 2015. Online: https://bit.ly/28NmW12.

Virtual Water: Online: https://bit.ly/2xVCBGW.

What Is Success in a City? The Economic Power of Talented People – Richard Florida. Online: https://bit.ly/2zC28XJ.

World Airline Map. *SquidHammer*, 5 March 2009. Online: https://bit.ly/2zC4yWe.

World Economic Forum: The Global Competitiveness Report 2013–2014: Full Data Edition. World Economic Forum, Geneva, 2013.

World Economic Forum: Geopolitics vs Globalization: How Companies and States Can Become Winners in the Age of Geo-economics. 2015. Online: https://bit.ly/1JRBTge.

World Economic Forum: Geo-economics: Seven challenges to globalization. 2015. Online: https://bit.ly/1JRBTge.

World Urbanization Prospects: United Nations, New York. Online: https://bit.ly/2zBCOkF.

Zurich and Lausanne Unis Launch 43 Startups. *The Local.ch*, 6 January 2016. Online: https://bit.ly/2NMEPU1.

INDEX

ABOUT THE AUTHOR

Norbert Csizmadia is a world traveller, Hungarian geographer and expert in economic strategy, geostrategy, regional and urban development, and geopolitics. He is the former State Secretary for the Ministry for National Economy and a former Executive Director of the Central Bank of Hungary in charge of economic strategy and planning. He is President of the Board of Trustees at Pallas Athéne Innovation and Geopolitical Foundation and is Chief Editor of *Hungarian Geopolitics* (*HUG*) magazine.